WHAT IS
CHRISTIANITY?

WHAT IS CHRISTIANITY?

A Dynamic Introduction

DENNIS M. DOYLE

Paulist Press
New York / Mahwah, NJ

Graphics from "The Global Religious Landscape," Pew Research Center, Washington, DC (December, 2012) http://www.pewforum.org/2012/12/18/global-religious-landscape-exec/ and "Global Christianity—A Report on the Size and Distribution of the World's Christian Population," Pew Research Center, Washington, DC (December, 2011) http://www.pewforum.org/2011/12/19/global-christianity-exec/. Reproduced by permission of the Pew Research Center.

Bly, Robert. Excerpt from "Surprised by Evening" in *Silence in the Snowy Fields* © 1962 by Robert Bly. Reprinted with permission of Wesleyan University Press.

The Scripture quotations contained herein are from the New Revised Standard Version: Catholic Edition, Copyright © 1989 and 1993, by the Division of Christian Education of the National Council of the Churches of Christ in the United States of America. Used by permission. All rights reserved.

Cover image (background texture) by R-Studio/Shutterstock.com
Cover design by Tamian Wood
Book design by Sharyn Banks

Library of Congress Cataloging-in-Publication Data

Names: Doyle, Dennis M. (Dennis Michael), 1952– author.
Title: What is Christianity? : a dynamic introduction / Dennis M. Doyle.
Description: New York : Paulist Press, 2016. | Includes index. | Description based on print version record and CIP data provided by publisher; resource not viewed.
Identifiers: LCCN 2016009357 (print) | LCCN 2016007055 (ebook) | ISBN 9781587686207 (Ebook) | ISBN 9780809149933 (pbk. : alk. paper)
Subjects: LCSH: Christianity—Essence, genius, nature. | Catholic Church—Doctrines. | Theology, Doctrinal.
Classification: LCC BT60 (print) | LCC BT60 .D69 2016 (ebook) | DDC 230—dc23 LC record available at http://lccn.loc.gov/2016009357

ISBN 978-0-8091-4993-3 (paperback)
ISBN 978-1-58768-620-7 (e-book)

Published by Paulist Press
997 Macarthur Boulevard
Mahwah, New Jersey 07430

www.paulistpress.com

Printed and bound in the United States of America

For Pat, Tom and Andrea,
Mike and Kyla, Patrick and Ally,
Chris, Maggie Jane, and Annie

CONTENTS

Contents

Contents

ACKNOWLEDGMENTS

I thank first of all my amazing wife, Pat, who read and skillfully critiqued various drafts of every chapter of this book. I thank also three more people who read and critiqued the entire manuscript: my editor, Chris Bellitto, whose guidance throughout every phase of the conception and writing was invaluable; William Collinge, whose many corrections and suggestions greatly improved the quality of the text; and Josh Wopata, my current graduate assistant, who devoted much time and energy to this work. I thank also my Dayton colleague, Meghan Henning, a Bible scholar who gave me feedback on all three chapters on Scripture; my Augsburg colleague, Kerstin Schlögl-Flierl, a scholar of moral theology who gave me feedback on all three chapters on Christian Life; and Sue Sack, a hospital chaplain and scholar who offered observations on multiple chapters. Thanks go to several people who have read and commented on one or more chapters: Judith Summer, Martin Blay, Tyler DeLong, Tinamarie Stolz, and Lysander Nelms. Thanks to those who have often discussed with me various topics related to this book, especially Bill Portier, Silviu Bunta, Cyril Orji, Jana Bennett, Mike Barnes, Vince Miller, David Hammond, Tony Godzieba, Jim Heft, Trecy Lysaught, Rick Gaillardetz, Hans Hafner, Martin Leiner, Vladimir Latinovic, Gerard Mannion, and the late Jeff Gros. I thank Jeremy Langford for his encouragement regarding a starter project long ago, and I thank Jim Heft and Deb Bickford of the University of Dayton for funding a course reduction in support of that starter project. I thank Dan Thompson and Jason Pierce of the University of Dayton for a course reduction in spring 2015. I thank the government of Bavaria and the University of Augsburg for supporting me with a research stipend in summer 2015. I also thank Charles Carroll for his ongoing support for my work. I thank Kornelia Hödl and her family for their welcoming support during my stay in Augsburg. Last, but certainly not least, I thank Thomas Schärtl not only for his leading role in securing for me my summer research stipend, but also for the many conversations we have had related to the topics covered in this book, as well as for the hospitality he and his wife, Manuela, showed to me in summer 2015.

Chapter 1

INTRODUCTION

At its core, Christianity has to do with love and commitment. Sometimes during a televised football game, someone will hold up a sign reading "John 3:16." If you look up the passage, it reads, "For God so loved the world that he gave his only Son, so that everyone who believes in him may not perish but may have eternal life." Christians believe that God's love and commitment have been expressed through the death and resurrection of Jesus Christ. They seek to live out the meaning of God's love and commitment within the context of relationships. Christians are in relationship with each other through their relationship with God. Christian churches and communities find their origins in the community founded by Christ among his disciples. The presence of the Holy Spirit provides the point of continuity between the communities of today and the original Christian community.

This text is being written primarily for use in academic courses in colleges and universities. Can faith perspectives and commitments be studied academically? Is participation in a faith tradition inherently subjective? If theology is a search for understanding that presupposes faith, should it be ruled out of the academic classroom? How can one possibly think that one can approach topics such as love, commitment, God, relationships, the meaning of life, and eternity in an academic manner?

One way might be to limit our discussion to history. Another approach might be to focus exclusively on perspectives from the social sciences. Would that mean, then, that we would rule out perspectives that are based on faith?

Christian theology occupies a central place in this textbook. Contemporary theology is itself interdisciplinary in that it includes concepts and methods drawn from a range of disciplines. The author of this textbook is both a Christian believer and an academic. Specifically, I belong to the Catholic Church.[1] I speak from a particular perspective. I cannot claim to be completely without bias, but I can pledge to be as open-minded, critical, inclusive, and fair a person as I reasonably can be. I have tried my best to make this book both Catholic and ecumenical, to explore Christianity in a way that not only Christians but also people of various faiths and worldviews can understand what is being said and feel included in any discussion about the material.

Treating My Own Faith Academically as I Treat Others

Once in an introductory religious studies course, at the beginning of a study of Buddhism, I led a group of first-year college students through a Buddhist meditation. At first, they were told to try to clear their minds and focus on breathing. Gradually, they were asked to identify thoughts that would enter their mind and then dismiss them. Finally, they were instructed to identify particular thoughts as either *wants* or *aversions* before they dismissed them.[2]

The meditation exercise took just a few minutes. We then had a discussion about what connected this particular form of meditation with Buddhism. Students were able to recognize that a key element of Buddhism was what to do with desire. Wants and aversions are both types of desire: one is a desire to have, and the other a desire to flee. The meditation allowed students to objectify their desires by naming them. They were thus able to challenge any illusions that they might otherwise have that they are a "self" constituted by desires. They were practicing, in a most initial way, a meditation that gave them control over desires through being able to dismiss them. At the end of that class, there were a few students who had been significantly struck by the experience. They asked me if there were any Buddhist places in the local area to which they could go to learn about and engage in Buddhist practices.

There were also a couple of other students, devout Catholics, who were upset with me because I had introduced Buddhism in such an attractive manner in an introductory class at a Catholic university. They thought that I should not be in the business of turning students into Buddhists. I replied that I was just trying to treat Buddhism academically. In my judgment, you are not communicating much about Buddhism if your students do not get some insight into why Buddhism is attractive and fulfilling to those who practice it. I was not preaching Buddhism but only trying to get my students to understand it. What good would it be to have students learn objectively about the Four Noble Truths and the Eightfold Path if they had no way of connecting with it experientially in the most positive of ways?

I think the same way about introducing students to Christianity. We will cover many points of criticism and analysis. Throughout this textbook, however, I try to present Christianity in such a way that one can catch a glimpse of what Christian faith means to those who believe and practice it.

The Approach of This Textbook

This introductory chapter will be followed by four sections of three chapters that will focus on a basic element of Christianity: Scripture, Tradition, Sacraments, and Christian Life. A major theme of this textbook is that no one of these four elements can be understood apart from reference to the other three elements. For this reason, even though the focus and emphasis will shift, all four elements will be present to some degree in all four sections.[3]

INTRODUCTION TO CHRISTIANITY	
Scripture	The Bible; sacred writings for Christians
Tradition	Christian faith as authentically handed down and lived out in history
Sacraments	Ritual ways of relating to God and receiving Christ's grace
Christian Life	Living out the Christian faith through spiritual and moral practices

What Is Christianity?

Christianity is the religion of those who are followers of Jesus Christ. *Christ* can be translated as "Messiah" or "the anointed one." *Jesus Christ* is a title given to Jesus of Nazareth, a Jew who lived in Palestine (now Israel) in the first century CE. Calendars that stem from Christian Europe, including many global calendars today, divide their years according to the year of Jesus' birth.

Jesus was born in Bethlehem about 4 BCE.[4] His family moved to Nazareth in Galilee, an area in Palestine at the northern tip of the Dead Sea. In the Gospels, he is said to be the son of a carpenter, Joseph. His mother's name was Mary. They were Jewish.

We know little about the first thirty years of Jesus' life. Starting about 27 CE, Jesus began a public ministry that would last for about three years. He preached about the unconditional love of God as well as the coming of God's kingdom. He performed healings and exorcisms and had many followers. Jesus spoke of a special relation he had with God, whom he called "Abba" or "Father." He promised to send to his followers the Holy Spirit, whom Christians have come to identify, along with the Father and the Son, as one of three persons in the one God. He had struggles with both the Jewish and the Roman leaders. About the year 29 CE, at the age of thirty-three, Jesus was tortured and put to death by crucifixion. His followers proclaimed that he was risen from the dead.

The disciples of Jesus carried their message throughout the Mediterranean world, down the Nile, through the Middle East, and all the way to India. Wherever they went, they founded Christian communities. These Christian communities were sometimes persecuted and had their own internal struggles, but their members believed themselves to be bonded with each other in the love of God through Christ and the Holy Spirit. By the end of the second century, a basic structure of organization emerged within Christianity that was centered around bishops.

Christianity has existed throughout history in many forms. Is Christianity so varied and complicated that one cannot really talk about it as one thing? Is there such a thing as Christianity? Should one just drop the term and speak instead only of Lutherans, Orthodox,

Methodists, Pentecostals, Catholics, and so on? My position is that there is such a thing as Christianity. I belong to a particular church, but it is important to me that I am a Christian. Being a Christian is something that I share with the other 2.2 billion Christians in the world. Christianity is a global religious phenomenon and needs to be studied as such. To study Christianity, however, does require that one not consider it in the abstract but rather investigate the various Christian traditions and the details of their development.

Christianity as a Global Phenomenon

Today, Christianity spans the globe, and numerous and interesting global elements can be traced throughout its history. Early on, Christianity spread throughout the Middle East and the Mediterranean area, going as far south as Ethiopia and as far east as northwest India. In the late fourth century CE, Christianity became associated institutionally with the Roman Empire, which itself encompassed what would later constitute the Latin West and the Byzantine East.

Diversity and division within Christianity will be addressed in chapter 7. Some general background on this important topic, however, needs to be given in this first chapter.

In 1054, the Great East-West Schism divided the Christian Church into the Orthodox Church and the Catholic Church. The Orthodox Church has several centers or patriarchates, but at the time of the schism, the main one was Constantinople (now Istanbul). Most Orthodox have lived in what is now the Middle East and Eastern Europe and have spoken Greek, Slavic, or other Middle Eastern languages, including Russian.

The Catholic Church was centered in Rome, and most of its adherents at that time lived in the Latin West. The European continent of the Middle Ages (800–1400) is known as Christendom, comprising many regions, operating with feudal structures, and ruled by kings, dukes, earls, counts, and other aristocrats. The great majority of the population was Catholic. The Catholic Church and its hierarchy functioned as the glue that held the society together.

Protestants trace their beginnings to the Reformation of the early sixteenth century. Martin Luther (1483–1546) and John Calvin (1509–64) were among its great figures. Many qualifications need to be made about those here being lumped together as "Protestants." The Pew Research Center offers the following chart:[5]

Denominations of Protestants

Denominational family	PERCENTAGE OF ALL PROTESTANTS
Historically pentecostal denomination	10.8%
Anglican	10.6
Lutheran	9.7
Baptist	9.0
United churches (unions of different denominations)	7.2
Presbyterian or Reformed	7.0
Methodist	3.4
Adventist	2.7
Congregationalist	0.5
Brethren	0.5
Salvation Army	0.3
Moravian	0.1
Other (independent, nondenominational and others)	38.2
Total	**100.0**

Source: Pew Forum analysis of World Christian Database. Historically pentecostal denominations include the Assemblies of God and the Church of God in Christ. Many members of the pentecostal movement belong to independent churches that are not part of historically pentecostal denominations. United churches are unions of several Protestant denominations. Examples include the Church of South India, the Church of North India and the United Church of Zambia. Figures may not add exactly due to rounding.

We can see from the chart above that no one Protestant tradition has anything near a majority. Lutherans, Presbyterians, and Baptists readily self-identify as Protestant, though some Anglicans do not. Many of the 38.2 percent listed above as "Other" self-consciously draw their structures and practices from sources independent of the historically organized churches. Many of those evangelical Christians who describe themselves as non-denominational also call themselves Protestants, but many other non-denominational churches do not, particularly those of a Pentecostal approach.

In the sixteenth through the eighteenth centuries, Western Christianity, both Catholic and Protestant, was thought of mainly as a Eurocentric religion. Global exploration and conquest, driven by political and economic motives, was accompanied by a large missionary expansion of Christianity to the Americas and Asia. In the nineteenth and early twentieth centuries, European colonization reached its heights. By 1878, Europe controlled two-thirds of the earth's land surface. The colonists brought not only Christianity but also various aspects of European culture. European colonization can boast of many great achievements in its history, but the cost in terms of human exploitation was enormous. In many places around the globe, Christianity still struggles to overcome the reputation left by its colonialist legacy and its continuing effects.

Today, Christianity is truly a global religion. About 31.5 percent of the world population is Christian.[6] A study published in 2013 shows that in 1970, 57 percent of the world's Christians lived in either Europe or North America. By 2020, that figure is projected to be 34 percent, with most of the shift in numbers being toward the global South, especially Africa and Latin America.[7] Asia is its own story, with a considerable number of Christians in the Southeast, especially the Philippines, but low percentages elsewhere.

About 50 percent of the world's Christians are Catholic; 37 percent are Protestant; 12 percent are Orthodox; and a little over 1 percent belong to churches that self-identify as Christian but, due to serious doctrinal differences, are often not recognized as Christian by the major denominations. These churches include Jehovah's Witnesses, the Church of Jesus Christ of Latter-Day Saints (Mormons), and Christian Science.[8]

Pentecostalism is a large worldwide Christian movement that grew out of the Holiness Movement in the United States. The Holiness Movement itself grew out of nineteenth-century Methodism. Methodists account for a small percentage of the world's Christians today, but they have had a large impact on contemporary Global Christianity. Their founding figure, John Wesley (1703–91), was an Anglican priest who intended the Methodist movement to remain a movement of renewal within the Anglican Church rather than become a church itself. However, after Wesley died, Methodism did become a church. Pentecostalism is a mainly independent movement that emphasizes the gifts of the Holy Spirit such as prophesying, speaking in tongues, and healing. Many Pentecostals interpret their movement as a fresh outpouring of the Holy Spirit rather than something historically allied with Protestantism. A movement related to Pentecostalism, but more associated with historical and mainline churches, is the Charismatic Renewal, which emerged in the 1960s and which also emphasizes the gifts of the Holy Spirit. Many members of the Charismatic Renewal are Catholics. If one adds together the number of Pentecostals and Charismatics in the world today, one arrives at a figure close to six hundred million.[9] That means that close to one quarter of all Christians in the world today are connected with these Spirit-emphasizing styles of belief and worship.

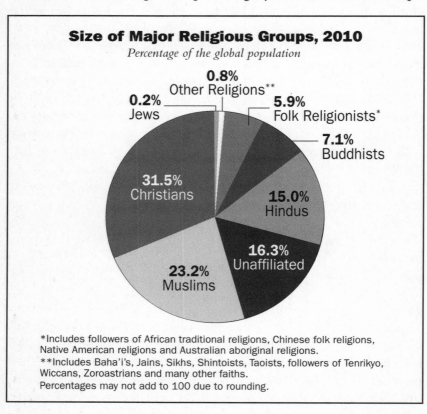

Size of Major Religious Groups, 2010
Percentage of the global population

0.8%
Other Religions**

0.2%
Jews

5.9%
Folk Religionists*

7.1%
Buddhists

31.5%
Christians

15.0%
Hindus

16.3%
Unaffiliated

23.2%
Muslims

*Includes followers of African traditional religions, Chinese folk religions, Native American religions and Australian aboriginal religions.
**Includes Baha'i's, Jains, Sikhs, Shintoists, Taoists, followers of Tenrikyo, Wiccans, Zoroastrians and many other faiths.
Percentages may not add to 100 due to rounding.

In addition to the 31.5 percent of the world population that is Christian, 23.2 percent are Muslim; 16.3 percent are religiously unaffiliated; 15 percent are Hindu; 7.1 percent are Buddhist; 5.9 percent practice traditional folk religions, and 0.8 percent belong to a variety of other faiths, such as the Baha'i faith, Jainism, Sikhism, Shintoism, Taoism, and Zoroastrianism.[10] Jews constitute 0.2 percent of the world population.

Christianity in a World of Many Religions

A young woman I know, Laura, once spoke of a course she took in college on world religions. Laura had been raised Catholic. She has come to think, however, that what religion one belongs to usually has more to do with what region of the world one was born in than any other factor. She wants to believe in a religion, but it is hard for her to believe that any one religion is the *right* one.[11]

Laura raises a fundamental religious question, which is whether Christians should think of Jesus as God for Christians only, or for Hindus and Muslims as well. If she really believes that Jesus is God, should she live in the hope that someday the entire world will be converted to Christianity? If she finds herself living in a world that she accepts as pluralistic and which she believes is ultimately healthy, does that mean that she must affirm that no one religion has all the final answers? If Laura is comfortable that Hindus remain Hindu and Muslims remain Muslim, does her comfort represent on some basic level an acknowledgment of the ultimate acceptability of their beliefs in a way that neutralizes the Catholic beliefs with which she grew up?

In order to consider such questions further, I will introduce four basic models or categories, representing different ways that Christians conceive of the relationship between Christianity and other world religions.[12] By considering these models, we may find out that Laura has more options open to her than she thought she had.

FOUR MODELS FOR RELATING CHRISTIANITY WITH OTHER WORLD RELIGIONS	
Exclusive	Christianity is true and other religions are false
Inclusive	Christianity offers the highest view; other religions are good but not the highest.
Mutuality	All religions offer good things; all are incomplete; no one religion is complete truth.
Coexistence	Christianity is the fullness of truth; no final judgments about other religions; open to dialogue with all.

Exclusive Model

This is the view that Christianity offers the only true revelation from God. All other religions are, at worst, absolutely false and, at best, misleading. Many Christians have held some form of this position, though the matter is historically a very complex one with many variations.[13] For centuries, the majority of Christian missionaries, Catholic and Protestant, have believed that those whom they have baptized and who have persevered in faith will go to heaven and that those who remain unbaptized will not be saved. The Catholic Tradition provides examples both of strong statements concerning the necessity of belonging to the Church in order to be saved and also subtle theological and pastoral loopholes that leave a door open to different interpretations.

I once heard an Evangelical preacher on the campus of a state college announce that Hindus were going to hell; Buddhists were going to hell; Jews were going to hell; and Muslims were going to hell. That man was an exclusivist in a most radical way.

Inclusive Model

This had been the favored position of mainline Protestants and Catholics over the last fifty years. It is the position that sees the great religious traditions of the world as good and even as basically revelatory, but which recognizes Jesus Christ as the highest and fullest expression of God's revelation. It was the position expressed by

Catholics at the Second Vatican Council (1962–65). Speaking specifically of Hinduism, Buddhism, and of other religions, the Council said,

> The Catholic Church rejects nothing that is true and holy in these religions. She regards with sincere reverence those ways of conduct and of life, those precepts and teachings which, though differing in many aspects from the ones she holds and sets forth, nonetheless often reflect a ray of that Truth which enlightens all men. Indeed, she proclaims, and ever must proclaim Christ "the way, the truth, and the life" (John 14:6), in whom men may find the fullness of religious life, in whom God has reconciled all things to Himself. (*Nostra Aetate* 2)

Read within its historical context, this 1965 statement represents a revolutionary shift from an official stance of exclusivism to an embrace of inclusivism, and it should be appreciated as such. Read within the context of the contemporary global community with its pluralistic pressures, one cannot help but notice the tension between a Christian "fullness" and other religions that "reflect a ray of that truth that enlightens all men." For Christians, the advantage of an inclusive model is that it allows one to embrace other religions as positive paths to God without sacrificing the ultimacy of Christ.

Mutuality Model

The mutuality model looks upon all major world religions as basically good but incomplete. All religions are thought to have available within them the presence of the Divine, or the absolute. No one religion has a corner on the market when it comes to the ultimate meaning of life. Religions are fundamentally equal when it comes to providing a helpful, comprehensive worldview.

Many academic approaches to religion employ a comparative method that builds upon the mutuality model. As a method, it is considered neutral. One uses categories such as scripture, beliefs, rituals, moral codes, and community structures to compare different religious traditions with one another. The mutuality model also seems to work well in the political realm in democratic societies. All religions are to be treated as equal.

Many Christians adopt the mutuality model in the academic and political realms but find it inadequate when it comes to faith and theology. When a mutuality model is adopted theologically as a faith position, the equal status automatically granted to all faith traditions becomes problematic. The mutuality model calls for a radical reconsideration of traditional religious understandings. Christians, for example, believe that God became a human being in the person of Jesus Christ, and that God remains present within Christian communities in the person of the Holy Spirit. Christians admit that a full comprehension of their faith is not possible in this life, but few would think that the lack of full comprehension makes Christian revelation anything less than fully true in itself.

Coexistence Model

The coexistence model represents a refusal to choose among the other models. The exclusive model has the obvious difficulty of being negative toward non-Christian religions. The inclusive model, though relatively more positive, can end up with the same difficulty. The mutuality model, from a Christian standpoint, has the difficulty of at least implying that Christ is not God in a way that is categorically above all others.

When it comes to Christ and Christianity, the coexistence model affirms an unsurpassable uniqueness. When it comes to other faith traditions, it insists that we cannot make final comparisons and judgments. There may even be a certain incommensurability between Christianity and other faith traditions; that is, it can be like comparing apples and oranges. Take Buddhism, for one of the easiest examples. Who is to say that Buddhism is ultimately a path either to God or to what Christians call salvation? Most Buddhists would feel quite uncomfortable with that terminology, not to mention the concepts. The same might be said in reverse. Is the Buddhist experience of Enlightenment something for which Christians are searching?

It is not hard to discern profound similarities among the great religious traditions of the world, yet the differences also remain great.

The inclusive and mutuality models have many assumptions that are difficult to account for. In recent years, the coexistence model has been growing in popularity. In my opinion, it is a necessary balancing act that holds in tension the two demands of being faithful to the core belief of the Christian Tradition and meeting the urgent need of the emerging global community for mutual respect and openness.

How can we get seemingly contradictory points to fit together? Most religious people believe that their faith tradition calls for nothing less than an ultimate commitment. Yet many of these same people believe that one must live with a respect for other people and their traditions that is infinitely deep and open-ended. In our complex world of today, many people find that they need to hold together points that might seem at first to be contradictory. The idea of "points held in tension" is a theme that will arise frequently in this textbook.

The next three chapters will focus on the topic of Scripture.

FOR FURTHER REFLECTION

1. What place do faith perspectives have in an academic course on religion?

2. How can it be that people of other faiths or who are non-religious can be fully included in a conversation focused on Christianity?

3. Are you surprised to find out that Christians constitute about one-third of the world population? What do you make of that?

4. Do you think that what most people believe depends more upon geographic location and their family of origin than on personal reflection and commitment?

5. Why might some people find it difficult to reconcile believing in a particular religion with living in a pluralistic society?

6. What are some of the advantages and disadvantages of using a "models" approach to address an issue such as the relationship among world religions?

7. For each of the four models, say briefly what you think would motivate an enthusiastic defender of that model to choose it.

8. Which model most appeals to you? Why?

9. Is the coexistence model a cop-out or does it display a willingness to live with a mystery beyond final human understanding? Or is it something else?

10. Can you think of an example from your own life in which you experienced "points held in tension"?

FOR FURTHER READING

Center for the Study of Global Christianity. *Christianity in Its Global Context, 1970–2020: Society, Religion, Mission*. South Hamilton, MA: Gordon-Conwell Theological Seminary, 2013.

Dupuis, Jacques. *Toward a Christian Theology of Religious Pluralism*. Maryknoll, NY: Orbis Books, 2001.

Knitter, Paul. *Introducing Theologies of Religion*. Maryknoll, NY: Orbis Books, 2002.

Pew Research Center. A Non-Partisan Fact Tank located in Washington, DC. http://www.pewresearch.org/.

Ratzinger, Joseph. *Truth and Tolerance: Christian Belief and World Religions*. San Francisco: Ignatius Press, 2005.

Second Vatican Council. *Nostra Aetate*. October 28, 1965. http://www.vatican.va/archive/hist_councils/ii_vatican_council/documents/vat-ii_decl_19651028_nostra-aetate_en.html.

Sullivan, Francis. *Salvation outside the Church? Tracing the History of the Catholic Response*. Mahwah, NJ: Paulist Press, 1992.

GLOSSARY

Academic study of religion: an interdisciplinary approach to the study of religion, not based in a particluar point of view in favor of any one religion.

Anglican: a worldwide communion of episcopal churches (based on apostolic succession through bishops) that has historical roots in the

Church of England. Anglicans strive to provide a middle way that is both "catholic" and "protestant."

Catholic: the Church that is led by Catholic bishops throughout the world with the pope as their head. Slightly over 50 percent of the world's Christians belong to the Catholic Church. The word *catholic* means "universal."

Christendom: a label for medieval Europe that stresses how society was held together by the Catholic Church.

Eastern Catholic churches: churches in countries dominated by Orthodox churches that maintain adherence to the pope in Rome.

Ecumenical: related to achieving deeper visible unity among the various Christian traditions.

Evangelical: a term initially used to distinguish Protestant churches—with their focus on the message of the Bible—from Catholic churches. Now used to label a large number of Protestant and Free Churches that are Bible-based.

Free churches: churches that stay clear of close connections with governmental bodies in contrast to the Catholic, Orthodox, and Protestant churches that have a history of being established churches.

Global South: a general term used to name those countries that lie to the south of more industrialized, developed neighbors; it stresses their material poverty yet richness of culture.

Methodist: churches that trace their origin to the movement associated with John Wesley. There are also Wesleyan churches.

Orthodox: ancient Christian churches rooted mainly in the Middle East and Eastern Europe, with traditions that both parallel and differ from those of Catholic churches. The word *orthodox* means "right-teaching."

Pentecostal: churches that belong to a quickly growing global movement that focuses on the gifts of the Holy Spirit.

Pluralism: describes a society in which many religions and world-views are present and active.

Presbyterian: a major branch of the churches that trace their origins to the theology of John Calvin.

Protestant: churches that trace their origins to the Protestant Reformation in Europe in the sixteenth century.

Roman Catholic: the largest of the churches that comprise the Catholic Church.

Theology: an interdisciplinary approach to the study of religion that presupposes a particular faith perspective; faith seeking understanding.

NOTES

1. Throughout this book, I will speak of the Catholic Church. Some Christians prefer that this use of the word *Catholic* always be modified by the word *Roman*. Many Anglicans, for example, call themselves "catholic." They resist allowing Roman Catholics to use the word *Catholic* in an unmodified sense, as if this important term only applies to them. On the other hand, there are also many Eastern Catholic churches that remain in full communion with Rome but who are not "Roman Catholic." Members of these churches resist having Roman Catholics refer always to the Roman Catholic Church when they mean to refer to the Catholic Church in a way that includes them also. I do not intend to offend anyone. In everyday ordinary language, people use the word *Catholic* to refer to the Catholic Church as led by the Catholic bishops and the pope. With some apologies, I will follow that usage.

2. I adapted this meditation exercise from Kevin Griffin, *One Breath at a Time: Buddhism and the Twelve Steps* (Emmaus, PA: Rodale, 2004), 28–29.

3. The interpenetration of the basic elements of Christianity is a common theological theme. I have been particularly influenced by the following authors and texts: Roberto S. Goizueta, *Caminemos con Jesús: Toward a Hispanic/Latino Theology of Accompaniment* (Maryknoll, NY: Orbis Books, 1995); Louis-Marie Chauvet, *The Sacraments: The Word of God at the Mercy of the Body*, trans. Madeleine Beaumont (Collegeville, MN: Liturgical Press, 2001 [French orig. 1997]); Pope Benedict XVI, *Deus Caritas Est*, http://w2.vatican.va/content/benedict-xvi/en/encyclicals/documents/hf_ben-xvi_enc_20051225_deus-caritas-est.html; David Matzko McCarthy and M. Therese Lysaught, *Gathered for the Journey: Moral Theology in Catholic Perspective* (Grand Rapids, MI: Eerdmans, 2007).

4. When the calendar based on the BC/AD chronology was constructed by Dionysius Exiguus in the sixth century, his intention was to make the birth of Jesus the beginning of the new era. His calendar was off by four years.

5. The Pew Research Center, "Global Christianity—A Report on the Size and Distribution of the World's Christian Population," Washington, DC (December 2011), http://www.pewforum.org/2011/12/19/global-christianity-exec/.

6. Pew Research Center, "The Global Catholic Population," Washington, DC (February 2013), http://www.pewforum.org/2013/02/13/the-global-catholic-population/.

7. Center for the Study of Global Christianity, *Christianity in Its Global Context, 1970–2020: Society, Religion, Mission* (South Hamilton, MA: Gordon Conwell Theological Seminary, 2013), 6. I derived these percentages from numbers listed in a chart in this publication.

8. Pew Research Center, "Global Christianity."

9. Ibid.

10. Pew Research Center, "The Global Religious Landscape," Washington, DC (December 2012), http://www.pewforum.org/2012/12/18/global-religious-landscape-exec/.

11. I tell more of Laura's story in "Young Catholics & Their Faith: Is Being 'Spiritual' Enough?" *Commonweal* 133, no. 15 (September 8, 2008): 11–15.

12. An excellent resource on this topic is Paul Knitter's *Introducing Theologies of Religions* (Maryknoll, NY: Orbis Books, 2002). My categories of exclusive, inclusive, mutuality, and coexistence correspond roughly with Knitter's categories of replacement, fulfillment, mutuality, and acceptance. Knitter explores these categories in much more detail and depth than space allows for here.

13. Francis Sullivan, *Salvation outside the Church? Tracing the History of the Catholic Response* (Mahwah, NJ: Paulist Press, 1992).

SECTION 1

SCRIPTURE

Chapter 2

THE BIBLE

The Christian Bible has two parts: an Old Testament and a New Testament. The Old Testament contains writings sacred to both Jews and Christians, whereas the New Testament is uniquely Christian. Both the Old Testament and the New Testament comprise many separate books. There are two senses in which the Bible can also be considered to be one book. First, it can be viewed as a collection, an official Christian anthology. Second, it can be regarded from the point of view of Christians who gradually, over the centuries, came to regard it and interpret it as one book. Taking both of these senses together, the Bible is a canon, an official collection of books received and accepted as having a special status for a particular community.

Many passages in the Old Testament are based on oral traditions before being written down. Nearly all of the books of the Old Testament were originally written in Hebrew, though parts of Daniel, Ezra, and one verse from Jeremiah were composed in Aramaic. The New Testament was originally written in Greek. Quantitatively, the Old Testament (Catholic and Orthodox versions) comprises a bit more than 71 percent of the Bible; the New Testament comprises a bit less than 29 percent. The authors of the New Testament, taken collectively, were familiar with most of the Old Testament books. They were deeply influenced by them, and they directly built upon them.

Christians believe that the Bible is the Word of God. It was written by many human authors over a period of many centuries. At the same time, though, in a deep sense, Christians believe it to be a book written by God "for the sake of our salvation" (*Dei Verbum* 11). It is a divinely inspired book that expresses God's revelation to human beings. Christians routinely call this book "The Holy Bible" or "The Holy Book." Christians do not think of the Bible as being simply a book like other books.

Still, as with so many elements crucial to Christianity, participants in various Christian traditions disagree about what it means to say that the Bible is the Word of God or that it is inspired. Some Christians, standing in reaction against modern challenges concerning the truth of the Bible, insist that it is literally the words of God, which is true in the plainest sense in which they can be read. Most Christians do not accept this literalist position, but there can be found a large spectrum of views among the majority. How to interpret the Bible will be a major focus in this chapter.

The Old Testament as Canon

The number of books contained in the Old Testament varies: The Eastern Orthodox version contains fifty books; the Catholic version forty-six; the Protestant version thirty-nine.[1] The actual writing of the Hebrew Scriptures took place from approximately 1000 BCE through the century before Christ.[2] In addition to a prehistory that stretches back to creation, it describes events that took place from about 1800 BCE until the Maccabean Revolt in 140 BCE and contains traces of oral histories that preceded the written accounts. A translation from Hebrew into Greek, done by Jewish scholars in Alexandria, Egypt, in the last couple of centuries before Christ, is known as the Septuagint. The Jewish canon, decided in the late first century CE, settled upon thirty-nine books, and is considerably shorter than the Septuagint. The Eastern Orthodox and Catholic versions are both based on the Septuagint and nearly the same; it is mainly the division and numbering of the books that differ.

Early Latin translations of the Old Testament included most of the books of the Septuagint. Many Church fathers of both the Greek and Latin worlds referred to a wide range of writings as sacred. When Jerome (c. 347–420) was commissioned by Pope Damasus to make a standard translation of the Bible in Latin (the Vulgate) at the end of the fourth century, he followed the Jewish canon and used original Hebrew sources for the Old Testament. Jerome did include many writings beyond the Jewish canon, but he identified them as such in prefaces he wrote for individual books. Many later editions of Jerome's translation did not include these prefaces. In practice, the range of books included in the Septuagint continued to be considered fully part of the Bible.

In the sixteenth century, the Protestant Reformers returned to the canon of the Jewish Bible, which they took to be more authentic. They labeled the additional writings found in Orthodox and Catholic versions the Apocrypha.[3] Most Protestant Bibles include the Apocrypha as an appendix, though there are also a number that exclude them entirely. At the Council of Trent (1545–63), the Catholic Church, in reaction to the Reformation, formally declared what Protestants call the Apocrypha to belong to the canon of scripture. Orthodox and Catholics have continued to include these writings within the body of the Old Testament but have been willing to acknowledge some distinction by referring to them as deuterocanonical, in contrast to those books that are protocanonical. Often today, this literature is called "intertestamental." This literature includes the Books of Judith, Tobit, the Wisdom of Solomon, Sirach, Baruch, and additions to the Books of Esther and Daniel (including the stories of Susanna and of Bel and the Dragon). The cultural impact of the Apocrypha in world art, literature, and music (especially hymnody) has been enormous.[4] Think of the number of people you have either known or heard of who are named Judith or Susanna.

New Testament authors, themselves writing in Greek, quoted most frequently from the thirty-nine books that would come to form the Jewish canon, and most of these quotes came from the Septuagint. In Matthew, for example, the Book of Isaiah is quoted: "Look, the virgin shall conceive and bear a son" (Matt 1:23; quote from Isa 7:14). The quote is from the Greek translation of Isaiah found in the Septuagint. In the original Hebrew, Isaiah refers not to a virgin but to a "young woman."

SOURCES AND VERSIONS OF THE OLD TESTAMENT		
Hebrew Scriptures	Sacred literature written in Hebrew; basic source of the Jewish Bible and various versions of the Old Testament	Written over a period of more than one thousand years in the centuries before Christ
Jewish Bible	39 books selected from the Hebrew Scriptures	Accepted as canon by some Jews near the end of the first century CE and by most Jews gradually over the next few centuries
Septuagint	Greek translation of Hebrew Scriptures that provides the basis of the Catholic and Orthodox versions of the Old Testament	Translation done by Jewish scholars in Alexandria, Egypt, completed in the first century BCE
Old Testament—Orthodox version	Contains the books found in the Jewish Bible plus other scriptures known as deuterocanonical	50 books based on the contents of the Septuagint
Old Testament—Catholic version	Also contains the books found in the Jewish Bible plus other Hebrew scriptures known as deuterocanonical	46 books based on the contents of the Septuagint; differs from the Orthodox version mainly in how books are divided
Old Testament—Protestant version	39 books; a return to the Jewish canon; begun by Martin Luther in 1525	Additional writings included in most versions but labeled "Apocrypha"

The books of the Jewish Bible are arranged in an order that differs significantly from the way in which Christians arrange the books of the Old Testament. First comes the Law (the Torah, the first five books, which were traditionally attributed to Moses). Then come the Prophets (though these include the Historical Books in the Christian Old Testament). Finally come the Writings (which are classified in the Old Testament as "Wisdom Literature"). In this arrangement, the last book of the Jewish Bible is 2 Chronicles. The final passages recount the time that the Babylonians destroyed the Temple in Jerusalem and then held the Jewish leaders in captivity (sixth century BCE). After nearly seven decades of exile in Babylon, the Jews are set free when Cyrus, the Persian king, conquers the Babylonians (539 BCE). The last lines tell of Cyrus's decree that the Jews are to return to Jerusalem to rebuild the Temple. Concluding at this point marks an appropriate end to the Jewish Bible.

The Christian versions of the Old Testament, with some differences among themselves, follow the arrangement of the Septuagint. Rather than the Law, the Prophets, and the Writings, they order the books as the Law (followed by the Historical Books), the Wisdom literature, and the Prophets. This arrangement is thought to reflect a grouping according to the past, present, and future, with the Prophets anticipating the coming of Jesus and the kingdom of God. Insofar as Christians have historically read the Old Testament in reference to and in anticipation of the New Testament, such a grouping of the books of the Bible may be considered an appropriate arrangement for any Christian reader.[5]

The New Testament as Canon

The New Testament contains twenty-seven books. Except for Paul, who wrote a number of the letters attributed to him, the actual names of the authors of the New Testament are not known with certainty. There are four Gospels, known as Matthew, Mark, Luke, and John. These are followed by an account of the early spread of Christianity, known as the Acts of the Apostles, written by the person who authored Luke. Then come twenty-one letters, fourteen of which have traditionally been attributed to Paul, two to Peter, three to John, and one each to James and Jude. The New Testament concludes with Revelation, attributed to John, which offers highly symbolic accounts of the end of time.

The writings of the New Testament contain references to oral and written sources, some of which date back to the time of Christ.

The books as they now appear were composed between about 52 CE and 100 CE. These writings contain two highly symbolic narratives of the birth of Jesus (about 4 BCE), but they focus mainly on Jesus' public ministry (c. 26–29 CE) and on the spread of Christianity until the martyrdoms of Peter and Paul in Rome (c. 67 CE). The Synoptic Gospels (Matthew, Mark, and Luke), when studied closely, yield some information about Christianity in the 80s and 90s. The Gospel of John and the letters of John can be mined for information about Christianity through the end of the first century.

The Hebrew Scriptures continued to function as sacred writings for Christians. The followers of Jesus proclaimed the Christian message for a long time before there emerged anything that could be called the New Testament. The oral and written sources that would be gathered into the New Testament were gradually treated as holy. They were proclaimed in liturgical settings, but their use was localized and varied. By the middle of the second century, the Gospels of Matthew and of John were used as liturgical texts alongside Old Testament texts in some Christian churches.

One of the driving factors in determining what would become the New Testament canon was the need to distinguish between authentic writings and those that promoted heretical beliefs. During the second half of the second century, there were pronounced conflicts between Christians who united under the leadership of bishops as catholic and orthodox and other groups, whom these Christians labeled "Gnostics" and considered to be heretical. The Gnostics were quite varied in their beliefs and practices, but many of them were described by Christian authors as spiritual elitists who claimed to possess a secret knowledge of the true meaning of the sacred writings. They believed in elaborate mythologies by which the material world was created by dark forces lesser than God and by which the human quest was to release the pure spirit within the human from the material realm. Many of the Gnostics claimed belief in Christ without accepting the Incarnation, thinking that God would not take on something so corrupt as a human body. In some cases, such as the writings attributed to John, there was a thin line to tread, since the Johannine writings reveal some Gnostic tendencies of their own, primarily in the way that they contrast the world and its darkness with the light that comes through Christ. In spite of such tendencies, however, the Johannine writings unequivocally affirm that God is the creator of all that exists and that, in Christ, the Word became flesh.

Persecutions of Christians in the late third and early fourth centuries provided another important motivation for Christians to clarify which writings would belong to a canon. Many of the Christians who were executed during these persecutions were those who refused to hand over the sacred writings to Roman authorities who would desecrate them.[6] Persecutions ended when, in 313, the Emperor Constantine (c. 272–337) issued the Edict of Milan, granting religious tolerance to Christianity and other religions. Constantine later ordered that Eusebius of Caesarea (c. 260–before 341) produce fifty copies of the Christian Scriptures, which he did from 334 to 346. Although there are no extant copies, similar collections from mid-century probably reflect the same ordering of books, which is very similar to that of the present-day New Testament. An extra book, the Epistle of Barnabas, was included, while 1–2 Titus, Timothy, Philemon, and Revelation were missing. The evidence is that in the time of Constantine, there was already widespread, though not perfectly uniform, agreement among Christians as to the makeup of the New Testament. A local church council in Laodicea (360–63) approved a list of books. In 367, Athanasius of Alexandria (c. 296–373) listed in a letter the twenty-seven books that are accepted today. The same list was approved by local councils in Hippo (393) and in Carthage (397).[7] By the first decade of the fifth century, the New Testament as known today was accepted throughout the Latin West and the Greek-speaking East.

Translations

In the early Christian centuries, various Christians spoke various languages, but most lived in areas where the official public language was either Greek or Latin. The New Testament was written in Greek. By the second half of the fourth century, Latin translations of all of the books of the New Testament were available, but they were of relatively poor quality. Jerome was mentioned above for his translation of the Old Testament, done mainly from original Hebrew sources. For the New Testament, Jerome translated the Gospels by revising an old Latin version with reference to the earliest Greek manuscripts. Most of the rest of the New Testament was done as a revision of the old Latin by translators other than Jerome. Jerome is the main, but not the sole, author of the Vulgate, which became the standard Latin version of the Bible up until recent centuries. The Vulgate is written in simple, beautiful Latin, though its accuracy as a translation does not meet modern standards.

Until the sixteenth century, virtually every educated person who read the Bible did so either in Greek or in Latin. Renaissance scholars, above all Erasmus (1466–1536), produced highly improved versions of both the Greek and the Latin texts. With the invention of the printing press (credited to Johannes Gutenberg in Germany in 1450, though earlier versions were known in China and in Korea) and the consequent rise in literacy came various translations of the Bible into vernacular languages. Popular translations of the Bible were also associated with movements of Church reform, because the medieval Church of great cathedrals, privileged clergy, high masses, pilgrimages, relics, devotions to the saints, processions, and purgatory did not appear to match up well with the plain sense of Scripture.

Martin Luther (1483–1546) published the first German translation of the New Testament in 1522, completing the Old Testament in 1534. Luther's Bible was so powerfully written that it had a major impact on the development of modern German.

Many of Luther's translations were criticized by defenders of the Catholic Church who judged that, on controversial points, he was more interested in promoting his views than in accuracy and precision. For example, for Romans 3:26 the Vulgate has "*Arbitramur hominem justificari ex fide absque operibus.*" A strict transliteration into English reads, "We hold humans to be justified by faith and apart from works." A transliteration of Luther's text into English reads, "We hold that human beings are justified without the works of the law **alone** through faith."[8] Luther had added the word "alone." This addition appeared suspicious to Luther's critics, however, because one of Luther's anti-Catholic slogans was that Christians are saved "by faith alone" in contrast to the Church's emphasis on the need for both faith and good works together. Luther claimed that German idiom and usage demanded that the word "alone" be used in order to clarify the exact meaning of the text. It should be clarified here that Luther taught that good works are extremely important, but that they should not be mixed in conceptually with the justification that comes through Christ as a free gift. Luther wanted to avoid any implication that Christians earn and merit their salvation. In German-speaking countries today, both Protestants and Catholics use a contemporary ecumenical version of the Bible that remains heavily influenced by Luther's language.

William Tyndale (1494–1536) obtained a copy of Luther's New Testament in 1522 and began his own translation into English based on the original Hebrew and Greek sources. His work was denounced and burned as containing "untrue translations." To defenders of the Catholic Church of his time, Tyndale's translation was interpreted as being anticlerical and anti-organized church. What a Catholic would read in the Vulgate as the word *church* (*ecclesia*), Tyndale translated from the Greek (ἐκκλησία) as "congregation." Tyndale was part of a movement that was claiming that the true Church is invisible, not the visible Catholic Church. What a Catholic would read as the phrase "do penance" (*paenitemini*), Tyndale translated from the Greek (μετανοεῖτε) as "repent." Tyndale's translation thus challenged the Catholic practice of reserving official forgiveness to the sacrament of penance. Tyndale's Bible served as a foundation for several English translations to follow. Tyndale became an enemy of Henry VIII, the head of the Church of England, for opposing the annulment of the king's first marriage on the grounds that divorce was unscriptural. Reportedly, at the instigation of Henry, Tyndale was strangled and then burned at the stake in October 1536 on the charge of being a heretic.[9]

Catholics published an English version of the New Testament in 1582, followed by a two-volume version of the Old Testament in English in 1609–10. This Douay-Rheims Bible was translated from the Vulgate and used word choices that supported Catholic doctrine. Its vocabulary was Latinate and difficult to read. It was thoroughly revised in the mid-eighteenth century, continued to serve as the official Catholic translation past the mid-twentieth century, and is still in use today among a small number of Catholics.

The King James Version of the Bible (KJV) was commissioned by James I in 1604 and published in 1611. Like the works of Shakespeare, it is considered a literary masterpiece and had a major impact on the development of modern English. The rhythms of the prose of the KJV flow throughout the English literature produced over the past four hundred years. Some Protestants still use the KJV today. There is also in use an updated version that drops the *Thee*'s, *Thou*'s, and *Whosoever*'s. For most Bible readers, however, the KJV itself, whether in its original or updated version, is no longer used because it lacks the accuracy of modern translations. Serious students of English literature, however, would do well to be familiar with this work.

Today, there exist many critical editions of the Bible translated into every major language in the world. The BibleGateway website (www.biblegateway.com) gives readers direct access to original Hebrew and Greek versions, fifty different English translations, and a large number of translations in other languages. In this text, we use the New Revised Standard Version (NRSV).

A Fourfold Method of Interpretation: Literal, Analogical, Moral, Anagogical

All written texts are subject to interpretation by their readers. Many of the great texts of world literature are highly symbolic in the modes of thinking that they express. What might appear on the surface to be contradictory or impossible to a later generation calls for an interpretation that goes beyond the surface.

Allegorical interpretation, which offers an alternative to a surface, or literal, interpretation, is a common way of trying to get at a meaning that goes beyond the surface. An allegory is a story that uses symbolic characters representing ideal principles or virtues to tell a moral tale. An allegorical play, for example, might have characters named Envy, Anger, Sloth, Justice, Prudence, and Temperance.

Some passages in the Old Testament already contain an allegorical interpretation of other passages written earlier.[10] For example, in Genesis 32:22–32, Jacob wrestles all night with a man who knocks his hip out of joint and then renames him Israel. In a literal interpretation, that man turns out to be God. Later generations, however, could not be content with a story that suggests that Jacob actually wrestled with a man who turns out to be God. Hosea 12:3–5 allegorizes the story by stating that Jacob wrestled with an angel. Wrestling with an angel comes to be understood as a symbol for wrestling with God.

Philo of Alexandria (c. 20 BCE–50 CE), who lived during the time of Jesus, is the best known among Jewish scholars who interpreted the Hebrew Scriptures in an allegorical manner. Philo thought that the true meanings of "heaven" and "earth" in the Genesis Creation stories refer to the mind and the senses. Likewise, "Adam" symbolizes the human mind and "Eve" the sense perception. The "Garden" is divine virtue, and the "fall" is from virtue. The work of Philo, a devout Jew, was mostly rejected by the rabbinic tradition as being more influenced by Platonism and other contemporary modes of thought than by Jewish tradition. His thoughts about God and his methods of interpretation had a significant impact, however, upon early Christian thinkers.

The authors of the New Testament interpreted the Hebrew Scriptures as prophetic literature that found its fulfillment in Christ and the Church. Paul interpreted Jesus as the savior who set right what had been lost through the fall, writing, "For just as by the one man's disobedience the many were made sinners, so by the one man's obedience the many will be made righteous" (Rom 5:19). Luke depicts Jesus as interpreting himself as fulfilling the prophecies in Isaiah concerning one who will come to bring good news to the poor and set the oppressed free (Isa 61:1–2; 58:6; Luke 4:16–21). Mark portrays Jesus as interpreting himself as the one about whom Daniel prophesied would return as a judge at the end of time (Dan 7:13–14; Mark 13:26–27).

In the Gospel of John, Abraham's willingness to sacrifice his son, Isaac, symbolizes God's actual sacrifice of his own Son, Jesus. Jesus carries his cross in the way that Isaac carried the wood for his own sacrifice (John 19:17). John the Baptist depicts Jesus as the Lamb that is sacrificed in the place of Isaac by saying, "Here is the Lamb of God who takes away the sin of the world!" (John 1:29).[11] There are literally hundreds of examples of passages in the New Testament that either build directly upon or allude to passages in the Old Testament.

FOURFOLD METHOD OF INTERPRETING CHRISTIAN SCRIPTURE		
Literal	What the words mean in their plainest sense	The basic story line
Allegorical	What the words symbolize in a philosophical, psychological, or spiritual sense	How all things lead to Christ
	What words, persons, things, or events typify, especially the prefiguring of the New Testament in the Old Testament	
Moral (or Tropological)	What words, persons, things, or events symbolize in regard to virtue	How Christians should live
Anagogical (or Eschatological)	What words, persons, things, or events symbolize in regard to the future	What Christians can look forward to

The early Church fathers developed a fourfold method of Scripture interpretation in close harmony with the way in which the New Testament was composed. The four levels of interpretation are literal, allegorical, moral, and anagogical. This fourfold method continued to be used and developed through the Middle Ages and well beyond. The literal meaning of Scripture is what a passage appears to say on the surface, which is often puzzling. Did God actually move about in the Garden with Adam and Eve? Since God is Spirit, such could not be so in the most literal of senses. Such language must be figurative. Yes, in some sense, God moved about in the Garden with Adam and Eve, but one cannot take the passage too literally. Early interpreters did believe that the literal level of Scripture was true, but they also accepted that the actual meaning of the literal level was often very mysterious.

Beyond the literal level, the Church fathers were aware of an allegorical meaning of Scripture. They were less inclined than Philo to use an allegorical method that was philosophical or even psychological. Their most common form of allegorical interpretation was typological. The Church fathers interpreted persons, things, and events in the Old Testament as representing symbolic types of things that would be fulfilled in the New Testament. And so for the Church fathers, the three angels that visit Abraham symbolize the Trinity. Noah's Ark symbolizes the Church. Again, the examples run into the hundreds.

The fourfold method of interpreting the Scriptures included also a moral level of meaning and an anagogical level of meaning. The moral, or tropological, level was seen already in Philo when he interpreted various elements of the Garden of Eden and of the story of the fall as expressing the truth about divine and human virtue. The anagogical, or eschatological, level of meaning refers to truth about the end of times or eternity.

Scripture scholar James L. Kugel says that few images in the Old Testament easily fit into all four levels of interpretation, but he offers the example of the city of Jerusalem as one that conveniently does.[12] On a literal level, Jerusalem is an actual city that one can still find on a map or even visit today. On an allegorical level, Christian commentators have interpreted the idea of dwelling in the city of Jerusalem as symbolizing belonging to the Church. On a moral level, some Christian interpreters have taken the city of Jerusalem to represent the individual's soul in its ideal state, a spiritual condition toward which each person should strive. Finally, on an anagogical level, the city of Jerusalem has been interpreted as the eternal city of God to be revealed at the end of time.

Academic Approaches to Biblical Studies

With the rise of modern methods of scholarship have come modern methods for studying the Bible. Especially over the past two centuries, biblical scholars have been developing methods of studying Scripture that draw together tools from history, archaeology, comparative cultural studies, linguistic analysis, and many other disciplines. This approach is called the "historical-critical method." The various tools that make up the historical-critical method have been labeled as types of criticism, not in a negative sense but in the sense that they strive for a critical distance not tied to the presuppositions of a particular faith community. Most biblical scholars use the historical-critical method to study each book of the Bible as a separate work in its own context, and even find that individual books have their own complex history of composition, with many stages of editing stretching in some cases over centuries. The results of biblical scholarship are often controversial and highly debated, perhaps especially among biblical scholars themselves. Even matters that are considered mostly settled often stand upon a majority consensus that retains elements of speculation.

Source criticism attempts to uncover various layers of authorship and editing that underlie a particular text. A source, in this context, could refer to one person or to a number of persons. Scholars examine consistencies and inconsistencies in elements such as vocabulary, factual claims, and style in order to distinguish the writing of one source from another. Most educated speakers of English, for example, could easily distinguish between samples of Old English, Elizabethan English, and contemporary English. Most could distinguish between passages representing British and American English, and some can identify Boston English in contrast with Chicago English.

In the first five books of the Old Testament, known as the Torah or Pentateuch, scholars have identified an early Yahwist or "J" (from the German *Jahwist*) source who probably wrote around 900 BCE. There are various sources that wrote and edited over the next several centuries. Throughout most of the twentieth century, biblical scholars would speak confidently about an Elohist or "E" source, and a Deuteronomist or "D" source, but more recently, the matter appears to be more complicated. Most scholars still agree about a Priestly or "P" source that made significant additions and edits to the Pentateuch around the time of the Exile (587–538 BCE) or soon after.

Form criticism focuses on identifying the many genera of literature found in the Bible in connection with the function of these types of expression within particular communities. They find a mixture of myth, history, rituals, poetry, aphorisms, letters, and many other forms. Scholars have identified Galatians 3:28 as likely part of an early baptismal rite: "There is no longer Jew or Greek, there is no longer slave or free, there is no longer male and female; for all of you are one in Christ Jesus." The line in Galatians that precedes this one refers to baptism: "As many of you as were baptized into Christ have clothed yourselves with Christ." Similar words in 1 Corinthians 12:13 include the word *baptized*: "For in the one Spirit we were all baptized into one body—Jews or Greeks, slaves or free—and we were all made to drink of one Spirit." The use of similar wording in Romans 10:12 and Colossians 3:11 indicates that Paul is drawing upon a familiar formula. For many readers, the link with an early baptismal formula enhances the theological meaning and importance of Galatians 3:28.

Redaction criticism highlights the particular theological emphases indicated by the patterns of choices made by those authors and editors who put a text into its final form. To redact means to revise or edit. The Gospel of Luke and the Gospel of Matthew both draw upon the Gospel of Mark as one of their major sources. Often, lines taken from Mark appear in those Gospels with changes that indicate a consistent pattern in each author. Take, for example, the passages in each Gospel that first mention John the Baptist and the baptism of Jesus (Mark 1:2–11; Matt 3:1–17; Luke 3:1–22). Matthew adds a polemic against the Pharisees and the Sadducees not found in either Mark or Luke. This passage is consistent with Matthew's frequent insistence that it is Jesus, not the Pharisees or Sadducees, who provides the correct interpretation of the Torah. Luke adds words implying that Jesus' vision of the dove descending and his hearing of a voice from heaven saying, "This is my beloved Son" were publically observable events. In Mark and Matthew, they could easily be interpreted as referring to a personal experience of Jesus. This is consistent with Luke's frequent attention given to the physical and bodily aspects of events.

Literary criticism can be found in various forms, such as textual, reader response, and rhetorical. **Textual criticism** aims at establishing the most authentic text from a number of variants. For example, most scholars agree that the original Gospel of Mark ended at verse 16:8 and did not contain any stories of appearances of Jesus after he had died. The verses that appear in Mark's present form after 16:8 are stories that were added to later editions of the text. **Reader response criticism** focuses on reading scriptures with an emphasis on how the passages in the Bible are structured to have a particular impact on the audience. Some reader response critics have argued that it is appropriate that the original text of Mark ends at 16:8 with the story of the empty tomb. They find in the empty tomb story a fitting climax to the thematic development and literary structure of the Gospel as it had unfolded up to that point. The ending leaves each reader in a position of needing to respond to the reality of finding the tomb to be empty. **Rhetorical criticism** focuses on how language can carry a range of meanings, moods, and tones in various cultural situations. We may be familiar with the title Messiah, having often heard Jesus referred to as the Messiah. A contemporary reader might think Messiah refers directly to Jesus' divinity as the Son of God, but for Matthew's Jewish readers, Messiah was more immediately understood in *political* or *revolutionary* terms, meaning that Jesus was the long awaited one who would liberate them from political oppression.

Canonical criticism is radically distinct from other types of biblical study. Some biblical scholars see it as belonging to an entirely different subfield because it does not bracket out theology, that is, the perspective of particular faith communities. On the contrary, canonical criticism brings together historical-critical tools with an explicitly theological perspective. Scholars using canonical criticism read the books of the Bible not only individually, but also as a part of the entire canon of the Bible as well as within the long traditions of biblical interpretation throughout the history of Christianity. It is true that from a purely historical point of view, the Bible cannot be read simply as if it were one book with one author. From a theological point of view, though, the Bible can be read within the context of faith communities that have received and interpreted it over the course of centuries as a book that expresses the Word of God for the sake of our salvation.

The Bible as Interpreted within Living Faith Communities

All written sources take on their actual meaning within a context of interpretation. The Bible is no exception but rather provides perhaps the greatest example of this principle. In the first chapter, we explained that the Bible, Tradition, Sacraments, and Christian Living constitute four elements of Christianity that need to be understood in relation to each other. Already in this second chapter, there has been an undertow of how the Bible cannot be understood apart from Tradition, Sacraments/Liturgy, and Christian Life.

The Bible needs to be understood within the context of Tradition. The Christian story that the Bible tells could not easily be derived directly from the text, apart from the faith communities that have interpreted it through the centuries. If someone on a desert island who had never heard of Christianity were given a Bible in their own language and studied it from cover to cover, they would probably not come very close to grasping any of the familiar contemporary versions of the Christian message. A reader needs to bring with them a set of presuppositions that would provide something of a lens for finding such a coherent meaning. These presuppositions consist in the lived experience and history of Christians as expressed in various verbal and nonverbal ways and passed down through the generations as Tradition.

The Bible also needs to be understood within the context of Liturgy. For most Christians throughout most of history, the most usual way to encounter the scriptures was to hear them proclaimed within the context of prayer and Sacraments. Much Christian education has been connected with reflection on the meaning of Scripture in preparation for the reception of Sacraments. Biblical passages take on particular meanings when grouped together with other passages and then heard and reflected upon in a context intended to facilitate Christian formation.

The Bible needs, moreover, to be understood within the context of Christian Life. There were Christians living out the message of the Bible before there existed anything like the New Testament as we

37

know it today. Christian Life and proclamation informed the very writing of the New Testament as its various works gradually, over centuries, were gathered into the canon (approved collection) that exists today. For Christians today, there is a back and forth, mutually informing relationship between their lived experience of faith and their interpretation of the Bible.

FOR FURTHER REFLECTION

1. Christians say that the Bible is the Word of God, but they can mean different things by that phrase. Explain at least two different meanings.

2. Briefly name and explain the four levels of meaning found in the Bible by early and medieval Christians.

3. Name and briefly explain any three types of the historical-critical method for studying the Bible.

4. Being as generous as possible, explain what someone might be trying to say with these words: "We don't interpret the Bible. We just read it for what it says."

5. What does it mean to say that the Bible takes on its meaning as it is interpreted within the context of faith communities?

6. Why has the academic study of the Bible posed challenges to traditional understandings?

FOR FURTHER READING

Coogan, Michael David. *The Old Testament: A Very Short Introduction.* New York: Oxford University Press, 2008.

Hayes, Christine Elizabeth. *Introduction to the Bible.* New Haven: Yale University Press, 2012.

Hoppe, Leslie J. *Priests, Prophets, and Sages: Catholic Perspectives on the Old Testament.* Cincinnati, OH: St. Anthony Messenger Press, 2006.

Kugel, James L. *How to Read the Bible: A Guide to Scripture, Then and Now.* New York: Free Press, 2007.

McDonald, Lee Martin. *Formation of the Bible: The Story of the Church's Canon*. Peabody, MA: Hendrickson Publishers Marketing, 2012.

GLOSSARY

Allegorical: a type of biblical interpretation in which characters or events referred to on the literal level of a text are taken to be symbolic of meanings on a figurative level.

Anagogical, or Eschatological: a type of biblical interpretation in which characters or events referred to on the literal level of a text are taken to be symbolic of future events or realities.

Apocrypha: writings included in the Orthodox and Catholic versions of the Old Testament and which are usually included in Protestant versions as an appendix; also known as deuterocanonical or intertestamental literature.

Canonical criticism: an approach to interpreting the Bible that reads each book as a part of the entire canon of the Bible as well as within the long traditions of biblical interpretation throughout the history of Christianity, thus including explicitly theological perspectives.

Douay-Rheims Bible: an English translation of the Bible done from the Vulgate (OT 1609–10; NT 1582) that served as the official Catholic English version up through the mid-twentieth century.

Fourfold method: an approach to interpreting the Bible used by early and medieval Christians to include literal, allegorical, moral, and anagogical levels of meaning.

Historical-Critical method: an approach to interpreting the Bible that attempts a scientific or historical point of view detached from the presuppositions of any particular faith tradition. It exists in various forms of criticism such as Form Criticism, Redaction Criticism, and the like.

Johannine: belonging to those New Testament writings that had traditionally been attributed collectively to John.

SCRIPTURE

King James Bible: the official Protestant English translation of the Bible from 1610 until modern times, still admired for its literary qualities.

Literal: the most basic or plain sense of what is expressed in a biblical text.

Moral, or Tropological: a type of biblical interpretation in which characters or events referred to on the literal level of a text are taken to be symbolic of moral principles or virtues.

Septuagint: a translation from Hebrew into Greek done by Jewish scholars in Alexandria, Egypt, in the last couple of centuries before Christ.

Typological: a form of allegorical interpretation that focuses on how a character or event in an earlier text can prefigure something in a later text; an approach often used by Christians when interpreting characters or events in the Old testament as prefiguring Christ.

Vulgate: a Latin translation of the Bible completed by Jerome and others in the late fourth century CE.

NOTES

1. Charts that outline the various versions of the Hebrew Scriptures and the Old Testament are readily available online. A reliable one can be found at http://catholic-resources.org/Bible/Heb-Xn-Bibles.htm.

2. To be precise, not all of the Hebrew Scriptures are in the Catholic Old Testament; also, some of the deuterocanonical books were written in Greek.

3. The term *Apocrypha* refers here to the additional books included in the Catholic and Orthodox canons. Sometimes, however, the term is used to refer to a much wider body of literature, related to the biblical texts in some way but not included in anyone's canon.

4. For a discussion of the influence of the Apocrypha in English-speaking lands, see "Introduction to the Apocrypha," in *The New Oxford Annotated Bible with the Apocrypha*, Revised Standard Version, ed. Herbert G. May and Bruce M. Metzger (New York: Oxford University Press, 1973), xviii–xx.

5. The Book of Malachi was put last in the Old Testament because of an apparent reference to John the Baptist in its closing lines.

6. The English word *traitor* is derived from the Latin word *traditor*, which literally means one who "hands over" a sacred scroll or text.

7. Material in this paragraph is drawn from Lee Martin McDonald, *Formation of the Bible: The Story of the Church's Canon* (Peabody, MA: Hendrickson Publishers Marketing, 2012), 88–100.

8. "Wir halte das der mensch gerecht werde on des gesetzs werk allein durch den glauben." Martin Luther, "An Open Letter on Translating," translated from "Ein sendbrief D. M. Luthers. Von Dolmetzschen und Fürbit der heiligenn," in *Dr. Martin Luthers Werke* (Weimar: Hermann Boehlaus Nachfolger, 1909), Band 30, Teil II, 632–46, by Gary Mann and revised and annotated by Michael D. Marlowe, June 2003, http://www.bible-researcher.com/luther01.html. The contemporary version of the Luther Bible reads, "So halten wir nun dafür, daß der Mensch gerecht werde ohne des Gesetzes Werke, allein durch den Glauben."

9. See "Tyndale Bible," Wikipedia.com, http://en.wikipedia.org/wiki/Tyndale_Bible.

10. "Allegory in the Old Testament," Jewishencyclopedia.com, http://www.jewishencyclopedia.com/articles/1256-allegorical-interpretation.

11. These examples are used by James L. Kugel in *How to Read the Bible: A Guide to Scripture, Then and Now* (New York: Free Press, 2007), 20.

12. Ibid., 23.

Chapter 3

THE HEBREW SCRIPTURES

The previous chapter examined traditional and modern methods for studying the Bible. It then emphasized that the Bible needs to be understood within the context of Tradition, Liturgy, and the Christian Life. The present chapter, after clarifying some terminology, will focus on selected passages from the Hebrew Scriptures in relation to modern methods, Tradition, Liturgy, and Christian Life.

The Old Testament is divided into the five books of the Pentateuch, the Historical Books, the Wisdom Writings, and the Prophetic Books. The Pentateuch begins with the story of creation and the fall of humankind. It narrates a blend of myth and history, beginning with Adam and Eve, and then telling the stories of Cain and Abel; Noah and the Flood; Abraham, Sarah, and Hagar, as well as Isaac, Jacob, and Ishmael; Joseph and the exile to Egypt; Moses and the Exodus from Egypt; and then up to the wandering in the desert for forty years. The Pentateuch contains many famous stories such as the Tower of Babel, Abraham's willingness to sacrifice his son (Isaac), the prophetic dreams of Joseph, the plagues, the parting of the Red Sea, and the giving of the Ten Commandments. Much of the Pentateuch is devoted to explaining the many laws that God gave to the Israelites. The Pentateuch ends with the death of Moses after he led the Israelites to the brink of the promised land of Canaan.

The Historical Books begin with the conquest of Canaan and the establishment of Israel as a kingdom and carrying on through and beyond the time of exile in Babylon (586–538 BCE). They contain stories of Saul, David, Solomon, and many other historic figures, including women such as Esther and Ruth. The Wisdom Writings, such as Psalms, Proverbs, and Job, have connections with the history of Israel but tend more toward expressing universal wisdom that any human being can relate to directly. The Prophetic Books parallel the time period covered by the Historical Books as they express the prophets' visionary pronouncements and religious and social criticism.

Hebrew Scriptures, the Jewish Bible, and the Old Testament

The Hebrew Scriptures provide the material for both the Jewish Bible and the Old Testament. The Jewish Bible and the Protestant Old Testament contain exactly the same books, but the books are arranged differently. The Catholic and Orthodox Bibles, which are very close but not identical in material and arrangement, include additional writings that most Protestant Bibles place in an appendix they label the Apocrypha. These writings are also known as deuterocanonical and intertestamental. They had functioned as sacred writings for the Jews, but had not been in the final canon of the Jewish Bible.

For most practical purposes today, the Jewish Bible and the Old Testament are basically the same book. As mentioned in chapter 2, the fact that the Jewish Bible and the various versions of the Old Testament differ in arrangement has some significance in that the Jewish Bible ends with a reiteration of the task of rebuilding the Temple in Jerusalem, whereas the Old Testament ends with the Prophetic Books that look forward to important events in the future. What most differentiates the Jewish Bible from the Old Testament, however, are the various ways in which these canons have been interpreted. The Jewish Bible is about the history and faith of the ancient Jews and their relationship with God. Christians have traditionally interpreted the Old Testament as being not only about the history of the Jews, but also, on other levels, about the preparation for and the foreshadowing of the coming of Christ. The Old Testament as interpreted within is a crucial element of Christian faith.

How we label these sacred writings is important. For many centuries, most Christians regarded Judaism to be the religion of the Old Testament, something outdated and surpassed. Although this view remains entrenched in many corners of the Christian world, in its most basic form, it is no longer acceptable to most educated Christians, who reject it as inadequate, inaccurate, and offensive for many reasons. Most Christians today acknowledge that God does not take back the original covenant made with Israel but remains faithful to it. Judaism did not stop developing, as some Christians might think, with the coming of Christ.

Jacob Neusner, a Jewish scholar who is a prolific author, expresses this point eloquently:

> While the world at large treats Judaism as "the religion of the Old Testament," the fact is otherwise. Judaism inherits and makes the Hebrew Scriptures its own, just as does Christianity. And just as Christianity rereads the entire history of ancient Israel in the light of "the resurrection of Jesus Christ," so Judaism understands the Hebrew scriptures as only one part, the written one, of "the whole Torah of Moses, our rabbi."[1]

The various forms of Judaism today find significant roots not only in the Hebrew Scriptures, but also in later sacred texts. Throughout the last two millennia, Jews have amassed an extensive literature of commentaries and reflections such as the Mishnah, the Talmud, and the Midrash, as well as other religious and intellectual writings in medieval and in modern times, just as does Christianity.

Judaism exists today as a vibrant faith tradition that has developed in many ways since the first century CE. At that time, what had been a religion of patriarchs, priests, prophets, and kings transformed into a religion of rabbis, philosophers, and scholars. Jews are not stuck in a prehistoric tradition that became petrified after the time of Christ. Contemporary Judaism—be it Orthodox, Conservative, or Reform—maintains its own identity and meaning that is not dependent upon Christianity.

In this text, I will use the terms *Hebrew Scriptures*, *Jewish Bible*, and *Old Testament*, not interchangeably, but as they are most appropriate in each context.

Traditional and Modern Methods of Interpretation: Creation, Evolution, and Genesis 1

The methods of modern scholars have often come into conflict with the traditional understandings associated with faith-based approaches. At the same time, however, there have been frequent and often fruitful attempts by many scholars to blend sincere faith with rigorous academic study.

The opening chapters of Genesis, the first book of the Bible, have been at the center of many controversies. Christians who accept historical-critical approaches recognize that Genesis 1—3 contains two distinct Creation stories. Genesis 2:4b—3:24 was probably first written by the Jahwist (J) source around 900 BCE. Genesis 1:1—2:4a was probably written by the Priestly (P) source in the postexilic period, somewhat after 538 BCE. The opening chapter of Genesis, then, is thought to have been written much later than the story of Adam and Eve.

Was the world created in six days? Were human beings made directly by God as an entirely unique species apart from any chain of natural evolution? Were Adam and Eve real people who interacted with God in the Garden of Eden?

As discussed in chapter 2, ancient and medieval Christian theologians were aware of various layers of meaning in Scripture. In addition to the literal sense of a passage, there could also be an allegorical meaning, a moral meaning, and an anagogical meaning related to the end of time. When Augustine (354–430) read Genesis, he was aware that six days did not necessarily mean six periods of twenty-four hours, though he thought that the passage does express the order of God's Creation. Likewise, Augustine knew that God, whom he believed to be utterly transcendent, did not actually walk in the Garden of Eden, but that the passage expressed in an accessible way the truth that there was a special mode of communication between God and our first parents. Still, Augustine did believe that Adam and Eve were historical figures and that, even though God forbade them, they ate of the fruit of the Tree of the Knowledge of Good and Evil. In fact, Augustine thought that apart from some figurative expressions, the Bible always told the truth about events that took place in human history. In principle, though, Augustine was not what one could label in the contemporary sense a literalist, that is, one who insists that every text in the Bible is true in every way, including the historical and scientific senses.

New historical and scientific challenges to traditional understandings of the Bible have appeared in recent centuries along with the coming of the modern world. Charles Darwin's claims about evolution, in particular, cast doubts about biblical accounts of Creation and the genesis of human beings. Many liberal Protestant theologians embraced the new science and reinterpreted the Bible accordingly. Fundamentalism arose as a broad-scale Christian movement in the United States in the early twentieth century in reaction to theological liberalism. The most famous biblical controversy of that period was the 1925 trial in Tennessee of a substitute teacher, John Scopes, accused of teaching evolution in the schools. Similar controversies continue today in the movement to have Creation Science taught in public school as an alternative theory alongside the theory of evolution.[2]

Neusner explains that contemporary Jewish interpretations of Genesis 1 draw upon rabbinic readings from the first millennium and, while these often overlap with moderate and liberal Christian readings, they do not overlap with Creation Science ones. The early rabbis, he relates, were convinced that the only factual information conveyed by the story is that God created the world. The rabbis held it arrogant to think that the verses revealed scientific facts that are beyond human understanding.[3] Neusner continues this rabbinic tradition by limiting his interpretation to basic theological themes such as the goodness of God, the order and goodness of the world, and the making of human beings in the image and likeness of God.

The themes that Neusner stresses are quite compatible with those stressed in moderate and liberal Christian circles. Most Jews and Christians hold that the teaching of Genesis, properly understood, is not incompatible with standard scientific claims about evolution. The Creation story of Genesis 1 was never intended to be a modern scientific treatise but is more along the lines of a primordial myth that establishes that God is the Creator of all that is, that everything that God made is good, and that human beings are made in the image and likeness of God. Scientific views are acceptable as long as these views do not overstep their own boundaries by pushing materialistic or deterministic views that are antireligious.

Does the traditionalist Creation Science view of Genesis 1 or the Jewish and majority-Christian view stand more in line with traditional belief? Jewish scripture scholar James L. Kugel argues that traditional biblical interpretation operated in accordance with four basic assumptions:

1. That the Bible is fundamentally a cryptic text. That is, the surface meaning contains puzzling elements and even apparent contradictions.

2. That the Bible is a book of lessons directed toward people in one's own time (in whatever century it was being read at that moment).

3. That the Bible ultimately contains no contradictions or mistakes and so must be interpreted in ways that go beyond the surface meanings.

4. That the Bible is essentially a divine text.[4]

Ancient and medieval interpreters accepted the first assumption because, at least on the surface, the Bible does contain many apparent contradictions or mistakes. Precisely because they believed that the Bible properly understood contained no errors, these interpreters were driven to seek out deeper levels of meaning or even come up with explanations beyond the texts themselves. Creationists might argue that modern interpretations open to scientific evolution violate the third and fourth assumptions. Modern interpreters might argue in return, however, that Creationists violate the first assumption. Rather than treating the most basic level of meaning in the text as mysterious and in need of further interpretation, Creationists defend the surface level as the fundamental truth. In response to the challenges posed by modern history and science, no modern person can read the scriptures in exactly the same way as ancient and medieval scholars. Those who reject the claim that creationism is really a science usually do so on scientific grounds.

Interpreting Scripture within the Context of Different Traditions

Creation and the Trinity

There is one major way in which traditional Christian readings of Genesis 1 have differed from Jewish readings. Christian interpretation finds Christ present at Creation. Christian belief that Christ is divine required a further belief that God is not only the Father but also the Son. The Christian experience of God present among them in a continuing way required also a belief in God as the Holy Spirit. Christians share with Jews the belief that God is one, but they believe further that there are three persons in one God. God as the Father, the Son, and the Holy Spirit is called the Trinity.

Christian interpreters have read hints of the Trinity in the opening three verses of Genesis. The second verse of Genesis speaks of a *ruach elohim* that swept over the waters. For this Hebrew phrase, the Vulgate has *spiritus Dei*, or "Spirit of God." "Spirit of God" is also the translation found in the Douay-Rheims Bible (1610), the King James Version (1611), and even the Revised Standard Version (1952). The New Revised Standard Version (1989) has "while a wind from God," but lists in a footnote "*while the spirit of God* or *while a mighty wind*" as alternative readings. The Hebrew word *ruach* can mean "breath," "wind," or "spirit." Most biblical scholars today think that *wind* is most appropriate, and even those who think that *spirit* works better do not think that the human author of the original text intended to speak of the Holy Spirit. My point here, though, is that Christians have traditionally interpreted the phrase as referring to the Holy Spirit, and whether or not the original human author intended this meaning has not been considered relevant. Christians have believed that God's revelation through Christ sheds new light on the meaning of the writings that now form the Old Testament, which they came to believe was all about preparing for Christ's coming.

Christians have found Christ present in Genesis 1 in God's creating by speaking words. Trinitarian theology sees Jesus as the Word eternally begotten by the Father, and the Holy Spirit as the love between the Father and the Son. Genesis 1:3 reads, "Then God said, 'Let there be light'; and there was light." Each further element of Creation is preceded by "And God said…" According to this traditional Christian reading, the Father, the Son, and the Holy Spirit all exist eternally beyond time; time is itself a creation. At the birth of Christ, the Word became incarnate.

Genesis 2:4b—3: Tribal Initiation and Original Sin

The Story of Adam and Eve in Genesis 2:4b—3 provides another example of how an Old Testament story can receive different interpretations. In this case, we will begin with a speculative reading from the perspective of cultural anthropology, and then consider interpretation in Jewish and Christian Tradition.

Read from the Point of View of Cultural Anthropology

For brevity's sake, we will refer to this story as Genesis 2—3. The author of Genesis 2—3, the Yahwist or J source, wrote it about 900 BCE. There may have been more than one author involved in this stage of authorship/editing, and some material may have been borrowed or is very old, but there does seem to be a distinct style such that the hand of one very talented author predominates in this material.

Genesis 2 tells a story about how God, during the time of the creation of the world, made Adam by breathing his own breath into some earth. God places Adam in a garden and gives him the task of cultivating it. God then makes Eve from Adam's rib to be his helper. Next, God instructs them not to eat from the Tree of the Knowledge of Good and Evil.

Genesis 3 then tells of a serpent conversing with Eve. Eve eats the forbidden fruit and gives some to Adam. They become ashamed to be naked. God discovers their disobedience. Adam blames Eve, and Eve blames the serpent. God declares that Eve will experience pain in childbirth and that the man will earn his bread through toil and sweat. God makes them leather garments, then banishes them from the garden.

On a simple level, the story of Adam and Eve is a story of movement from innocence to experience. A very small child knows no shame in being naked. Only with some age and social exposure do most of us need to wear clothes to feel comfortable in public. It is also when we are children that we are told to obey, and when we disobey, we get in trouble. Ancient societies did not recognize a lengthy period of adolescence. When one is a child, one is cared for, but as an adult, one marries. As is reflected in the punishments given to Adam and Eve, men take on the responsibility of heavy labor, and women come to know the pains of childbirth.

A standard textbook of cultural anthropology, designed for a first-year course, recounted that a tribal leader from New Guinea, upon hearing the story of Adam and Eve read aloud, remarked that it was a typical story of initiation.[5] In other words, when heard out of a Jewish or Christian context, it sounded like a story that young members of a tribe would hear during ceremonies of initiation into adulthood.

Other elements in the story may reflect other, larger patterns of the kind discussed in textbooks in cultural anthropology and ancient history. Historians describe what they call the Neolithic revolution that took place between approximately ten thousand and eight thousand BCE. It had the following characteristic shifts:

- From food gathering to food producing
- Rise in population
- Division of labor
- Increase in innovation: wheel, plough
- Increase in cultural sophistication
- Increase in exchange of goods and ideas
- Development of cities (c. 3000 BCE)

The patterns are very large indeed, and any comparisons with the story of Adam and Eve will be rather general. Still, Adam and Eve go from collaborating in cultivating and gathering food in the Garden to a new situation in which the man earns his bread by the sweat of his brow. There is a new division of labor as well as a new, unequal differentiation of the roles of the sexes. There is a new shame in nakedness. Women now have pain in childbearing. The exile from the Garden thus brought with it new responsibilities and new hardships.

Read from the Point of View of Jewish and Christian Faith Traditions

Jews and Christians see in Genesis 2—3 the story of the first sin. What was the nature of the first sin? Traditional interpretations have offered several ways of labeling it. Disobedience is often mentioned. So also is pride, understood here as not accepting human limitations but rather insisting on taking the place of God. Some early desert monks, known for their fasting, identified the first sin as gluttony. The presence of a serpent and the reference to the pain of childbirth have led some to speculate that the first sin is of a sexual nature.

Both Jews and Christians have interpreted Genesis 2—3 as telling a story that stands opposed to dualistic or Gnostic traditions. These dualistic traditions hold that if both good and evil exist, then both good and evil must ultimately come from the creative forces. There must be lower creative forces in addition to an all-good God. These lower forces are responsible for the creation of the material world and its evils. Jews and Christians hold, in contrast, that God, the Creator of all that exists, is all-good and all-loving. Everything that God creates is good. God creates a universe in which sin and evil can occur, but God is not directly responsible for moral evil. Sin enters the world through the choice of human beings.

Jews and Christians have traditionally differed, however, in whether Genesis 2—3 tells the story of what in Christian doctrine is known as original sin. Original sin interprets the transgression of Adam and Even as having plunged humankind into a state of being alienated from God that is passed down from generation to generation. Original sin distorts basic desires and motivations as they had existed in the state of innocence. Human reason and freedom are impaired in a world filled with blame and mistrust. Original sin brings about a sick state of being that could only be remedied by a divine Savior.

One finds the earliest Christian expressions of the concept of original sin in the New Testament in the writings of Paul:

> For if, by the transgression of one person, death came to reign through that one, how much more will those who receive the abundance of grace and of the gift of justification come to reign in life through the one person, Jesus Christ. In conclusion, just as through one transgression condemnation came upon all, so through one righteous act acquittal and life came to all. (Rom 5:17–18 NABRE)

> For just as in Adam all die, so too in Christ shall all be brought to life. (1 Cor 15:22 NABRE)

Since Judaism, in contrast to Christianity, is not based on the need for a divine Savior, it is not surprising that most Jews have regarded Adam and Eve's transgression as the story of the first sin but not as original sin. Original sin in the sense of a state of being from which the human race needs to obtain redemption as merited by a savior is not a traditional Jewish concept.

Mid-twentieth-century Jewish philosopher Martin Buber (1878–1965) interpreted the eating of the fruit not as original sin but as the story of coming to awareness of the opposites inherent in the being of the world.[6] Creation issues in a series of dualities such as being and nonbeing, chaos and order, light and darkness, truth and falsehood. Buber argued that coming to an awareness of opposites includes a knowledge of good and evil and represents a new stage for human beings in history, with a new set of advantages and disadvantages. Human beings become closer to God; yet God, the Creator of all that is, transcends both being and not-being and comprehends them on a level still inaccessible to human beings, and so human beings also become more aware of their distance from God. Buber thought that Genesis 3 speaks deeply to the ambiguity of the human condition in a way that is relevant to all human beings.[7]

Mid-twentieth-century Jewish theologian Abraham Joshua Heschel (1907–72) discussed the incompatibility of original sin within a Jewish perspective:

> Though the Jewish view of life also embraces profound consciousness of sin, it focuses on sin in a concrete sense, as a personal act committed against the will of a personal Creator. And though the sins may be grave and many, the evil done is not irremediable. The Christian reference to an ineradicable and comprehensive sinfulness in the nature of every man can never strike root in the Jewish mind. A mighty evil impulse there is in him, but in opposition to it there is also the good impulse.[8]

Heschel was arguing against a particular Protestant reading of original sin that he explicitly attributed to Martin Luther (1483–1546) and to Søren Kierkegaard (1813–55). This is a view known as "total depravity," which holds that original sin wipes out all capacity for goodness in human beings. Heschel argued against views that do not leave sufficient room for talking about human merit in relation to pleasing God. Heschel would not agree with traditional Catholic positions either, but his arguments do have some parallels with official Catholic responses to the positions expressed by Protestant leaders at the time of the Reformation. Catholics held that the effects of original sin were serious, but they rejected Protestant claims about total depravity.

The debates about original sin among Christians at the time of the Reformation were part of a larger discussion of what it meant to be saved or justified by Christ. In the year 1999, the Lutheran World Federation and the Roman Catholic Church signed the "Joint Declaration on the Doctrine of Justification." The representatives of each Church did not agree to exactly the same positions. Rather, they expressed their positions in such a way that each was able to acknowledge what the other said as acceptable: "It does not cover all that either church teaches about justification; it does encompass a consensus on basic truths of the doctrine of justification and shows that the remaining differences in its explication are no longer the occasion for doctrinal condemnations."[9]

Lutherans and Catholics may still disagree somewhat in their interpretations of the meaning and significance of original sin, but they are in firm agreement in reading Genesis 2—3 as giving an account of it. For Christians, the nature of the first sin as original sin gradually emerged as they reflected upon what it meant to say that Christ redeemed them from sin. In other words, the first sin became original sin when read within the context of Christian Tradition regarding the redemption achieved through Christ.

Interpreting Scripture with a Focus on Liturgy: Exodus 1—13

We have seen how religious Tradition sets a context for the interpretation of stories in the Hebrew Scriptures. Exodus 1—13 serves as an excellent example of how the Old Testament is deeply connected with Jewish liturgy. The foundation ritual of the Jews, the central ritual that expresses their most basic identity as a group, is the Passover observance of the seder meal. Although the term *Passover* refers most directly to the tenth plague during which the firstborn sons of the Hebrews were passed over as the Lord (Yahweh) killed the firstborn sons of the Egyptians, the seder is the celebration of God's whole work of redemption as discussed in the first thirteen chapters of Exodus, which also includes the ten plagues of which the passing over was the tenth, climactic one. The liberation of the Hebrew slaves can also be thought of as a passing over from oppression to freedom to live with God alone as their ruler.

A common saying in the field of religious studies can aid in understanding Exodus as a foundation origin story: *The myth explains the ritual; the ritual acts out the myth.* My use of the technical term *myth* here is not intended to imply that there is no historical basis for the story of the Exodus.

The Myth Explains the Ritual

The first half of our formula is that *the myth explains the ritual*. The ritual is the Jewish celebration of the Passover meal, or seder. In Exodus 12:1–20, the Lord gives Moses and Aaron detailed instructions concerning how the celebration is to be carried out, not only for the first Passover night, but for all time. Moses then relays these instructions to the elders of Israel:

> "For the LORD will pass through to smite the Egyptians; and when He sees the blood on the lintel and on the two doorposts, the LORD will pass over the door and will not allow the destroyer to come in to your houses to smite you. "And you shall observe this event as an ordinance for you and your children forever. "When you enter the land which the LORD will give you, as He has promised, you shall observe this rite. "And when your children say to you, 'What does this rite mean to you?' you shall say, 'It is a Passover sacrifice to the LORD who passed over the houses of the sons of Israel in Egypt when He smote the Egyptians, but spared our homes.'" And the people bowed low and worshiped. (12:23–27 OJB)

When a Jewish child asks about the meaning of the Passover ritual, the proper response is to tell the story of the Exodus. That *the myth explains the ritual* in this case means that the story of the Exodus explains the celebration of the Passover. In this sense, the first thirteen chapters of the Book of Exodus can themselves be read primarily as an explanation of the reasons for the Passover ritual.

The Ritual Acts Out the Myth

The second half of our formula is that *the ritual acts out the myth*. The contemporary celebration of the Passover is a symbolic reliving of the Exodus experience. The seder begins with the youngest child asking, "Why is this night different from all other nights?"

Various elements of the meal recall distinct details.[10] Horseradish, for example, stands for the bitterness of slavery. Apples and nuts represent mortar and bricks. A roasted egg is a freewill offering. The lamb is of course the Passover lamb. Various vegetables symbolize life, hope, and redemption. Salt water recalls the tears often shed.

Unleavened bread, or matzoh, represents the type of bread used in the journey. Two somewhat competing explanations for the use of unleavened bread are given in Exodus. On the one hand, the escaping Hebrews use unleavened bread because they leave in the middle of the night and do not have time to let their dough rise (see 12:39). On the other hand, the Lord had already given Moses specific instructions that unleavened bread was to be used (see 12:13–20). Which came first? For the author of the text, there is no conflict between an event happening because of earthly contingencies and God having foreknowledge of that event.

The Passover celebration is both a memorial and an actual sacrifice. A contemporary Jew who takes part in this meal symbolically relives the Passover experience. It is thus not only Jews of the time of Moses who live through the Passover experience. It is also contemporary Jews who, by partaking of the seder, symbolically relive the Passover experience and make it their own. They belong to that people who were set free from slavery by God.

The Exodus and the Passover do not function apart from other stories and rituals important for Jewish identity. Within this larger context, however, it is this story that is most basic. In a most fundamental sense, a Jew is a member of the people called forth by God through Abraham, Isaac, and Jacob, whom God liberated from slavery in Egypt in order to give them the Law as they set out on their forty-year journey to the promised land of Canaan. To act out the story is to participate symbolically in the original experience and to make it one's own. To tell the story is to explain why the ritual is being acted out. Taken together, the acting out and the telling reinforce the identity of the Jews as God's chosen people.

Christians believe that they see a yet even larger meaning in the joining of the Old and the New Testaments. We have seen how Genesis 2—3 is interpreted differently by Jews and by Christians. We also saw that there is some pluralism of interpretation within each tradition as well. The story of the Exodus has also been interpreted in certain ways by Jews and then appropriated in various ways by Christians within a framework set by the New Testament. Christians have traditionally interpreted the story of Exodus as a prefiguring of the story of Christ.[11] Moses and the Law set the Israelites free from the tyranny of the Egyptians and free for relating with God as their only supreme ruler. According to Christian Tradition, Christ fulfilled the Law to set people free from sin and free for eternal communion with God. As will be explored in the next chapter, there are strong parallels between the seder as a celebration of the Passover event and the Eucharist as a celebration of the life, death, and resurrection of Christ.

Interpreting the Jewish Bible with a Focus on Jewish Life

The Jewish Bible cannot be understood apart from communities of faith who try to live out its teachings.

The communal relationship of the Jews with God is most deeply expressed in terms of a covenant.[12] The first mention of a covenant is with Noah, when God promises never again to destroy the world by flood and gives the rainbow as the sign of the agreement. God's covenant with Abraham makes him the father of a people who will always be special to God, and promises them the land of Canaan. The sign of this covenant is the circumcision of all Jewish males, that is, the cutting of the foreskin of the penis.

God continues and expands the covenant with Moses:

God also spoke to Moses and said to him: "I am the LORD. I appeared to Abraham, Isaac, and Jacob as God Almighty, but by my name 'The LORD' I did not make myself known to them. I also established my covenant with them, to give them the land of Canaan, the land in which they resided as aliens. I have also heard the groaning of the Israelites whom the Egyptians are holding as slaves, and I have remembered my covenant. Say therefore to the Israelites, 'I am the LORD, and I will free you from the burdens of the Egyptians and deliver you from slavery to them. I will redeem you with an outstretched arm and with mighty acts of judgment. I will take you as my people, and I will be your God. You shall know that I am the LORD your God, who has freed you from the burdens of the Egyptians. I will bring you into the land that I swore to give to Abraham, Isaac, and Jacob; I will give it to you for a possession. I am the LORD.'" (Exod 6:2–8)

After God liberates the people of Israel from their slavery in Egypt, the covenant is further sealed through the giving of the Law. The Pentateuch names 613 commandments, though the most encapsulated and well-known form of the Law is the Decalogue, the Ten Commandments given to Moses by God on Mount Sinai. The people are to keep the Law, especially the commandment to be faithful to God and to reject idolatry. Leviticus 26 gives a long list of God's threats concerning what will happen if the covenant is violated, including that they would perish among nations, though the possibility of repentance and restoration is also mentioned.

For the Jews, the law is both a legal contract and an expression of God's love. The connection between God and the people of Israel is a love relationship, often spoken of in terms of a marriage. When Israel is unfaithful to the covenant, the prophets label it adultery.

There are dozens of prophets in the Hebrew Scriptures. They had visions and dreams and they were recognized as inspired messengers of God. Even kings had to listen to the prophets. Predicting the future was not among their main tasks, though in the later centuries, prophets offered apocalyptic visions about the destruction of the world and the coming of a new world.

The prophets often chastised the people of Israel for their failures to live up to the covenant through their disobedience to the Law. Disobedience usually took the form of idolatry, the worship of other gods. Idolatry could take the form of participating in cultic ceremonies or using charms and amulets in the pursuit of favors, but any transgression of the Law was considered to be unfaithfulness to God.

Often idolatry was connected with social injustice in that the worship of other gods was manifested in the hypocritical pursuit of further riches and personal pleasure by the wealthy in the face of the poverty of their neighbors. Amos, a prophet of the eight century BCE, proclaims a message that expresses God's disgust with Jewish rituals when the Law is not being lived out:

> I hate, I despise your festivals,
>   and I take no delight in your solemn assemblies.
> Even though you offer me your burnt offerings and grain
>   offerings,
>   I will not accept them;
> and the offerings of well-being of your fatted animals
>   I will not look upon.
> Take away from me the noise of your songs;
>   I will not listen to the melody of your harps.
> But let justice roll down like waters,
>   and righteousness like an ever-flowing stream.
>   (Amos 5:21–24)

Amos prophesied the overthrow of the sanctuary, the fall of the royal house, and the captivity of the people, though he also left hope for the restoration of a Davidic king.[13]

The history of Israel is largely the history of God's faithfulness and Israel's wavering faith. Before there ever was a king, there was strong debate about whether Israel should have one. Rather than be like other peoples, those who opposed kingship thought they should allow God to remain as their only ruler. This position did not win out, as Saul, David, and then Solomon were anointed as kings, and Solomon built a great temple. There was always, however, some air of ambivalence about having a king. After Solomon, Israel split into a northern kingdom and a southern kingdom. In 722 BCE, the Assyrians conquered the northern kingdom and destroyed its capital, Samaria. In 586 BCE, the Babylonians conquered the southern kingdom, destroyed Jerusalem including the Temple, and carried the Jewish elite off to exile. The Babylonian exile ended in 538 BCE when the Persians conquered the Babylonians and sent the Jews back to

Jerusalem with the task of rebuilding the temple, which they did. The canon of the Jewish Bible ends with a reiteration of this task. The people of Israel do indeed rebuild the temple, but they never again achieved independence as a nation or had another king. By the time of Jesus, there are different factions within Judaism, each with its own set of expectations concerning the future.

To capture truly the spiritual depth of the Jewish Bible is far beyond the reach of this chapter, almost as far as the knowledge of God is beyond the reach of one who prays:

> O Lord, you have searched me and known me.
> You know when I sit down and when I rise up;
>   you discern my thoughts from far away.
> You search out my path and my lying down,
>   and are acquainted with all my ways.
> Even before a word is on my tongue,
>   O Lord, you know it completely.
> You hem me in, behind and before,
>   and lay your hand upon me.
> Such knowledge is too wonderful for me;
>   it is so high that I cannot attain it. (Ps 139:1–6)

What we have accomplished in this chapter, hopefully, is to have considered the interpretation of selected passages and concepts in the Hebrew Scriptures in relation to challenges of modern thought as well as in relation to the larger context of Tradition, Liturgy, and Jewish and Christian Life. In the next chapter, we will turn to the New Testament.

FOR FURTHER REFLECTION

1. What are the differences between the Jewish Bible and the various versions of the Old Testament?

2. What does it mean to say that Genesis 1 is a religious text and not a modern science text? Do you agree with the implications of this statement?

3. Why might a tribal leader from New Guinea think that Genesis 2—3 sounds like a typical story of initiation?

4. What points in Genesis 2—3 could be argued to mirror broadscale cultural shifts?

5. How can Genesis 2—3 be interpreted as addressing the question of the origin of evil?

6. What are key differences between any Jewish and any Christian reading of Genesis 2—3?

7. How can Christians possibly interpret Genesis 2—3 as a story about original sin if the story existed for centuries without anyone interpreting it in that way?

8. Explain how in Exodus 1—13, the myth explains the ritual, and the ritual acts out the myth.

9. How do the covenant and the Law reflect a relationship between God and the people of Israel?

FOR FURTHER READING

Anderson, Gary A. *The Genesis of Perfection: Adam and Eve in Jewish and Christian Imagination*. Louisville: Westminster John Knox Press, 2001.

Buber, Martin. *On the Bible: Eighteen Studies by Martin Buber*. Edited by Nahum N. Glatzer. New York: Schocken Books, 1968.

Coogan, Michael David. *The Old Testament: A Very Short Introduction*. New York: Oxford University Press, 2008.

Heschel, Abraham Joshua. *A Passion for Truth*. New York: Farrar, Straus and Giroux, 1973.

Hoppe, Leslie J. *Priests, Prophets, and Sages: Catholic Perspectives on the Old Testament*. Cincinnati: St. Anthony Messenger Press, 2006.

L'Heureux, Conrad E. *In and Out of Paradise: The Book of Genesis from Adam and Eve to the Tower of Babel*. New York: Paulist Press, 1983.

Neusner, Jacob. *Christian Faith and the Bible of Judaism: The Judaic Encounter with Scripture*. Grand Rapids, MI: Eerdmans, 1987.

———. *Confronting Creation: How Judaism Reads Genesis. An Anthology of Genesis Rabbah*. Columbia: University of South Carolina Press, 1991.

Trible, Phyllis. "Eve and Adam: Genesis 2—3 Reread." *Andover Newton Quarterly* 13 (1973): 74–81.

GLOSSARY

Babylonian exile: the period when the Jewish elite were held captive in Babylon (586–538 BCE) after the Babylonians defeated the southern kingdom and destroyed Jerusalem.

Covenant: a pact made between God and the people of Israel.

Creation Science: an approach to creation formulated by biblical fundamentalists to provide a challenge to the standard scientific theory of evolution.

Deuterocanonical: a term used by Catholics and Orthodox to refer to books in the Old Testament that are not part of the Jewish Bible, also known as the Apocrypha.

Fundamentalism: a Protestant movement started in the early twentieth century that interprets the Bible literally in reaction against theological liberalism.

Intertestamental: a term used mainly by Protestants to refer to books in the Old Testament that are not part of the Jewish Bible, also known as the Apocrypha.

Neolithic revolution: a period in human history (c. 10,000–8,000 BCE) when many humans shifted from being food-gatherers to being food-producers.

Original sin: an interpretation of the sin of Adam and Eve that sees it issuing in an inherited state of being from which humankind needs to be redeemed by a savior.

Passover: the tenth plague in Exodus; the story of the liberation of the Hebrew slaves from Egypt; and also the traditional celebration of the Exodus event.

Prophet: in Israel, a visionary who relates messages from God.

Seder: the traditional meal in which Jews celebrate the Passover.

Total depravity: a Protestant view of original sin that emphasizes the complete alienation of human beings from God and the comprehensive distortion of human reason and freedom.

Trinity: the three persons in one God, the Father, the Son, and the Holy Spirit.

NOTES

1. Jacob Neusner, *Confronting Creation: How Judaism Reads Genesis. An Anthology of Genesis Rabbah* (Columbia: University of South Carolina Press, 1991), vii.

2. There is even today a Creation Museum in Newport, Kentucky, just across the Ohio River near Cincinnati, Ohio. The Creation Museum, aimed at children, displays exhibits that offer an alternative to an evolutionary worldview. One exhibit depicts dinosaurs alongside of human beings as if they actually existed in the same period (other than in Jurassic Park)!

3. Jacob Neusner, *Christian Faith and the Bible of Judaism: The Judaic Encounter with Scripture* (Grand Rapids, MI: Eerdmans, 1987), 14.

4. James L. Kugel, *How to Read the Bible: A Guide to Scripture, Then and Now* (New York: Free Press, 2007), 14–17.

5. I have not been able to find the textbook in which I read this point many years ago.

6. Martin Buber, *Good and Evil* (New York: Charles Scribner's Sons, 1952), 73–74.

7. Martin Buber, *On the Bible: Eighteen Studies by Martin Buber*, ed. Nahum N. Glatzer (New York: Schocken Books, 1968), 6–7. German original segment published in 1936 from lectures given in 1926.

8. Abraham Joshua Heschel, *A Passion for Truth* (New York: Farrar, Straus and Giroux, 1973), 254.

9. See paragraph 5 of Lutheran World Federation and the Catholic Church, "Joint Declaration on the Doctrine of Justification," http://www.vatican.va/roman_curia/pontifical_councils/chrstuni/documents/rc_pc_chrstuni_doc_31101999_cath-luth-joint-declaration_en.html.

10. A basic and useful description of a seder can be found in the popular children's book written by Lynn Sharon Schwartz, *The Four Questions* (New York: Puffin Pied Piper Books, 1989).

11. See Jay Casey, "The Exodus Theme in the Book of Revelation against the Background of the New Testament," in *Exodus: A Lasting Paradigm*, ed. Bastiaan M. F. van Iersel et al. (Edinburgh: T&T Clark, 1987), 34–43.

12. For a study of the various covenants, see Scott Hahn, *A Father Who Keeps His Promises: God's Covenant Love in Scripture* (Cincinnati: Servant Books, 1998).

13. "The Book of Amos," *The Catholic Study Bible*, ed. Donald Senior et al. (New York: Oxford University Press, 1990), 1126.

Chapter 4

THE NEW TESTAMENT

The New Testament is a written witness to the faith of those who held that Jesus of Nazareth is the Son of God, the Messiah, who, through his death and resurrection, fulfilled all that the Old Testament had led up to and prepared for.

Jesus as the Fulfillment of the Old Testament

The Hebrew word *Messiah* means "anointed one." The Greek word for Messiah is *Christ*, a term that is related to the word for the oil of anointing, *chrism*. In the Old Testament, there are three types of people who are anointed: priests, prophets, and kings. Of the three parts of the Jewish Bible—the Law, the Prophets, and the Writings—the first two parts can be subdivided into the Priestly, the Kingly, and the Prophetic Books. As the Messiah, or Christ, Jesus was interpreted as having fulfilled all aspects of the Old Testament promises and prophecies. That Jesus is a prophet is stated by some of his followers in Matthew 21:11 and in Luke 24:19. Jesus is identified as a king—ironically—in his entry into Jerusalem, in his conversation with Pilate, in the way he is mocked by his torturers, and in the sign atop the cross on which he died, which read in three languages, "Jesus the Nazarene, King of the Jews." Jesus is a priest in the way that he presides at the Last Supper but, above all, in the way that he offers the sacrifice of his own life in order to usher in the kingdom of God.

Christians read their experience of Christ as the fulfillment of the Hebrew Scriptures back into Jewish history. Some Jews had maintained a hope that God would rescue the people from their conquered state and through a chosen leader restore the greatness of the

Jewish kingdom. The prophet Daniel spoke of an "anointed one" who would be cut down (9:26). According to the logic of Christianity, now that the fulfillment has arrived, one can look back and see just what the Jews had been waiting for.

Judaism of biblical times, however, was not a religion based primarily on the hope for a messiah. Most biblical Jews did not think of their religion as radically incomplete but rather as in need of reform and restoration. The various subgroups within Judaism at the time of Jesus—the Sadducees, the Pharisees, the Zealots, and the Essenes—had their own expectations about the future, but none of them thought that a restoration of the kingdom would involve anything like God taking on flesh and sacrificing himself for the salvation of humankind. The Sadducees wanted to keep what limited power they had been granted within the provincial Roman state. The Pharisees wanted to reform daily practice, and they believed in the resurrection of the dead. The Zealots looked for a military revolution and victory. The Essenes thought that in their radical asceticism, they were living out the presence of the kingdom of God.

Interpreting Jesus as the fulfillment of the Old Testament is a critical key to the meaning of Christianity and to the message of the New Testament. This message is that Jesus' death and resurrection represent the culmination of God's revelation, which had been received through the prophets. Paul refers to this original message:

> For I handed on to you as of first importance what I in turn had received: that Christ died for our sins in accordance with the scriptures, and that he was buried, and that he was raised on the third day in accordance with the scriptures, and that he appeared to Cephas, then to the twelve. Then he appeared to more than five hundred brothers and sisters at one time, most of whom are still alive, though some have died. Then he appeared to James, then to all the apostles. Last of all, as to one untimely born, he appeared also to me. (1 Cor 15:3–8)

The early Christians envisioned the death and resurrection of Jesus as having been foreshadowed in every Old Testament event and in every prophecy that referred to Israel's destruction and future restoration, of which there were many.

Using a contemporary Bible, a quick glance through the reference notes to the stories of Christ's passion in the Gospels will show that Old Testament allusions and parallels abound. Mark emphasizes how Jesus' offering of bread and wine as his body and blood at the Last Supper is a Passover meal. Matthew tells the story of the passion of Christ with specific allusions to Isaiah's story of a suffering servant who will be led to slaughter like a lamb, be pierced as an offering for sin, and who bore the sins of many (see Isa 52:15—53:12). Luke portrays Jesus himself as quoting Isaiah's story of the suffering servant: "For I tell you, this scripture must be fulfilled in me, 'And he was counted among the lawless'; and indeed what is written about me is being fulfilled" (Luke 22:37; Isa 53:12). John explains that when the soldiers do not tear the garments of Jesus but rather cast lots to divide it among themselves, they fulfill the prophecy that reads, "They divided my clothes among themselves, and for my clothing they cast lots" (John 19:24; Psalm 22:18). Regarding the resurrection, Matthew depicts Jesus as saying, "Just as Jonah was three days and three nights in the belly of the sea monster, so for three days and three nights the Son of Man will be in the heart of the earth" (Matt 12:40; Jonah 1:17—2:9). These few specific examples just scratch the surface of the many connections made. The New Testament writers believed that in the death and resurrection of Jesus, a new covenant with God had been forged.

On the one hand, one cannot understand the origins of Christianity without knowing that the earliest Christians were Jews who found the fulfillment of their tradition in Christ. On the other hand, however, it is of utmost importance in contemporary times to avoid the error of "supersessionism," the one-sided belief held by some Christians that the once-valid Jewish faith became invalid because it has been superseded by Christianity. At the Second Vatican Council (1962–65), the Catholic Church proclaimed its belief that the covenant between God and Jews is not merely a thing of the past:

God holds the Jews most dear for the sake of their Fathers;
He does not repent of the gifts He makes or of the calls He

issues—such is the witness of the Apostle. In company with the Prophets and the same Apostle, the Church awaits that day, known to God alone, on which all peoples will address the Lord in a single voice and "serve him shoulder to shoulder" (Soph. 3:9). (*Nostra Aetate* 4)

This point about the continued covenant is deeply linked with the Catholic Church's explicit rejection of persecution of Jews, much of which historically had been perpetrated by Christians:

In her rejection of every persecution against any man, the Church, mindful of the patrimony she shares with the Jews and moved not by political reasons but by the Gospel's spiritual love, decries hatred, persecutions, displays of anti-Semitism, directed against Jews at any time and by anyone. (4)

Point and Counterpoint in the New Testament

The twenty-seven books that make up the New Testament are united in their testimony to Jesus as the Son of God and the Messiah who completes the Hebrew Scriptures. They differ, however, in the precise understandings they offer for these beliefs and their implications. The authors represent a range of voices and various points of view on a number of important matters. The mysterious character of the Christian faith, which can be accepted and lived as truth yet whose full comprehension is beyond human beings, included a number of points to be held in tension. Christianity is both the continuation of Judaism and a discontinuous break from it. Jesus is both a human being who is made divine by his resurrection and the eternal Word of the Father who became a human being. There is only one God, but God is the Father, the Son, and the Holy Spirit. The kingdom of God is both here and yet to come. Those who are not with us are against us, but those who are not against us are with us. We are saved by faith, not works, but faith without works is dead. Rome is the evil empire, but all legitimate authority is to be obeyed.

The New Testament contains various emphases that can be held together within a living Tradition of interpretation. Individual New Testament authors may place significantly greater stress on one side of these points than on the other. Overall, though, not only the New Testament as a whole but, for the most part, the individual books achieve some kind of balance on these matters. For example, all of the Gospels strongly affirm that Jesus is both fully human and fully divine. The Synoptic Gospels (Mark, Matthew, and Luke), though, focus on Jesus as a human being who comes to be recognized as God; the Gospel of John focuses on Jesus as God who has taken on human flesh. It seems to be a good interpretative strategy to read the Synoptic Gospels and the Gospel of John as offering complementary points of emphasis within the New Testament canon.

CHRONOLOGY OF ORAL AND WRITTEN MATERIALS IN THE NEW TESTAMENT					
c. 29 CE	Death of Jesus				
30s and 40s	Sayings of Jesus (written)	Stories of Jesus' exorcisms and healings	Stories of Jesus' passion	Liturgical formulas used by Christians	
50s	Letters of Paul				
70s to 100 CE	Synoptic Gospels	Acts of the Apostles	Letters attributed to Paul	Catholic Letters	Book of Revelation
After 100 CE	Gospel of John	Letters of John			

Jesus died about 29 CE. There exist a range of oral sources and at least one written source that precede any of the completed books of the New Testament. Many of these sources may date back to the time of Jesus. The written source is a book of the sayings of Jesus, known as "Q," which was drawn upon extensively by Matthew and Luke.[1] Other sources include passion narratives and stories of Jesus' miracles. All of the writings of the New Testament make some use of prior sources. A particular New Testament book completed later than another book may still contain materials that go back to the earliest witnesses.

The authentic letters of Paul, that is, those actually composed by him, were written in the 50s CE and are the earliest complete books of the New Testament. 1 Thessalonians, the earliest of these, was probably written in 51, over twenty years after Jesus' death. In his letters, Paul taught that through baptism, one enters into the death and resurrection of Christ. One becomes a member of the Body of Christ who contributes one's gifts to the community and who shares in the joys and suffering of all members. Christian communities were expected to live by strict moral standards as they awaited the return of Christ at the end of time, which was expected to happen imminently. Those who belonged to Christ would rise up to be with Christ and be saved from the wrath of God.

There are some points of development in the thought of Paul in the five years between 1 Thessalonians and his Letter to the Romans. The early Paul thought that those who died before the second coming of Christ would still await the time of Christ's coming to be raised up collectively with those who are saved. In Romans, Paul expresses his belief that one who dies goes directly to be with Christ. Also in Romans, Paul contradicts his earlier belief that the Jews are now rejected with his belief that God remains faithful to his covenant with the Jews and that the Jews will all be converted by the end of time.

Paul places so much emphasis on the significance of God's raising of Jesus from the dead that he hardly ever mentions anything about Jesus himself or what Jesus said and did. The Gospel of Mark, probably written soon after 70 CE, can be seen as providing a kind of supplement to Paul's letters.[2] Mark still tells of Jesus' death and of the discovery of the empty tomb, signifying his resurrection. In leading up to this climax, however, Mark also speaks of Jesus being baptized by John, his teaching, his performing exorcisms and healings, his relationship with his disciples, and the details of his passion. Paul's focus on God working salvation through the death and resurrection of Christ is completed by Mark's focus on the man, Jesus of Nazareth, and his powerful words and deeds. The Gospels of Matthew and

Luke, written in the 80s or even 90s CE, draw upon Q and other sources as they add infancy narratives, the Sermon on the Mount (or Plain), many more parables, more extensive and detailed allusions to the Old Testament, and resurrection appearance stories. Matthew and Luke also engaged in detailed editing of Mark's materials. In their many additions and changes, they are both supplementing Mark and continuing to supplement the letters of Paul. Matthew draws out the complexities of the relationship between Judaism and Christianity and connects salvation with the living out of a universal ethic. Luke stresses the mission of Jesus to the lost and the disenfranchised, and he very pointedly addresses issues concerning the rich and the poor.

THE TWENTY-ONE LETTERS IN THE NEW TESTAMENT	
Letters of Paul	1 Thessalonians, Galatians, Philippians, 1 Corinthians, 2 Corinthians, Romans
Disputed letters attributed to Paul but probably not written by him	2 Thessalonians, Ephesians
Letters attributed to Paul but not written by him (Pseudepigraphical)	Colossians, Philemon, 1 Timothy, 2 Timothy, Titus; Hebrews is not directly attributed to Paul but is implicitly so
Catholic (addressed to all) Letters	James, 1 Peter, 2 Peter, Jude
Letters of John	1 John, 2 John, 3 John

The pseudepigraphical letters of Paul, that is, letters attributed to him but not written by him, were for the most part written by his coworkers, or those in Pauline communities who have preserved an oral tradition and who feel secure that they are communicating the message of Paul. These letters go beyond Paul, however, in extending or applying his thought, or even in correcting what are taken to be misunderstandings or misapplications of Paul's letters. The pseudepigraphical letters stress, even more than Paul himself, the harmony between Judaism and Christianity, the desire for peaceful coexistence with the State, the importance of domestic harmony, and the need for clear structures of authority in the churches. Many readers find the Christian vision expressed in these pseudepigraphical letters to be narrower and less engaging than the vision expressed in the letters written by Paul.

The Catholic Letters (considered "catholic" or "universal" in that they are not addressed to one particular community) even more directly offer counterpoint to the teaching of Paul. First Peter, in contrast to Paul, emphasizes the need for resistance when public authorities are oppressive. Second Peter addresses the criticism made against Christians that the end times have not yet come, even though they had been expected imminently. The author explains that to God, one day is like a thousand years, and Christians must be patient, for the end will come suddenly when no one expects it. Although Paul himself simply emphasized that the end is near, the author attributes his own positon to Paul.

The Gospel of John and the three Letters of John are not all written by the same person, but they seem to stem from communities that belong to the same stream of Christianity, known as the Johannine tradition. The language of the Gospel of John is highly symbolic. Jesus is depicted as the all-powerful and all-knowing God who has become incarnate. Jesus knows all things, predicts all things, and is in control of all things. In the first half of the Gospel, Jesus' divinity is revealed clearly through seven wondrous signs, such as the turning of water into wine at the wedding feast of Cana and the raising of Lazarus from the dead.[3] In the second half of the Gospel, John turns his attention to the main event, the "hour" for which Jesus had come, his passion, death, and resurrection. Jesus reveals to his disciples the plan of his Father, and then remains in charge throughout his own suffering and death as he carries out his mission. Whereas the Synoptic Gospels had offered a counterpoint to Paul, the Gospel of John offers a counterpoint to the Synoptic Gospels. That is, the Synoptic Gospels supplemented Paul's almost exclusive focus on what God had accomplished through the death and resurrection of Jesus by emphasizing the life of the man Jesus, what he taught and what he did. The Gospel of John offers a counterpoint to the Synoptic Gospels by highlighting that the God-ness of Jesus was present all along and by shifting the focus back to Jesus' death and resurrection as his most glorious accomplishment.

The New Testament thus gathers together many points and counterpoints in its witness to Jesus as Messiah and Son of God. As will be discussed in chapter 6, ecumenical councils in later centuries will clarify frameworks of interpretation that are sometimes present in these texts as vague presuppositions, such as that Jesus is fully human and fully divine and that there are three persons in one God. It is possible for an individual reader to pit some of the New Testament books against each other and read them as contradictory. Within a living faith tradition that holds these works to be sacred texts, however, these works are heard as a back and forth conversation that articulates, in a sometimes untidy and messy manner, the mystery of the Christian faith.

Interpreting the New Testament with a Focus on Ritual

As was shown in the previous chapter in connection with the Old Testament, interpretation of the writings of the New Testament requires some attention to the rituals that establish and reinforce a people's most basic identity. Baptism and Eucharist together constitute the foundation rituals of Christianity.

Baptism

The Acts of the Apostles depicts the apostles and other initial Christian disciples receiving the Holy Spirit on the day of Pentecost. Peter then proclaims the gospel that Jesus had risen from the dead in fulfillment of the Scriptures. When the crowd asks what they should do, Peter replies, "Repent, and be baptized every one of you in the name of Jesus Christ so that your sins may be forgiven; and you will receive the gift of the Holy Spirit. For the promise is for you, for your children, and for all who are far away, everyone whom the Lord our God calls to him" (Acts 2:38–39). Throughout the Acts of the Apostles, anyone who accepts that Jesus is the Messiah is promptly baptized.

The Acts of the Apostles, however, is an idealized historical reconstruction written by Luke more than six or seven decades after the death of Jesus. Scholars dispute the early history of baptism and the forms that it might have taken, but the ritual is attested to significantly in many places in the New Testament. Paul references baptism in his letters and reports that he had baptized some himself. Mark portrays John the Baptist as saying of Jesus, "I have baptized you with water; but he will baptize you with the Holy Spirit" (Mark 1:8). Matthew portrays the risen Christ as giving the eleven (the twelve apostles minus Judas) the mission: "Go therefore and make disciples of all nations, baptizing them in the name of the Father and of the Son and of the Holy Spirit" (Matt 28:19). The Gospel of John shows Jesus declaring, "Very truly, I tell you, no one can enter the kingdom of God without being born of water and Spirit" (John 3:5).

There is no exact Old Testament parallel to baptism. Biblical Jews had a ritual of purification that involved washing with water, but it was performed frequently, not just once. Christian baptism functions more like circumcision, a one-time ritual that marked the recipient as a member of the faith community. There is some evidence of point and counterpoint in the New Testament concerning the necessity of baptism for eternal salvation in that a passage such as John 3:5, quoted above, can be held in tension with Matthew 25:31–46, in which people are saved who did service for the Son of Man, even though they did not know it, whenever they fed the hungry, gave drink to the thirsty, or visited the imprisoned.

Eucharist

The Eucharist, or Lord's Supper, in its recounting of the words of the Last Supper and its sharing of the bread and wine, both narrates and acts out the basic Christian story. As with baptism, scholars dispute the Eucharist's exact origins and the different forms it had taken in the earliest times. The Acts of the Apostles speaks several times of the earliest Christian communities participating in "the breaking of the bread." In 1 Corinthians, Paul speaks of the Eucharist as a tradition he had received from the Lord, and he tells of Jesus' words at the Last Supper designating the bread and wine as his own body and blood. Apparently, the Corinthian Eucharist was being celebrated within the context of a large bring-your-own feast. Paul admonishes the wealthy among them that they should eat at home rather than feast in front of the poor without sharing. The main theme of 1 Corinthians is that Christians must live out a unity in Christ that transcends all divisions, and that baptism and Eucharist are signs of this unity.

Paul's understanding of the Eucharist is deeply bound up with his understanding of the Christian community as the Body of Christ. In Paul's vision, the Body of Christ is Jesus' body that died on the cross and then rose again from the dead. It is also the body that is received in the Eucharist. But the Body of Christ is now also made up of all of the members of the Christian community. All of the faithful members of Christ will themselves rise up bodily on the coming Day of Judgment. Paul believed that membership in the Christian community is participation in the death and resurrection of Christ (See Rom 6:5 and 8:17; 2 Cor 1:5; Phil 3:10).

The Gospel of Mark can be read with a focus on how it explains the meaning of the original celebration of the Last Supper as well as the reason why Christians have continued to celebrate it. It is an example of the saying explained in chapter 3, that "the myth explains the ritual, and the ritual lives out the myth." Mark thus shows some similarities in structure and function to Exodus 1—13. One could almost envision a Jewish-Christian child of the early 70s CE asking a parent, why do we celebrate the Lord's Supper? The Gospel of Mark could issue in response. As the Passover meal commemorates the covenant God made with Abraham and Moses and relives symbolically the experience of the Exodus, so the Eucharist commemorates the new covenant and relives symbolically the Last Supper as well as the life, death, and resurrection of Jesus the Christ. As Jewish people of today symbolically participate in the Exodus experience when they eat the seder meal and so make that experience their own, so Christians of today symbolically participate in the life, death, and resurrection of Jesus Christ and so make that experience their own.

Addressing Objections to Celebrating the Eucharist

The Gospel of Mark contains many responses to objections that people of his time, Christian and non-Christian, might raise concerning why Jesus should be the subject of liturgical worship that was reserved for the divine. If Jesus is Son of God and Messiah, why did he teach about the coming reign of God and not about himself? Why did he not restore Israel to its former glory? Why do many who follow him receive suffering and death as their reward?

Many verses in Mark address the topic of Jesus concealing his identity. Taken collectively, these verses are known as "the messianic secret." Mark shows in individual cases how Jesus was trying to avoid crowds or to avoid being misunderstood. In other places, though, Mark portrays a Jesus who does his best to reveal himself but is misinterpreted, especially by his own disciples. A key point in the Gospel is that Jesus cannot be properly understood until after his resurrection from the dead.

Mark makes sure that his readers know who Jesus is, and there are many characters along the way who recognize his identity. In the very first line of the Gospel, Mark proclaims Jesus' identity directly to the reader: "The beginning of the good news of Jesus Christ, the Son of God." John the Baptist knows who Jesus is. At Jesus' baptism, a voice from heaven declares that Jesus is "my Son, the Beloved" (1:11). The demons whom Jesus cast out recognize him as the Son of God. The people whom Jesus heals seem to get the point. The Jewish leaders who oppose Jesus understand very well the implications of who Jesus is. At the crucifixion, a Roman centurion (of all people!) exclaims, "Truly this man was God's son! " (15:39). At the end, an empty tomb and a promise that Jesus will meet the disciples in Galilee make clear that death is not the end of the story for this man Jesus.

The disciples appear throughout the Gospel as those who misunderstand Jesus. Jesus' corrections of their misunderstandings serve to instruct Mark's readers about the true meaning of discipleship. Mark 8:27—10:45, focused directly on the identity of Jesus, serves as a critical central section of the Gospel framed by two different stories of Jesus healing a blind man. The author framed the passage in this manner in order to emphasize that it represents something eye opening that the audience should come to see. When Jesus asks Peter, "Who do you say that I am" (8:29), Peter is able to answer that Jesus is the Christ, but then it is quickly shown that he does not at that time understand what his own claim really means. Peter likely associated the title of Christ or Messiah with the one who will lead Israel into its glory. When Jesus instead connects his identity as the Christ with his upcoming suffering and death, Peter has a hard time of it. Later in the Gospel, Peter will deny Jesus three times. When Jesus is crucified, all of the male disciples have fled; only the women remain.

Mark's Gospel consistently contrasts the stratified ranks of human society with the inclusive and all-embracing reign of God. Women are frequently depicted as those on the margins of society who give loyal service to Jesus and to whom Jesus reaches out and offers acceptance.[4] In 5:25–34, for example, Jesus, unknowingly at first but then approvingly, heals a woman who has an unclean flow of blood who had come up from behind and touched his cloak. By Jewish purity laws, this woman was an outcast. Jesus' response is to say, "Daughter, your faith has made you well." In 7:24–30, a non-Jewish woman, a Syrophoenician, approaches Jesus and begs him to drive a demon from her daughter. He agrees after she haggles with him. Both of these scenes represent the breaking down of social barriers, those that divide the so-called unclean from the clean, and those that divide the Greek from the Jew. In 15:33–41, as Jesus dies on the cross, the scene is shared by various women disciples with the Roman centurion who recognized that Jesus was the Son of God. In Mark's Gospel, the reign of God challenges the status of worldly powers, and the discipleship of women functions as a powerful theme in support of building community based on mutuality and reciprocity and inclusion of women and men in contrast to the pursuit of status and power.

The members of Mark's community were probably being persecuted and experiencing real suffering and death. Some members of the community may have started to feel discouraged and to lose hope. They were, think many scholars, people who needed encouragement to accept the humility and suffering and persecution that goes along with being a disciple of Christ. A strong part of Mark's message is that suffering and death for the sake of Christ is not a sign that you are doing something wrong, but rather a sign that you are doing something right in your following of Jesus.

Mark's Gospel thus explains not only why Christians celebrate the Eucharist but also what it means to be a follower of Christ. In his own way, Mark reinforces the theme stressed by Paul that partaking of the Eucharist entails entering into the suffering and death of Christ that will eventually lead to the resurrection.

Interpreting the New Testament with a Focus on Christian Life

Already in this chapter, the topic of Christian Life (morality and spirituality) has unavoidably arisen, since it would be very difficult to speak about Scripture, Tradition, and ritual completely apart from it. Reflecting upon Tradition brought with it the question of the Law and its relationship to a spiritual life that is more than the Law. Explaining the meaning of the Eucharist required some idea of what it means to live as a disciple of a man who died on a cross in a world based on status and power.

Morality and spirituality give rise to many points and counter-points that need to be held in tension. This tension can be found already throughout the Old Testament, in which the Law is the gift of a loving God. Just following rules and performing rituals, therefore, is not enough. Faithfulness to God is also a matter of the heart. Deuteronomy repeats three times the commandment to "love the LORD your God with all your heart, and with all your soul, and with all your might" (Deut 6:5; 10:12; 13:3).

The prophets chastise the people of Israel not only for idolatry and corruption but for spiritual apathy. Ezekiel, prophesying during the time of the Babylonian exile, expresses the Spirit of God saying, "I will give them one heart, and put a new spirit within them; I will remove the heart of stone from their flesh and give them a heart of flesh, so that they may follow my statutes and keep my ordinances and obey them. Then they shall be my people, and I will be their God" (Ezek 11:19–20). Jeremiah also prophesies about the return from exile. He foresees a new covenant, declaring that the Lord says, "I will put my law within them, and I will write it on their hearts; and I will be their God, and they shall be my people" (Jer 31:33).

Christians interpreted the prophecies in Ezekiel and Jeremiah as applying to the new covenant through Christ. Paul engages in some word play when he refers to the Christians of Corinth as his own letter of recommendation, "written not with ink but with the Spirit of the living God, not on tablets of stone but on tablets of human hearts" (2 Cor 3:3). Paul often sounded very strict in his firmness that Christians not violate basic moral rules regarding idolatry, sexual behavior, and justly settling legal disputes among themselves, but he did not think that Christians were to be bound by the Jewish ritual laws. He contrasted the law of the flesh with the law of the Spirit and thought that a Christian will refrain from immoral things, not because they are against the law, but because they have "crucified the flesh with its passions and desires" as the Spirit guides them to live in "love, joy, peace, patience, kindness, generosity, faithfulness, gentleness, and self-control" (Gal 5:22–24).

Jesus is portrayed in the Gospels as dramatically continuing the dynamic between respect for the Law and going beyond the Law in Love. Jesus teaches that love of God and love of neighbor sum up the Law. He says that he has come not to abolish the Law but to fulfill it. He tells a rich young man that in order to be saved, he must keep the commandments; beyond that, though, he can sell everything that he has and follow Jesus.

Mark depicts Jesus as radically inclusive of people on the margins of society.[5] Jesus healed the lepers and the unclean. He worked on the Sabbath. He violated ritual purity laws. He ate with tax collectors and sinners. He feasted and had a certain air of extravagance about him. He disregarded boundaries of gender, ethnicity, and class. Jesus taught in parables about the kingdom of God, a kingdom in which basic worldly values and expectations are turned upside-down.

The Sermon on the Mount (Matt 5—7) presents a formulation of Jesus' teaching as a radical ethic. It begins with the eight beatitudes, which call "blessed" the poor in spirit, the peacemakers, and those who are reviled and persecuted for Jesus' sake. Jesus then makes several pronouncements that take the form of "you have heard it said," quoting the Law, followed by "but I say to you." The Law says not to murder, but Jesus says that whoever is angry with a brother or sister will be liable to judgment. The Law says not to commit adultery, but Jesus says that anyone who even looks at a woman with lust has already committed adultery with her in his heart. The Law says, an eye for an eye and a tooth for a tooth, but Jesus says not to resist the evildoer, and if someone strikes you on your right cheek, then turn to them the other. Jesus has much to say in the Sermon on the Mount about avoiding the hypocrisy of those who practice religion publicly but not with sincerity. He advises not to store up one's treasures on earth, but rather in God's kingdom; for where your treasures lie, there lies your heart. He teaches not to judge so that you will not be judged, and that the measure that you use to judge others will be used to judge yourself. And not only should you treat others as you would like to be treated, but you should love your enemies and do good to those who hate you.

Many scholars think that Jesus probably did not give the Sermon on the Mount as one teaching, but that Matthew assembled it from various groups of sayings in the Q source. Most of the sayings appear also in Luke but are spread out in various places in Luke's Gospel. Still, the Sermon on the Mount likely contains many teachings as well as an overall spirit that go back to Jesus. Its deeply striking and unsettling nature has called forth a wide variety of interpretations. Thomas Aquinas interpreted the Sermon using a distinction between rules that all Christians should follow and evangelical counsels that are directed to those who take religious vows and live a more radical lifestyle. Martin Luther thought the Sermon functioned to convince the hearer that no one can fulfill the Law, and that all must have faith in Christ in order to be saved. Some of the more radical Reformers connected the Sermon with pacifism and with rejection of the political establishment.

Some modern interpreters have labelled the Sermon an interim ethic intended for people who were convinced that the end of the world is very near, but not an ethic that can be lived out for the long run in a practical way. As will be discussed further in chapter 12, Leo Tolstoy, the Russian novelist, focusing on Jesus' teaching not to resist the evildoer, saw in the Sermon a call to a radical pacifism and a non-violent resistance to oppression. In chapter 11, we will examine how Friedrich Nietzsche, the German philosopher, read Tolstoy's interpretation and used it as a basis for his portrayal of Jesus in *The Antichrist*, claiming that modern Christians are hypocrites who do not really follow the teaching and example of Christ. Modern pacifists such as Mahatma Gandhi, Dorothy Day, and Martin Luther King have all drawn inspiration from Tolstoy in their interpretation of the Sermon and of Christianity. Most traditional interpreters of the Sermon on the Mount have seen in it a call to a radical change of heart, but have not drawn political conclusions from it.

Concern for the poor and warnings to the rich run throughout the Gospels. It is a topic concerning which some points and counterpoints can be found. All three of the Synoptic Gospels portray Jesus as saying, "It is easier for a camel to go through the eye of a needle than for someone who is rich to enter the kingdom of God" (Mark 10:25; Matt 19:24; Luke 18:25). But then in all three Gospels Jesus adds that with God, all things are possible. In Luke (16:19–31), Jesus tells the story of a rich man who ate well every day and the poor man Lazarus who had sores and who lay outside his gate hungry. The scene then shifts to Hades (the Greek term for the abode of the dead), from where the rich man looks up to see Lazarus with Father Abraham. He begs to have Lazarus just put a drop of water on his tongue.

A story that offers something of a counterpoint about riches and poverty is found in Mark (14:3–9), a version of which appears also in Matthew (26:6–13) and in John (12:1–8)—but not in Luke—in which a woman anoints Jesus with costly oil. When some disciples complain about the cost and suggest that the oil should be sold and the money given to the poor, Jesus replies, "Let her alone; why do you trouble her? She has performed a good service for me. For you always have the poor with you, and you can show kindness to them whenever you wish; but you will not always have me."

Throughout the entire Bible, however, the balance of point and counterpoint falls heavily on the side favoring social justice in the relationship between the rich and the poor.

The Prologue to the Gospel of John

The brief Prologue that opens the Gospel, verses 1–18, is thought by many scholars to have been a hymn sung in the Johannine communities about the role of the Word in creation and how the Word became flesh. Some think that the interspersed lines about John the Baptist were added to the hymn.

The Prologue places the Word of God who became flesh in Jesus at the beginning before all of creation. That the opening words of the Prologue, "In the beginning," parallel the opening words of Genesis is no accident. Nor is it an accident that both opening passages focus on the contrast between light and darkness. The Word that will become flesh in Jesus is in the presence of God at the moment of Creation and is God. The exact meaning of this passage for the author and his audience is of course complex and the subject of much speculation. Whether the exact doctrine of Christ's preexistence is already expressed here or results from later interpretation is a subject of debate. But the wheels of interpretation are set in motion. As the Jews came to believe that the God who rescued them from their slavery in Egypt is the same God who made the heavens, the earth, and human beings, so Christians came to believe that the Jesus Christ who had walked among them and whom they encountered as risen from the dead was both fully human and fully divine. They came to believe that Jesus is both one of us and one with God. He was present with the Father and the Holy Spirit at the moment of Creation.

Did Jesus Think of Himself as God?

There is no clear scholarly consensus concerning how Jesus understood his own identity. There is a wide range of speculation, some of it challenging of traditional Christian doctrine. Some nineteenth-century biblical scholarship suggested that Jesus' own public preaching was more about the coming of the kingdom of God than about himself. Some contemporary schools of thought basically assume that Jesus made no assertions about his own divinity but rather that such claims were made up by his followers. Such assumptions, however, are themselves highly speculative.[6]

Numerous scholars argue for the likelihood that Jesus had a very intimate experience of God as Father or Abba. He saw himself in a special way as God's representative and he foresaw his own death and even his resurrection as being tied in with the ushering in of the reign of God. Jesus envisioned the apostles as judges over the twelve tribes of Israel and himself as over the apostles. He spoke in a way that placed his own authority above the Law of Moses. It is a credible position to hold that Jesus himself gradually came to a self-understanding in continuity with the ways Christians came to understand and express his identity and mission in Scripture and Tradition as the decades and centuries passed.[7]

Our three-chapter section on Scripture now comes to an end. The following three chapters will turn our focus to Tradition.

FOR FURTHER REFLECTION

1. Why is some knowledge of the Old Testament important for understanding Christian beliefs about Jesus?

2. How can the Synoptic Gospels be interpreted as supplementing and giving a broader context to the letters of Paul?

3. How can the Gospel of John be interpreted as offering a counterpoint to the Synoptic Gospels?

4. Explain how the Gospel of Mark connects the core Christian narrative with the celebration of the Eucharist.

5. How is the role of women disciples a significant theme in Mark's Gospel?

6. Describe how Mark thinks that Christians should not understand the meaning of discipleship. Then describe how they should understand the meaning of discipleship.

7. Explain the tension in the New Testament between affirming the Law and going beyond the Law.

8. How does the Prologue of the Gospel of John relate to the opening chapter of Genesis?

9. Give examples of how the New Testament can be read as a conversation that reflects a point and counterpoint of different points of view.

10. What is at stake in the question of whether or not Jesus thought of himself as God?

FOR FURTHER READING

Brown, Raymond. *An Introduction to the New Testament*. New York: Doubleday, 1997.

Johnson, Luke Timothy. *The Real Jesus: The Misguided Quest for the Historical Jesus and the Truth of the Traditional Gospels*. San Francisco: HarperSanFrancisco, 1996.

Loewe, William P. *The College Student's Introduction to Christology*. Collegeville, MN: The Liturgical Press, 1996.

Miller, Susan. *Women in Mark's Gospel*. London: T&T Clark International, 2004.

Reiser, William. *Jesus in Solidarity with His People: A Theologian Looks at Mark*. Collegeville, MN: The Liturgical Press, 2000.

Rhoads, David M., Joanna Dewey, and Donald Michie. *Mark as Story: An Introduction to the Narrative of a Gospel*. Minneapolis, MN: Fortress Press, 1999.

Sloyan, Gerard S. *What Are They Saying about John?* New York: Paulist Press, 1991.

Theissen, Gerd. *The Fortress Introduction to the New Testament*. Translated by John Bowden. Minneapolis: Fortress Press, 2003.

GLOSSARY

Baptism: ritual of initiation into the community of Christians, performed with either pouring of or immersion in water and the saying of the words, "I baptize you in the name of the Father, the Son, and the Holy Spirit."

Body of Christ: Jesus' own body that was crucified and risen; all of the members of the Christian community taken collectively.

Christ: the Greek word for the Hebrew *Messiah*, meaning "anointed one."

Eucharist, or Lord's Supper: the Christian ritual that remembers and represents symbolically the Last Supper as well as the life, death, and resurrection of Jesus.

God the Father: God as addressed intimately by Jesus as *Abba* or "papa"; God as loving creator and ruler of the universe.

Holy Spirit: the Wisdom, Power, or Love of God working through the prophets, in Jesus, in the Christian community, and in each Christian.

Johannine Tradition: a stream of New Testament tradition that includes the authors of the Gospel of John, the three letters of John, and the Book of Revelation.

Messiah: Hebrew word for the "anointed one" who was expected to restore the kingdom of Israel.

New covenant: the new relationship with God that Christians believed had been forged through Jesus' death and resurrection.

Passion: the events in Jesus' life beginning with his entry into Jerusalem and concluding in his death on the cross. The passion includes Jesus' agony in the Garden, the Last Supper, his betrayal and trial, his being tortured, and his carrying of the cross.

Pentecost: The fiftieth day after the resurrection of Jesus when the Holy Spirit descended upon the apostles and other disciples.

Pseudepigraphical letters: writings that are attributed to an author who did not actually compose them.

Q source: from the German word *Quelle*, or source, the early written collection of sayings of Jesus that served as an important source for both Matthew and Luke; no manuscript exists, but the source has been reconstructed by scholars.

Resurrection: Jesus' rising from the dead. Also, the general rising from all human beings from the dead for the last judgment at the end of time.

Sermon on the Mount: a striking and unsettling discourse of Jesus found in Matthew 5—7.

Son of God: a title given to Jesus that in various stages meant a messenger of God; the adopted son of God; the man conceived by Mary through the Holy Spirit; the Word of God present at Creation.

Synoptic Gospels: the three Gospels that can be viewed together or compared concerning their accounts of the life of Jesus: Mark, Matthew, and Luke. The Gospel of John is notably different from the Synoptic Gospels in chronology and structure.

NOTES

1. There are no extant copies of Q. Scholars reconstruct it by working with the materials in the Synoptic Gospels. A few scholars challenge whether Q ever existed.

2. I got the basic idea of later New Testament writings supplementing, clarifying, or correcting earlier writings from Gerd Theissen, *Fortress Introduction to the New Testament*, trans. John Bowden (Minneapolis: Fortress Press, 2003). Most of my chronology of the writings also comes from this text.

3. The full list of the seven wondrous signs are (1) changing water into wine at the wedding feast of Cana, (2) the cure of a royal official's son, (3) the cure of a paralytic at a pool, (4) the multiplication of loaves and fishes, (5) walking on the water of the Sea of Galilee, (6) the healing of a young man born blind, and (7) the raising of Lazarus from the dead.

4. Susan Miller, *Women in Mark's Gospel* (London: T&T Clark International, 2004).

5. William Reiser, *Jesus in Solidarity with His People: A Theologian Looks at Mark* (Collegeville, MN: The Liturgical Press, 2000), 107–19.

6. Luke Timothy Johnson, *The Real Jesus: The Misguided Quest for the Historical Jesus and the Truth of the Traditional Gospels* (San Francisco: HarperSanFrancisco, 1996). Johnson demonstrates the questionable historical basis for many skeptical claims about Jesus.

7. There are many sources that will argue for some version of the general position I have outlined here. See, for example, E. P. Sanders, *The Historical Figure of Jesus* (London: Allen Lane, The Penguin Press, 1993), 238–81; N. T. Wright, *Who was Jesus?* (Grand Rapids: Eerdmans, 1993), 97–103; Raymond E. Brown, *An Introduction to New Testament Christology* (New York: Paulist Press, 1994); and Gerald O'Collins, *Christology: A Biblical, Historical, and Systematic*

Study of Jesus (Oxford: Oxford University Press, 1995). William P. Loewe gives an accessible explanatory account of how Jesus' growing self-awareness of his identity and mission could be continuous with later Christian doctrine in *The College Student's Introduction to Christology* (Collegeville, MN: The Liturgical Press, 1996), 82–85.

SECTION 2

TRADITION

Chapter 5

CHRISTIAN TRADITION

Christian Tradition, in a basic sense, can be understood as the entirety of the faith in all of its aspects as it has been revealed by God and authentically handed down and lived out by Christians in all times and in all places.

We will use the phrase "the Christian Tradition" in a positive way, focusing on a shared reality that is articulated and expressed in different ways within different Christian communities. A tradition is something that is handed down and lived out. The Christian Tradition hands down the heritage of the past, shapes the world of the present, and envisions the goals of the future. In this sense, the Christian Tradition constitutes the entire shared reality of what it means to be a Christian. Tradition, in this sense, includes Scripture, doctrine (church teaching), Sacraments, and moral teaching and practice. This understanding lends itself well to a core theme of this textbook: Tradition cannot be understood apart from Scripture, Sacrament, and Christian Life.

Christian Tradition needs to be understood in connection with the belief that Christianity is a revealed religion. Christians hold that the Christian faith ultimately comes from God. It is not something that Christians have simply made up for themselves.

Various Qualifications Concerning the Term *Tradition*

The concept of tradition has been for some Christians a controversial category. Several qualifications need to be kept in mind.

TRADITION

First, when we speak of the Christian Tradition, we should remember that we are using the phrase in a somewhat idealized sense. Is there really a single, unified entity that can be called "the Christian Tradition?"[1] Of course, we can say there are many Christian traditions. And the word *tradition* can mean many things. For example, just for starters, *tradition* can refer to a custom or it can refer to a particular faith tradition.

Second, Christian revelation happens within the context of an ongoing relationship between God and Christians in history. In this regard, revelation is God's self-communication with human beings. It is not, at root, an object or set of propositions but a personal encounter with God. The faith by which Christians believe is, first of all, a response to God's offering of God's own self. Revelation thus has both subjective and objective dimensions. The objective dimensions exist because the personal relationship is expressed in concrete ways in history. There is not only the faith *by which* Christians believe, but also the faith *that* Christians believe. On its subjective side, faith entails a trusting and loving relationship with the God who first loves us. On the objective side, faith entails the acceptance of beliefs, rituals, scriptures, and customs as they are handed down and lived out. Sometimes the word *Tradition* is used only to name the objective side of revelation in abstraction from the subjective side. At other times, though, the word *Tradition* is used to name both dimensions of faith at the same time, referring to the objective side in a way that conceives of the beliefs, rituals, scriptures, and customs as they are actually being lived out in the context of a relationship with God. Orthodox and Catholics have historically emphasized the meaning of *Tradition* in this latter sense.

Third, some Christians, not without their reasons, routinely use the word *Tradition* in a negative sense. In the sixteenth century, many Protestant Reformers concluded that Tradition in the Catholic Church presented an obstacle to understanding the Gospel message. Martin Luther declared that Christians should give ultimate trust to Scripture alone rather than to sometimes-corrupt human authorities. Luther himself retained many aspects of traditional faith and practice, but he rejected specific elements such as mandatory belief in purgatory, the sale of indulgences, and cultic devotion to the saints.

I recently had lunch with a Baptist minister. When I told him that I was writing about Tradition, he said, "First you need to look to Scripture. You know, Jesus rejected tradition." I replied rather defensively, remarking that Paul says that he hands on to us what had been handed on to him by the Lord, and that Jesus himself had said, "I come not to abolish the law but to fulfill it." The minister agreed that there are many angles from which to view what Jesus did and many interpretations that can be legitimate for different people to hold. I was struck by the way in which the minister's first reaction to the word *Tradition* reflected a negative view that is distinctive to his own faith community. My own Catholic presuppositions reflect an emphasis on Tradition. His Baptist presuppositions reflected an emphasis on Scripture.

A tradition is something shared, but the Christian Tradition is expressed and lived out in many ways within communities that are divided from each other. On the one hand, it will be important to remember that the Christian Tradition does not exist in some abstract and ideal manner apart from the particular ways in which it is embodied. On the other hand, each Christian shares with all other Christians the reality of being a Christian.

Perhaps the exchange I had with the Baptist minister reflects the type of point and counterpoint conversation that in previous chapters, we had found in Scripture itself. A conversation is perhaps one of the best metaphors for thinking about what Tradition is and the way in which things are actually passed down in history. Very rarely does a single line in Scripture constitute by itself a final word in Christian belief. Various points of view are represented by various voices. When official truth claims are made by church leaders or councils, they often reflect what has emerged from the back-and-forth banter of the many voices. I do not intend to take a position that truth is relative, and that it is not possible for one person to be correct and the other to be wrong. In matters as complex and mysterious as divine revelation and the human interpretation of it, however, it is often the case that the full truth is somewhat beyond us. In matters of faith, it is possible to be convinced that something is true while at the same time acknowledging that one does not have full comprehension of it. In many cases, it is best if all parties in a debate try to leave some room for the Holy Spirit.

The rise of modern science and historical criticism in the centuries that followed the Reformation has added to negative attitudes concerning Tradition and authority in general. The actual practice of religious traditions in our world, including Christianity, has often been ambiguous, sometimes quite negative. The history of Christian persecution of Jews in many ways, times, and places stands out as a stark example of a religious tradition lived out in a terrible and inauthentic manner.[2] In many parts of the modern world, the word *tradition* has gotten something of a bad intellectual reputation. There is a tendency to contrast tradition with science and reason. In a provocative short story by Shirley Jackson, "The Lottery," a person chosen by lot is stoned to death by the people of a village.[3] Why? Because of tradition! Used in this sense, the word *tradition* means a custom carried out mindlessly with no thought and with no knowledge of the reason why it is done. If that is all tradition is, then there is no reason why anyone would want to have anything to do with it. Jackson's story, a critique of small-town life in mid-twentieth-century America, does not have to be interpreted as a condemnation of all tradition but can be rather an invitation to think deeply about what tradition is and how it should—and should not—be lived out.

The various qualifications that need to be made concerning the use of the word *tradition* should be kept in mind even as we settle on an operative definition for this textbook. Here, Christian Tradition refers most directly to the entirety of the life that Christians share as it has been passed down through the centuries and as it is lived out today within the context of a relationship with God revealed as Father, Son, and Holy Spirit.

Christian Tradition and the Social Construction of Reality

Christian Tradition is both received and reshaped by each generation. It functions objectively as a set of shared presuppositions that make it very real for those who accept the basic beliefs and values of their faith community. It constitutes the world of meaning in which Christians live, being present in their fundamental beliefs, values, and practices.

Understanding what the Christian Tradition is and how it functions can benefit from some reflection upon the way in which reality is socially constructed. Natural scientists might study rocks, trees, birds, amoebae, quarks, the process of evolution, or the theory of relativity. Not everything natural scientists study is immediately visible, though quite a bit of it is. Social scientists investigate things such as institutions, customs, rituals, values, and practices. Scholars in the humanities focus even more directly on language, art, symbols, and narratives that express and shape the realities within which we live.

It is a widely shared assumption in the social sciences and the humanities today that what we experience as reality is "constructed." A system of justice, an educational organization, a marriage—these realities do not simply exist with the formidable objectivity of a rock. We have courtrooms, classrooms, and chapels, but the objectivity of what actually happens in these institutions rests upon deeply shared beliefs and values. The legal system, education, and marriage are very real, and their existence transcends any particular individual. Their objectivity, however, does depend upon the shared presuppositions of those who participate in them and those who continue to shape them.

Paper money provides a good example of what is meant by the social construction of reality. Money has power in that you can use it to buy things. But money works that way because it is a shared symbol that people believe in and value. The money of one place does not usually work immediately in another place. And if you found yourself on a desert island or on the moon, your money would be worthless. After all, money is nothing in itself; it is just a symbol that can only work if you are in a place where other people accept that particular symbol system. In itself, it's just a piece of paper. Very few of us, however, would take out a one-hundred-dollar bill and use it to light a grill. The fact that people do live in large communities in which there are shared beliefs and values makes money take on a reality and power that goes beyond just being a piece of paper.

U.S. citizens experience the United States of America as a socially constructed reality. Citizens share fundamental beliefs about the founding of the nation and of its great leaders. Social commentators even speak of how the stories, rituals, and symbols associated with the United States constitute a kind of "civil religion."[4] There are monuments to leaders and statues of heroes. There are parades on the Fourth of July displaying many patriotic symbols and followed by fireworks. The National Anthem, "The Star-Spangled Banner," is sung before every game of baseball, the national pastime. Students in school recite the "Pledge of Allegiance to the Flag." There are deeply held values expressed in stories and sayings connected with self-reliance, the rugged individual, equal opportunity, lifting oneself up by one's own bootstraps, and being practically minded.

As shared presuppositions change over decades and centuries, they become contested and reinterpreted. Some can vanish and new ones can appear. For centuries, most people in the Western world thought that in a marriage, the man should automatically be the head of the household, but the majority of modern people in the West no longer accept that view. It is possible that in some parts of the modern world, the number of shared beliefs and values continually becomes fewer and fewer, but they still exist and are still important. Very few citizens of the United States would disagree with the basic presupposition that citizens have a right to freedom of speech, even if they understand the applications and limits of this right differently. The objectivity that rests upon shared presuppositions may be distinguishable in some ways from the objectivity of a rock, but these presuppositions are neither less objective nor less real. Saying that justice, education, and marriage are socially constructed is one way of distinguishing these realities from rocks. Reality as socially constructed consists in the world of meanings and values that is passed on from a preceding generation and is received and reshaped by each succeeding generation.

CHRISTIAN TRADITION AS DIVINELY REVEALED AND AS A SOCIAL CONSTRUCT	
Christian Tradition as divinely revealed	**Christian Tradition as socially constructed**
Accepted by believers as coming ultimately from God	received and reshaped by each generation
	functions as shared presuppositions
	constitutes the world of meaning in which Christians live

In many ways, the Christian Tradition can be fruitfully under-stood as a socially constructed reality. Christians believe, however, that Christianity is not simply humanly constructed, but is first and foremost something revealed by God. Like the Bible, though, the Christian Tradition mixes what is divine with what is undeniably human. Seeing the Christian Tradition as a socially constructed real-ity places a more immediate focus on the human dimensions than on the divine dimensions, but many Christians find it to offer a helpful viewpoint that can yield many insights into how their faith works.

Christian Tradition and Narrative

A film version of the life of Christ, *The Greatest Story Ever Told*, came out in 1965. I remember looking at the marquee of a local movie theater and thinking, "Are they saying that it's just a story?" In my seventh-grader imagination, there were only two possibilities: either there were things that really happened or it's just a story. Now, many decades later, I have no problem with regarding a story as something that expresses an interpretation of things that really hap-pened. I now think that the "Christian story" is among the most use-ful categories for talking about the Christian Tradition.

The phrase the "Christian story" (or narrative), like the cate-gory of the "Christian Tradition," needs to be used in a qualified sense. There is no one Christian story that exists completely apart from the many Christian stories in which it is expressed. In spite of its difficulties, however, we will use the phrase "Christian story" to refer to a narrative about the core meaning of Christianity as it is shared by most Christians. Again, as with the phrase "Christian Tradition," we can say that the Christian story is more than just something that is handed down from the past. It is also something that shapes the meaning of the present world in which Christians live, as well as how they imagine what they hope for in the future. For stories are not only tales that we tell but also dramatic scripts according to which we act out our lives (though often we find ourselves ad-libbing).[5]

A story still needs to be distinguished from what really happened. After all, some stories are false or misleading. Some true stories may be better than other true stories. Some stories may be better at bringing out the facts. Other stories may be better at bringing out the fuller meaning of what took place. In some cases, one can only get a full perspective by listening to a range of stories about the same happenings.

Once one gets into complicated events beyond the simple reporting of a minor fact, the question "What really happened?" cannot be completely separated from interpretation. In the world of meaning in which we live, interpretation is already happening as a dimension of any human event that takes place. What human beings think, believe, judge, and decide constitute an integral dimension of the event itself.

Think about a tale of romance. What does it take to tell a story about two people who fall in love? Beyond the observable facts, the storyteller must account for the expectations, fears, hopes, feelings, and decisions of those who fall in love, as well as of all of the other characters. The many presuppositions held by the storyteller about what love is must be considered, also.

The William Faulkner novel *As I Lay Dying* tells the story of a family in the southern United States from fifteen different points of view. These narrations contrast and conflict at points, but each narrator contributes a perspective that is important for the reader to grasp the novel's overall meaning. In a sense, each character is basically telling a true story influenced by personal biases and limitations. The reader is able to achieve a wider range of knowledge and insights than could have been gleaned if the story had been told by a single narrator.

The Christian story is not a work of fiction. Christians believe that the Christian story is an interpretation and expression of God's revelation as manifested in lived experiences and events. It is passed on in tales told by many witnesses and narrators whose own interpretations require further interpretation by their hearers and readers. Interpreting the story can be complicated. Most Christian communities have established authorities or, at the very least, rules and practices intended to safeguard the integrity of interpretation concerning matters of faith.

The Question of Truth

The Christian story informs and supports a way of life. But is the Christian story true? Religious belief cannot be proven by reason alone, but most believers would stop believing if their faith could be shown to be contrary to reason. Questions about the truth of the story are not matters that can be settled in a science lab or with a mathematical equation. Believers think both that religious belief is reasonable and that faith commitment includes existential and personal elements. For the most part, believers first judge the truth of their faith according to the testimony of others whom they trust. Often a person's first encounter with faith is within the context of their own family. At various times or stages, believers may test the truth of their faith according to how it proves itself out in everyday life, that is, according to the goodness it achieves and the love that it makes possible. Making judgments about religious truth is done not only by individuals but also by the faith communities that precede them and to which they belong.

Contemporary skeptics find in the fact that religious belief cannot be absolutely proven grounds for casting serious doubt upon the entire enterprise of religious believing. Yet there may be grounds that are at least as good for doubting what skeptics say about religious belief. Demanding that religious claims be proven according to modern standards of science wrongly categorizes those claims and places an artificial burden upon a person's faith, which it was never meant to carry.[6] As the early modern believer-scientist Blaise Pascal put it, "The heart has reasons that reason knows not."[7] Many believers think that in the next life, the essential elements of their faith will be confirmed but often in surprising ways that they neither could have anticipated nor fully comprehended in this life.

The Christian Story as an Overarching Narrative

The Christian story, as something that shapes the meaning of the lives of Christians, can be analyzed in comparison with what philosophers in recent decades have called "metanarratives."[8] I will not label the Christian story a metanarrative because metanarratives are usually described in terrible terms. I will instead call the Christian story an "overarching narrative."

A metanarrative is a master story that has a great impact on the lives of the people who live it out. It is a story that gives the final explanation of everything and to which all other stories must bend. Philosophers link metanarratives with totalitarianism, domination, and lack of openness. They accuse metanarratives of having functioned historically as tools for dominating people of other faiths and civilizations. The metanarrative of European superiority and progress that accompanied the conquest and colonization of much of the world, climaxing in the late-nineteenth and early-twentieth centuries, brought with it innumerable instances of abuse of native peoples, both individually and collectively. Marxism as lived out in the Soviet Union during the twentieth century functioned as a tool for repression and slaughter. The Nazi ideology of Aryan superiority and the destiny of the Third Reich resulted in many atrocities, including the attempted genocide and actual murder of six million of the Jewish people. In the eyes of some analysts, the U.S. metanarrative of democratic capitalism fueled and sustained the 2003 invasion of Iraq, with dire consequences being experienced well over a decade later.

Comparing the Christian story with metanarratives requires the navigation of some deep and dark waters. This is especially true since the role played by Christianity in world history, though often glorious and admirable, is not without serious blemishes. The history of the colonization of much of the world by Christian nations is a complicated one about which sweeping generalizations must be avoided. Conquerors and colonizers, however, often used modified versions of the Christian story in support of political and economic purposes.

The Christian story structures and shapes the lives of Christians. It offers an all-encompassing explanation for the fundamental meaning of life. The overarching narrative of the Christian story is beyond any one particular articulation of it, but it goes something like this:

> God, who is Father, Son, and Spirit, created the entire universe not out of necessity but out of love. Everything that God created is good. Human beings, made in the image and likeness of God, are called to live in eternal communion with God. But human beings fell into sin, something from which human beings cannot save themselves. After a long preparation over many centuries among the people of Israel, God became a human being in Jesus Christ. Christ died for our sins and rose from the dead. Soon afterward, the followers of Christ received the Holy Spirit at Pentecost and went forth to carry the gospel message over all the earth. For two thousand years, Christians have tried to live out this message, believing that their lives do not end in death but rather in eternal life with God.

There are many things left out in this brief summary, even elements considered essential by many Christians. A Pentecostal version might contain baptism in the Spirit. An Evangelical version might include the need to accept Jesus Christ as one's personal savior. A Catholic version might place more emphasis upon the need to belong to the Church that Jesus founded. For these Christians, such additions would represent not simply things that they would prefer to be added to the basic story, but rather things that they consider essential to the basic story itself.

Of particular concern in this textbook is the question of how authentic versions of the Christian story might be protected from co-optation and abuse. How can Christianity function for believers as an overarching narrative without becoming a totalitarian, controlling, and closed metanarrative? I will briefly mention three concepts that might be helpful in this regard: **mystery**, **point/counterpoint**, and **openness**.

Christian revelation communicates the **mystery** of God in a personal manner. *Mystery* in this sense does not refer to a puzzle to be solved but is rather more like a personal relationship with an intriguing someone about whom one has infinitely more to learn. The more Christians come to know God through Christ and the Holy Spirit, the more they realize that a full comprehension of God lies beyond their final grasp. Christians have encountered God through Christ and in the Holy Spirit, but God retains a mysterious character. Christians speak of the knowledge that they have through faith, but they also acknowledge that full comprehension of the truths of the faith remains far beyond their grasp.

The expression of faith entails a **point/counterpoint** discussion among various voices. Christian Tradition thus constitutes a kind of back-and-forth conversation that has been taking place over decades and even centuries. A single statement of a position rarely constitutes a full declaration of the whole truth. Mark supplements and balances off Paul; Matthew and Luke do the same for Mark; John adds his own counterbalancing witness to the overall discussion. Of particular relevance here is the example given in the previous chapter about how some passages in Scripture express the necessity of being saved by Christ whereas other passages point toward salvation in connection with a more universal ethic. In other words, one group of Christians might focus selectively on passages that declare that salvation comes only through Jesus Christ. Another group of Christians might focus selectively on passages that appear to say that various people might be saved by having lived lives based on charity and justice. In my judgment, though, Christians cannot simply choose one set of passages and dismiss the other set. All of these passages need to be read and interpreted in the light of the seemingly contrary passages. Much of the history of Christian theology can be understood as the working out of positions that do justice to the entirety of the Christian witness. Christian unity has been understood throughout most of history as allowing for and even requiring a great deal of diversity.

When thinking about how the Christian story can be guarded from functioning like a metanarrative in the negative sense, the need for **openness** becomes pressing. The most horrifying aspects of negative metanarratives are that they are totalizing, final, and closed. Vocal critics of society in Nazi Germany and in the former Soviet Union faced imprisonment and often death. The Christian story needs to be interpreted and lived out in today's world not only in a way that avoids totalizing, but in a way that directly confronts totalizing forces.[9] What Jesus taught about the coming of the kingdom of God is contrary to the wishes of those who lust for power, control, and domination. Jesus often spoke in parables with many layers of meaning that defied simplistic expectations. He commanded his followers to enter through the narrow gate, but rather than being narrow, his teaching was mind-expanding. In Luke 13:18–21, Jesus delivers two parables in four verses:

> "What is the kingdom of God like? And to what should I compare it? It is like a mustard seed that someone took and sowed in the garden; it grew and became a tree, and the birds of the air made nests in its branches." And again he said, "To what should I compare the kingdom of God? It is like yeast that a woman took and mixed in with three measures of flour until all of it was leavened."

In the first of these parables, the mustard seed is among the smallest of seeds, yet it grows into an expansive tree that houses birds. In the second parable, some biblical commentators think that "three measures of flour" is likely to be enough to feed an army. The kingdom of God may start small, but it is much greater and more wonderful than anything human beings are used to imagining. Other parables of Jesus evoke images of a kingdom of God in which the first will be last and the last first and in which those who take the last seat will be invited to sit at the head of the table. The Christian story told and lived in the style of Jesus will enlarge hearts and minds without being dominating or oppressive.

It is doubtful that any Christian, even the greatest of saints, has lived out the Christian story perfectly. But many Christians experience the Christian story as giving a meaning and direction to their lives that seems infinitely deeper and more fulfilling than anything they could have simply invented on their own. Many Christians, both individually and collectively, have lived recognizably holy lives within the context of this narrative.

Christian Tradition in a Pluralistic Society

We live in a secular age. We live in a world in which there are many, sometimes conflicting, narratives about the meaning of life and the proper ranking of values. Most Christians today support the basic idea of the separation of church and state, even if they differ about the precise implications of that separation. Churches cannot tell governments what to do, but churches can form individuals and communities with a significant impact upon the moral tenor of a nation.

Virtually all of us experience everyday life situations in which we think it best not to insert our own worldview, religious or otherwise. We do not want to drag faith into places where it does not belong, and we accept each person as a human being without regard to what their religion is. Those who do drag religion into places where it does not belong are seen at best as odd and at worst as fanatical.

Any consideration of the Christian Tradition as a socially constructed reality or as an overarching story needs to be qualified by further reflection on how most people today, including Christians, live within a multitude of narratives. Few Christians live in an environment completely shaped by Christian Tradition. Even Amish communities and Catholic monasteries are not hermetically sealed. Virtually everywhere, one encounters the pull of forces between the overarching narratives of faith communities and the overarching narratives of the modern world. Whether that pull is more positive or more negative is a question over which Christians themselves are divided.

In this chapter, we have considered the concept of the Christian Tradition from many angles. In the next chapter, we will turn our attention to one important dimension of Christian Tradition—church teaching, also known as doctrine.

FOR FURTHER REFLECTION

1. Explain how *tradition* is a word that is often used in an extremely positive way and often used in an extremely negative way.

2. What does it mean to think of Christian Tradition as a "socially constructed" reality?

3. Is thinking about Christianity in terms of the "Christian story" helpful? What qualifications and distinctions does one need to make in order to use the term fruitfully? What insights does it yield?

4. How can Christians best prevent the Christian story from being misused as a metanarrative in the negative sense?

5. What does it mean to say that most people today live within a multitude of narratives?

6. Why do many people experience the pull of forces between Christian Tradition and the modern world to be mostly negative? What could be positive about it?

FOR FURTHER READING

Berger, Peter L., and Thomas Luckmann. *The Social Construction of Reality: A Treatise in the Sociology of Knowledge*. Garden City, NY: Anchor Books, 1966.

Knitter, Paul. *Introducing Theologies of Religions*. Maryknoll, NY: Orbis Books, 2002.

Lyotard, Jean-François. *The Postmodern Condition: A Report on Knowledge*. Translated by Geoff Bennington and Brian Massumi. Minneapolis: University of Minnesota Press, 1984, reprint 1997.

TRADITION

Sullivan, Francis. *Salvation outside the Church? Tracing the History of the Catholic Response*. Mahwah, NJ: Paulist Press, 1992.

Thiel, John E. *Senses of Tradition: Continuity and Development in Christian Faith*. New York: Oxford University Press, 2000.

Tilley, Terrence W. *Story Theology*. Collegeville, MN: Liturgical Press, 2000.

Ware, Kallistos. *The Orthodox Way*. Crestwood, NY: St. Vladimir's Press, 1995, revised 1999.

GLOSSARY

Christian Tradition: the entirety of the faith in all of its aspects as it has been revealed by God and authentically handed down and lived out by Christians in all times and in all places.

Metanarrative: a master story that gives the final explanation of everything and to which all other stories must bend, usually functioning in a totalitarian, dominating, and closed manner.

Mystery: not to be understood as a puzzle that needs a clear solution. In relation to God, mystery is like a characteristic of a personal relationship in which the more one learns about someone, the more one becomes aware of the infinite depth of the other. In relation to revelation, mystery refers to things that believers can know to be true but that remain ever beyond their full comprehension.

Openness: when applied to an overarching narrative, it is the opposite of being totalitarian, dominating, and closed.

Overarching narrative: a story that gives the final explanation of everything but not necessarily having the negative characteristics attributed to metanarratives.

Point/Counterpoint: a characteristic of a conversation in which fuller understanding and deeper truth emerges from within a higher viewpoint generated by open exchange of ideas.

Revelation: what God has disclosed beyond anything that human beings could discover on their own without special help.

Social construction of reality: an understanding of what is taken to be reality as a shared world of meaning and values generated within the context of the common presuppositions of those who participate in that world and those who continue to shape it.

NOTES

1. There is a deep philosophical question at stake here, the relationship between "the one" and "the many." Often, whatever is "one" can also be considered in terms of its many dimensions or component parts. In such cases, though, in another sense, the many dimensions or parts form a unity. See Plato's dialogue *Parmenides*, in which Socrates reflects dialectically upon this most basic of philosophical paradoxes.

2. The history of the Jews is full of positive accomplishments and contributions but also includes many persecutions, including those by Christians. See Michael Brenner, *A Short History of the Jews* (Princeton: Princeton University Press, 2010).

3. Shirley Jackson, "The Lottery," *New Yorker*, June 26, 1948.

4. The concept of civil religion in the United States is most associated with Robert N. Bellah, *Beyond Belief: Essays on Religion in a Post-Traditionalist World* (New York: Harper and Row, 1970).

5. One scholar describes Christian discipleship as the living out of Christian Tradition using the analogy of a musical score being performed. There can be many performances along with many variations of what remains the same musical score. See Anthony J. Godzieba, "'...And Followed Him on the Way' (Mark 10:52): Identity, Difference, and the Play of Discipleship," *CTSA Proceedings* 69 (2014): 1–22.

6. John Henry Newman gives many examples of the ability of people to arrive at truth by commonsense judgments made in the context of everyday life in *An Essay in Aid of a Grammar of Assent* (London: Burns, Oates, and Co., 1874). Available as a Gutenberg e-book at http://www.gutenberg.org/files/34022/34022-pdf.pdf.

7. "Le cœur a ses raisons, que la raison ne connaît point." From *Pensées* (1669); Section IV: On the Means of the Belief, no. 277. *Point* is an emphatic version of *pas*.

8. Jean-François Lyotard, *The Postmodern Condition: A Report on Knowledge*, trans. Geoff Bennington and Brian Massumi (Minneapolis: University of Minnesota Press, 1984, reprint 1997).

9. Lieven Boeve argues for the need to present the Christian story as an "open narrative" that challenges hegemonic views in *Interrupting Tradition: An Essay on Christian Faith in a Postmodern World*, trans. Brian Doyle (Grand Rapids, MI: Eerdmans, 2003).

Chapter 6

CHRISTIAN DOCTRINE

Doctrine means "teaching" or "body of teachings." The first Christian teaching is the original gospel message as preached by the apostles. It is about the life, death, and resurrection of Jesus fulfilling the Old Testament prophecies and promises. We have addressed this original doctrine, the basic Christian story, in chapter 5. This chapter will focus on doctrine as church teaching beyond this initial proclamation.

Some Christian churches limit their body of teaching to what can be found in Scripture, and members of these churches can offer a point of view that will be critical of much of what is said in this chapter.[1] Orthodox, Catholic, and mainline Protestants accept some need for church teaching that provide additional guidelines for interpreting the meaning of Christian revelation.

Getting the Story Right

What has been said previously about Tradition can also be said about doctrine. Doctrine is an important, even essential element of Christian faith, but it needs to be understood within the context of other elements of Christian faith such as Scripture, Sacraments, and Christian Life. If abstracted from the whole, doctrine can receive distorted interpretation and inflated emphasis. Understood within the context of liturgy and life, doctrine functions as a key element in what unites Christians in their faith and practices. If, as discussed in the previous chapter, the Christian story structures the very reality within which Christians live, then it is very important to get the story right. Church doctrines can be understood as guidelines for inter-preting and living out the Christian story.

Many church teachings have been formulated in order to settle disputes either among Christians or between Christians and others. Often these doctrinal disputes have revolved around the identity and nature of Jesus Christ as God incarnate and as Savior. Who is this Jesus, and how is he related to God and to human beings? In the New Testament, Jesus is called "Christ," "Lord," "Son of Man," and "Son of God." Early Christian worship put Jesus at the center as if he were God. What did it mean to act as if Jesus is God? Claiming that both Jesus and the Father are God gave rise to the need for a doctrine of the Trinity. Working out doctrines about Christ and the Trinity were done in connection with the meaning of salvation and the ultimate end of life. The main points of emphasis in this chapter will be about the identity and nature of Jesus Christ as well as doctrines concern-ing the Trinity, the meaning of salvation, and the coming of the kingdom of God.

Church doctrine requires teachers who have authority. After Jesus, the original authority belonged to the apostles. After the apos-tles themselves died, there were various ways within Christian com-munities for continuing to identify the structures and means of authority. Some communities had bishops, others had elders, and others placed authority in charismatic leaders. By about the middle of the second century CE, there emerged a church-wide network of bishops who held authority in local churches and who recognized the authority of each other.[2] This fairly rapid identification and consolida-tion of authority took place in response to a crisis brought on by con-flicts between those who accepted the teaching of the Catholic bishops and various other groups of Christians whom the Catholic Christians considered heretical and who were labeled collectively as "Gnostics."[3]

One might think intuitively that those who historically were orthodox or catholic would tend to be strict or even rigid, and that those considered heretics would be lax. The reality, however, has tended to be otherwise. Heretics, especially of the Gnostic variety, have historically been unforgiving purists with little tolerance for anything less than perfect. They were spiritual elitists who claimed to know the real "truth" that is reserved for the few and hidden from the masses. Gnostics favored the spiritual world over against the material world and had great trouble believing that Christ was the Word made flesh. How could God take on a body if the material world constitutes that from which the Spirit needs to escape?

Creeds, Councils, and Christology

Gradually, disagreements would arise among the Catholic bishops themselves. Local and regional matters were decided by gatherings of bishops called synods. Issues of concern for the entire Church were settled in ecumenical councils, the first of which was summoned by the Roman Emperor Constantine and took place in Nicaea, in what is modern-day Turkey, in 325 CE. The Emperor Constantine wanted agreement on doctrine in order to stop political unrest and to bring unity to the Roman Empire. The divisions between the Arian bishops and the non-Arian bishops were not politically acceptable. The manner in which the Council of Nicaea was conducted was not a model of fair and open debate. Still, the Church fathers who were active in the early doctrinal disputes debated philosophical fine points neither for political purposes nor for intellectual sport but in order to get the story of salvation right.

| CHRISTIAN DOCTRINES EMPHASIZED IN THIS CHAPTER ||
Area:	The study of:
Christology	teachings about Christ
Trinitarian teaching	teachings about one God in three persons
Soteriology	teachings about the meaning of salvation
Eschatology	teachings about the kingdom of God and the last things

Several key doctrines about Christ were officially decided by the first four ecumenical councils of the third and fourth centuries. The Church of England priest and theologian Richard Hooker (1554–1600) offered a very schematic way of considering these four councils together. Although lacking in nuance, this chart based on Hooker's analysis[4] offers a helpful starting point for thinking about these councils. The various names and labels in the chart will be discussed below.

RICHARD HOOKER'S ANALYSIS OF THE FIRST FOUR ECUMENICAL COUNCILS			
Council	**Concerned**	**Asserting**	**Against the**
Nicaea 325	Christ's deity	True divinity	Arians
Constantinople I 381	Christ's humanity	Perfect humanity	Apollinarians
Ephesus 431	The conjunction of both	Indivisible union	Nestorians
Chalcedon 451	The distinction of one from the other	Distinction of natures	Eutychians

Many of the key teachings of the first two councils are contained in the Nicene Creed. What is today known as the Nicene Creed was actually issued not by the Council of Nicaea but rather by the later council, Constantinople I. Constantinople I built upon the brief creed issued at Nicaea as well as upon other sources. The Nicene-Constantinople Creed contains most of the elements of the Apostles' Creed with the exception of the phrases, "he descended into hell" and "the communion of saints." The exact origin of the Apostles' Creed is unknown, though it is widely accepted as being very early and as expressing the apostolic faith. A medieval legend has it that when the twelve apostles gathered together for the final time, they each contributed one of its twelve statements. The Apostles' Creed, however, does not easily divide into exactly twelve statements but rather has a structure that reflects belief in the Trinity.[5]

Like the Apostles' Creed, the structure of the Nicene Creed also reflects belief in the Trinity. A comparison of the two creeds will highlight what is distinctive to the Nicene Creed in a way that points toward the doctrinal disputes of the fourth century. The following translations of these creeds are taken from *The Catechism of the Catholic Church*, though a newer translation of the Nicene Creed is currently in use in Catholic masses in the United States.[6]

Christian Doctrine

THE APOSTLES' CREED

I believe in God,
the Father almighty,
creator of heaven and earth.

I believe in Jesus Christ,
his only Son, our Lord.

He was conceived by the
power of the Holy Spirit
and born of the Virgin Mary.

He suffered under Pontius Pilate,
was crucified, died, and was buried.
He descended into hell.

On the third day he rose again.

He ascended into heaven
and is seated at the right hand
 of the Father.
He will come again to judge
the living and the dead.

I believe in the Holy Spirit,
the holy catholic Church,
the communion of saints,
the forgiveness of sins,
the resurrection of the body,
and the life everlasting.
Amen.

THE NICENE CREED

We believe in one God,
the Father, the Almighty,
maker of heaven and earth, and of all that
is, seen and unseen.

We believe in one Lord, Jesus Christ,
the only Son of God,
eternally begotten of the Father,
God from God, Light from Light,
true God from true God,
begotten, not made,
one in Being with the Father.
Through him all things were made.
For us men and for our salvation,
he came down from heaven:

by the power of the Holy Spirit
he was born of the Virgin Mary,
and became man.

For our sake he was crucified
under Pontius Pilate;
he suffered, died, and was buried.

On the third day he rose again
in fulfillment of the Scriptures;

he ascended into heaven
and is seated at the right hand of the Father.
He will come again in glory
to judge the living and the dead,
and his kingdom will have no end.

We believe in the Holy Spirit,
the Lord, the giver of life,
who proceeds from the
Father and the Son.
With the Father and the Son
he is worshipped and glorified.
He has spoken through the Prophets.
We believe in one holy
catholic and apostolic Church.
We acknowledge one
baptism for the forgiveness of sins.
We look for the resurrection of the dead
and the life of the world to come.
Amen.

Already in the Apostles' Creed can be seen a proclamation of basic Christian beliefs formulated in a way to guard against certain heresies. "God the Father almighty, creator of heaven and earth," opposes the Gnostic claim that God created only the heavens, not the material earth. "Jesus Christ, his only Son, our Lord….conceived by the power of the Holy Spirit and born of the Virgin Mary" rejects the beliefs of those who deny either the divinity or the humanity of Christ. "He suffered under Pontius Pilate, was crucified, died, and was buried" counters those who thought that Christ only appeared to suffer and die, and that he did not really rise from the dead. "He will come again to judge the living and the dead" stands against the teaching of Gnostics who preach union with God through meditation and withdrawal from the world. The closing statements that connect the Holy Spirit with the holy catholic Church as well as with forgiveness and life everlasting counteract those Gnostic teachings that stress personal achievement over forgiveness and that reject the authority of the apostolic churches.

The Nicene Creed, while retaining a stance against Gnosticism, directs its main attention toward refuting Arianism. Arius (c. 250–336) was a priest from northern Africa who taught that the Word who became flesh in Jesus Christ was almost but not quite divine. Was the Word something created by God? Everything except God is created; only God is uncreated. As reflected in the decrees of the Council of Nicaea, debates about Arianism included questions about the Son, such as "Was there a time when he was not?" and "Was he made from nothing?" In Arius's view, God is the Creator of all things, and the Word, for all of its unique glory, is something created. Arius could accept most Christian claims about Jesus Christ up to but not including the claim in the opening of the Gospel of John that "In the beginning was the Word, and the Word was with God, and the Word was God." Arius could point to other lines in Scripture in which Jesus claims that the Father is greater than he is and in which he denies that he knows all things. Arius could say that the Son is very much like (*homoiousion*, or "similar in being") the Father, but he could not say that the Son is of an identical nature (*homoousion*, or "one in being") with the Father.[7] The difference in Greek was literally one "iota," the letter *i*.

Many bishops of the fourth century were Arians. This dispute was creating major political unrest in the Roman Empire.

Against the Arians, the Council of Nicaea decreed that Jesus Christ is "God from God, Light from Light, true God from true God, begotten not made, one in being (*homoousion*; consubstantial; of the same nature) with the Father."

Five and a half decades later, Constantinople I, still fighting against Arianism, mentioned the names of several heretical groups.

HERETICAL GROUPS NAMED EXPLICITLY AT THE FIRST COUNCIL OF CONSTANTINOPLE (381)[8]	
The Group	**The claim rejected as heretical**
Arians	The Son is very similar to but not identical in substance to the Father
Sabellians	There is one indivisible God with three modes of operation
Eunomians	The Son is "unlike" the Father
Pneumatomachoi, or Macedonians	The Holy Spirit is not divine
Marcellians	The "Son" is the Word regarded as incarnate, not the man Jesus Christ[9]
Photinians	Christ was a mere man
Apollinarians	The Word took on human flesh but not a human mind
Novatians, or "Cathars"	Lapsed Christians should not be received back into the Church; second marriages are unlawful
Montanists	The Holy Spirit speaks revelation through prophets in the present time

Constantinople I extended Nicaea's focus on the divinity of Christ to include also the divinity of the Holy Spirit, who, with the Father and the Son, is worshipped and glorified. It is this Holy Spirit who has spoken through the prophets but whose authority is now linked with the apostolic church. In this way, Constantinople I not only countered those who denied the divinity of the Holy Spirit, but also rejected the claims of independent prophets such as the

Montanists who claimed that their own authority through the Holy Spirit superseded that of the catholic Church.

Nicaea and Constantinople I were followed by the third and fourth of the ecumenical councils, Ephesus (431) and Chalcedon (451). The Council of Ephesus condemned the position of Nestorius, who refused to give Mary the title of "Mother of God" (Greek *Theotokos*), calling her only the "mother of Jesus." According to his opponents' interpretation, Nestorius's position implied an unacceptable division within Jesus between his divinity and his humanity. Nestorius was three times summoned to the council but did not show up. The Council of Ephesus taught that Mary, as the mother of Jesus Christ who is both divine and human, should appropriately be called the Mother of God. Today, it is debatable whether Nestorius's actual positions were treated fairly at the time.[10]

The Council of Chalcedon condemned the position of Eutyches (c. 380–c. 456), a priest and monk of the church of Constantinople. Eutyches first became known at the Council of Ephesus for his strong condemnation of Nestorius, but his fierce attacks made him sound as if he were at the opposite extreme. He claimed that in Jesus Christ there was a fusion of human and divine elements. He was taken to mean that in Christ, there is only one nature. The Council of Chalcedon decreed that in the one person, Jesus Christ, there are two distinct natures, one divine and one human. As with Nestorius, modern commentators question whether Eutyches's position was interpreted accurately and fairly at the time.

Through these first four ecumenical councils, a picture emerges: Jesus Christ is divine. He is also fully human. He is one person, Jesus Christ, not a mixture of two things. This one person has two natures, divine and human, that remain distinct within the one person.

If any of the christological heresies had been accepted, then the basic Christian story would be radically different from what it is. If the Word that became flesh is less than God, then God did not become a human being in order to save us. If the Word merely took on a human body but is not fully human, then again God did not become a human being in order to save us. If Mary cannot be called Mother of God, then Jesus Christ must be two different things at the same time, not one person who is both divine and human. If Jesus

Christ does not have two distinct natures, one divine and one human, but is rather a fusion of divinity and humanity, then he is neither fully God nor fully human, but rather a third thing, in-between.

The Christian story proclaims that Jesus Christ, the eternally begotten Son of God, became the Word made flesh. He taught wondrous things and did marvelous deeds. He suffered and died for our sins, and he rose from the dead. He sent his Spirit to be with us until the end of time when he will return to judge the living and the dead, and his kingdom will have no end. This is a story that does not work unless Jesus is both fully God and fully human, indivisible yet distinct, with neither mixture nor separation.

The Trinity

Trinitarian language and concepts can be found throughout the New Testament, but a formal doctrine of the Trinity, that the Father, the Son, and the Holy Spirit are three persons in one God, developed gradually over the early centuries along with the christological doctrines. One who reads Scripture through the lens of the doctrine of the Trinity can argue persuasively that the New Testament is saturated with a trinitarian perspective, but without such a lens, the conclusion is not so immediately obvious. As long as the full divinity of either Christ or of the Holy Spirit had remained in dispute, there could be no clear doctrine of the Trinity. The formal doctrine emerges in the Nicene Creed as approved by Constantinople I as well as in its direct statement that

> the Father, the Son, and the holy Spirit have a single Godhead and power and substance, a dignity deserving the same honor and a co-eternal sovereignty, in three most perfect hypostases, or three perfect persons.[11]

Once it is explicitly and clearly stated not only that Jesus is one in being with the Father, but also that along with the Father and the Son, the Holy Spirit is worshipped and glorified, there is no getting around the claim that in the one God, there are three persons.

More so than any other Christian doctrine, the Trinity is said to be a sacred mystery. We are dealing here with a truth that could not be attained through reflection on nature, through human reason, through human experience, or through mystical meditation. In addition, it is a truth that, even when revealed, remains beyond human comprehension. The doctrine is a statement of something that Christians maintain must be true if prior Christian doctrines, such as the divinity of Christ and of the Spirit, are also held to be true. Without the doctrine of the Trinity, for example, Jesus could only be understood as a great teacher or a prophet, not as God Incarnate. In terms of its genesis, then, the doctrine of the Trinity functioned as a secondary support for christological and pneumatological claims. Once the doctrine of the Trinity was formally decreed as Christian truth, however, it became one of the most central of Christian claims, and the theological speculation surrounding it became a vital part of Christian Tradition.

Many basic doctrinal terms and concepts about the Trinity were developed by Eastern, Greek-speaking theologians. Orthodox theology is known for starting with the relations among the three persons rather than with the unity of the one God. Athanasius (c. 296–373), the bishop of Alexandria, argued against the Arians and the Pneumatomachoi who denied, respectively, the divinity of Christ and of the Holy Spirit. The Cappadocian fathers, Basil of Caesarea (330–79), Gregory of Nazianzus (329–89), and Gregory of Nyssa (c. 332–95), carried forward and further developed Athanasius's thought. There are not three Gods, but rather three persons who "coinhere" as one being sharing in one divine activity.[12] Gregory of Nyssa played a leading role at Constantinople I. The Council's formulation about the Holy Spirit as "the Lord and Giver of life, who with the Father and Son is worshiped and glorified" comes close to being a direct quotation from the seminal work of Athanasius.[13]

In contrast to Eastern trinitarian theology, the Western approach emphasized the oneness of God before discussing the distinction between the three persons. Augustine of Hippo (354–430) best represents the early trinitarian thought of the Latin West. Augustine's own experience of conversion took place in 386, just five years after the Council of Constantinople. Before his conversion, he had read books by Neoplatonist philosophers that convinced him that the human mind, with its capacity for memory, perception, understanding, judging, and willing, was much greater than anything that could be observed in the visible world. Augustine came to think that, of all the things in creation, the human mind would be where the most clues could be found about what God is like.

As a Christian, Augustine carried this introspective method over into his trinitarian thought. Always careful to remind his reader of the limits of his speculation, he compared the three persons in one God to the operations of a human mind. One of his examples involved the interconnectedness of memory, knowledge, and will. Another explored memory, understanding, and love. Though Augustine did not claim to have explained the mystery, he asserted that he had at least given examples of how there can be three distinct things whose operation is inseparable.[14]

Soteriology and Eschatology

Soteriology refers to the study of the doctrine of salvation. In addition to clarifying doctrines about Christ, the Holy Spirit, and the Trinity, the Nicene Creed also emphasizes that Christ's mission was intended for the benefit of human beings: "For us men and for our salvation he came down from heaven," and "For our sake he was crucified under Pontius Pilate, suffered death, and was buried / On the third day he rose again in fulfillment of the scriptures." The Nicene Creed is here testifying to the drama of salvation. Christians believe that Christ's birth, death, and resurrection are not just abstract truths to be assented to and stored away in memory, but rather are events that accomplished something wonderful for human beings.

What are human beings *saved from*, and what are they *saved for*? The Nicene Creed speaks of "one baptism for the forgiveness of sins," for Christians are *saved from* sin because of Christ's death and resurrection. The Creed speaks further of "the resurrection of the dead / And the life of the world to come," for through Christ's death and resurrection, Christians are *saved from* death and *saved for* eternal life.

Athanasius connected doctrines about Christ with an understanding of the meaning of salvation. Concerning Christ, he argued that "he was made man that we might be made gods."[15] For Athanasius, to "be made gods" meant to share eternal happiness with God. Gregory of Nazianzus connected this understanding of salvation with the need for Christ to be both fully divine and fully human: "That which was not assumed is not healed; but that which is united to God is saved."[16]

Soteriology is closely linked with eschatology. Eschatology refers to the study of doctrines concerning the coming of the kingdom of God, the end times, judgment, and eternal life.

The coming of the kingdom of God was the main focus of the public teaching of Jesus as he is portrayed in the Gospels. In the Gospel of Mark, the first thing Jesus says is "the time is fulfilled, and the kingdom of God has come near; repent, and believe in the good news" (Mark 1:15). The Lord's Prayer exhorts, "Your kingdom come" (Matt 6:10; Luke 11:2). The main topic of most of Jesus' many parables is the kingdom of God, and he uses the phrase frequently when speaking with his disciples. When Jesus passes the cup of wine at the Last Supper, he says that he will not drink of the cup again until he is in the kingdom of God (see Matt 26:29; Luke 22:18). Most scholars agree that Jesus went to the cross with the conviction that his death was deeply connected with ushering in God's kingdom.

Jesus himself is named king, sometimes ironically, in several places in the New Testament. All four Gospels testify that Jesus was mocked as the "King of the Jews" and that a sign above his crucifix read, "The King of the Jews." Early Christians believed that the second coming of Jesus as Judge at the end of the world would happen imminently. But they also thought that, in an important way, the end times had already broken into this world. Christ, who fulfilled Scripture, was already installed as priest, prophet, and king of the universe.

Early Christians disagreed about how much legitimate power the Roman emperor had, but they were in complete agreement that Christ the King was infinitely above all earthly rulers.

When Ignatius of Antioch (born c. 50 CE, died between 98 and 117) appeared before the Roman Emperor Trajan for refusing to worship idols, the martyr claimed to have within him "Christ the

King of heaven."[17] Ignatius believed that everyone, including Trajan, would eventually have to answer to a higher judge. He had faith that by being loyal to Christ the King in his refusal to obey the emperor, he—like Christ—would be raised from the dead and live eternally in Christ's kingdom.

The Nicene Creed testifies that Christ rose from the dead, that he will return again in glory to judge, that his kingdom will have no end, and that there will be a future resurrection of the dead followed by a world to come. For Christians, the resurrection of Christ confirmed that there is a justice beyond this life, and that earthly powers do not ultimately have the final say. Death itself has been defeated. The peaceful, just, and humble know that God is on their side. The kingdom of God is in some ways already present in this life, but it will not be here in its fullness until the end of time as we know it.

The Meaning of Christian Doctrine for Today

The focus of this chapter so far has been on Christian doctrine as it emerged in the early centuries. We have seen that the Nicene Creed was mainly directed against Gnostics and Arians. The Councils of Ephesus and Chalcedon retained that focus and also addressed a range of other heresies. Of what value to Christians, if any, are these doctrines today? To some extent, this question will often be in the background as we engage the materials for the remainder of this textbook. I will address it only in an initial manner in this chapter.

The basic Christian story that God became a human being and died for the sake of our eternal salvation has an enduring meaning for Christians of all times and places. Orthodox theologian John Zizioulas explores the contemporary relevance of the doctrine of the Trinity. He finds in the fourth-century writings of the Cappadocian fathers an articulation of a Christian trinitarian experience of reality. God, who is prior to and greater than all of creation, is relational. Underlying all of reality is not some dull impersonal oneness or some neutral material framework but rather a communion of persons. Persons relating lovingly to each other is the basic stuff that precedes the created universe and out of which the created universe is made.

Christians learn that they are not limited to living their lives as isolated individuals but are rather called to live as beings in relation with each other.[18]

Catholic theologian Catherine Mowry LaCugna builds upon the work of Zizioulas to further express the relevance of the Trinity to everyday life: "Mutuality rooted in communion among persons is a non-negotiable truth about our existence, the highest value and ideal of the Christian Life, because for God mutual love among persons is supreme."[19] As it is with the three persons in one God, our human personhood exists always in relation with others. The doctrine of the Trinity helps us to realize that love is not simply some abstract concept but rather is something lived out in a real way in real relationships with the communion of persons that lie at the heart of all that is.

René Girard (1923–2015), a philosophical anthropologist whose studies focused mainly on literature, has explored the meaning of incarnation and salvation for our times. Girard had been a self-proclaimed agnostic until he wrote his first book (1961), which included a literary analysis of works by Dostoyevsky, at which point he became a committed Catholic.[20] Drawing upon world mythologies and literature, Girard claims that human societies worldwide are based on violence and ritual sacrifice.[21] Relatively innocent victims are identified as scapegoats and eliminated in order to protect those who rule by lies and intimidation. The Christian story has some similarities to other literature in that a victim is sacrificed, but the story is also unique in that that victim, as well as the witnesses, proclaim his innocence and name the injustice. According to Girard, the only victim who could possibly play this purely innocent role would have to be the incarnation of God, for all other human beings are tainted by the sinful world of scapegoating and violence.

Girard is not a theologian, but the theological implications of his work have been further developed by the Swiss theologian Raymund Schwager. Schwager brings out how Christians of today need to unmask the lies and manipulations of the powers of this world in order to reject violence and intimidation and instead speak the truth and take sides with those who have been victimized.[22] In other words, Girard and Schwager argue that God becoming a human being in order to save us has real effects that continue to be worked out in real ways in our world of today. Christ did not eliminate the manipulations of earthly powers from this world, but he put in place the possibility of recognizing and naming these manipulations and acting against them in love and forgiveness. People continue to be victimized, but Christians can choose to follow the way of Christ rather than the way of blaming and bloodshed. In this perspective, experiencing Christ in the face of those who are oppressed and abused is not some abstract ideal but one of the most concrete of realities.

M. Shawn Copeland, an African American Catholic theologian, applies the meaning of the incarnation and of Christ's death on the cross to our understanding of the history of slavery in the United States as well as to the later phenomenon of lynching.[23] Copeland believes that since God became "enfleshed" in Christ, those who follow Christ must have an "enfleshed" faith.[24] God valued the world so much as to become part of it, and so Christians must pay attention to what actually happens to people in this world, including what happens to their bodies. Christians should not focus on the "spiritual" in a way that ignores material and social realities. Copeland posits further that Christians should see, in the tortured bodies of African American slaves and in the bodies of the lynched, the tortured and crucified body of Christ. She calls for the people of the United States to reconfigure their historical memories in a way that appreciates the tortured slaves and lynched persons as martyrs who died for the sake of the freedom of all, and to remember the wounds on their bodies in a manner alike to the way that the glorious wounds on the body of the crucified Christ are remembered.

The contemporary implications of eschatology have been explored deeply by the German Lutheran theologian Jürgen Moltmann. Somewhat like Girard and Copeland, Moltmann holds that, through the suffering of Jesus, God has chosen to identify with victims. Moltmann's own emphasis is on how, using an eschatological perspective, all those who suffer can see in the suffering and death of Christ on the cross a sign of hope.[25] The future is both here and yet to come. Christians know that the story of the cross is followed by the story of the resurrection. Knowing the general framework of how the story ends—that the God of love, justice, and mercy triumphs for all eternity—deeply impacts our experiences and interpretations of the past and the present. Moltmann emphasizes further that the forgiveness offered by Christians opens up the possibility of the salvation of the perpetrators. Hope is not limited to the victims, but is ultimately for everyone. Moltmann's theology brings out how and why Christians of today, even in the face of suffering, need to live in hope for the future of this world and the next.

In the previous subsection, we had spoken of the martyrdom of Ignatius of Antioch and how he had chosen to be loyal to Christ the King rather than to the Roman Emperor. Girard, Schwager, Copeland, and Moltmann express the meaning of Christian doctrine in ways that can be linked with the opposition to oppressive earthly powers by martyrs of the twentieth and twenty-first centuries. Franz Jägerstätter, an Austrian Catholic farmer, contrasted loyalty to the Nazis with loyalty to the kingdom of Christ:

> Just as those who believe in National Socialism tell themselves that their struggle is for survival, so must we, too, convince ourselves that our struggle is for the eternal Kingdom. But with this difference: we need no rifles or pistols for our battle but, instead, spiritual weapons—and the foremost among these is prayer.[26]

Jägerstätter chose to go to his death rather than serve what he believed was an unjust war of aggression initiated by the Nazis.

Not every Christian is called to martyrdom, and perhaps few are called to the most radical forms of social activism. The ways in which Christian doctrine continues to inspire people to give of their lives in various ways, however, speaks to its continuing relevance for everyone in whatever their situation in life. As a popular song of some years ago put the question, "What if God was one of us?"[27] Contemporary Christians believe that the implications are myriad.

Doctrines have been formulated in the interest of Christian unity, for it is important that Christians share the same faith. Doctrines have also functioned, however, as a battleground upon which many divisive battles have been fought out. Divisions among Christians and attempts to heal those divisions will be the topic of the next chapter.

FOR FURTHER REFLECTION

1. Some Christians see no need for doctrine beyond what is already in Scripture. What might be some arguments in favor of there being a need for doctrine beyond Scripture?

2. Is it possible to hold that doctrine is very important, even essential, and still think that some people manage to be overly focused on doctrine?

3. Name and explain three ways in which the Nicene Creed, when compared with the Apostles' Creed, reveals some of the doctrinal issues at stake in the fourth century?

4. How is it that a clear declaration of the divinity of Jesus is linked with the need for a teaching like the doctrine of the Trinity?

5. What does it mean to say that doctrine is formulated in order to support a correct interpretation of the Christian story? Try to give an example or two.

6. How are doctrines about Christ linked with questions about the meaning of salvation?

7. How did early Christian belief in Christ the King have significance both for this life and for the world to come?

8. Is it more of a metaphor or more of a reality to speak about encountering Christ in the face of the poor or the suffering?

9. What does it mean to say that at the heart of all that is are persons in relation? What difference might that make?

FOR FURTHER READING

Bellitto, Christopher M. *The General Councils: A History of the Twenty-One Church Councils from Nicaea to Vatican II,* Mahwah, NJ: Paulist Press, 2002.

Hunt, Anne. *Trinity: Nexus of the Mysteries of Christian Faith.* Maryknoll, NY: Orbis Books, 2005.

Loewe, William P. *The College Student's Introduction to Christology*. Collegeville, MN: Liturgical Press, 1996.

Marthaler, Berard L. *The Creed: The Apostolic Faith in Contemporary Theology*. Mystic, CT: Twenty-Third Publications, 2007.

Volf, Miroslav. *After Our Likeness: The Church as the Image of the Trinity*. Grand Rapids: Eerdmans, 1998.

Zizioulas, Jean. *Being as Communion: Studies in Personhood and the Church*. Crestwood, NY: St. Vladimir's Seminary Press, 1985.

GLOSSARY

Apollinarianism: the Christian heresy that Christ had a divine mind within a human body but not a human mind, and therefore not a full human nature.

Apostles' Creed: an early formulation of Christian faith whose exact history is unknown but which is considered to be of apostolic origin.

Arianism: the heretical belief that the Word that became flesh in Jesus was created rather than unbegotten and therefore something less than God.

Christology: the study of doctrines concerning Jesus Christ.

Christ the King: a title given to Christ in the early centuries that relativized the authority of earthly rulers as well as the level of allegiance that is owed to them.

Doctrine: teaching, or body of teachings.

Eschatology: the study of the last things, Judgment, Heaven, Hell, and so on. Modern eschatology has focused on the concept of the kingdom of God as both here and yet to come.

Eutychianism: the Christian heresy that in Christ, the divine and human natures are so much in unity that they cannot be distinguished from one another.

Homoousion: Greek term for "one in being," or consubstantial. Term applied to the Son's relationship with the Father against those who claimed that the Son was *homoiousion*, or similar in being to the Father.

Incarnation: the Christian doctrine that God became a human being in Jesus Christ.

Kingdom of God: a key element of Jesus' public teaching; the reign of God in contrast to the reign of earthly powers; that which is breaking into this life whenever human beings do the will of God.

Montanism: a North African Christian heresy of the early centuries that placed the teachings of charismatic prophets above that of bishops.

Nestorianism: a heresy that denied the full unity of the divine and human natures of Christ.

Nicene Creed: a formulation of basic Christian teaching directed against a number of heresies and approved by the Council of Constantinople in 381 CE.

Resurrection: the Christian doctrine that Jesus Christ rose from the dead; also the doctrine that all human beings will rise to judgment.

Soteriology: the study of the doctrine of salvation.

Theotokos: Greek term for "Mother of God," applied to Mary in a way that affirmed that in Jesus Christ, the divine and human natures formed a unity.

Trinity: the Christian doctrine that in God, there are three persons, the Father, the Son, and the Holy Spirit.

NOTES

1. Curtis Freeman traces out Baptist views of the creeds as he offers his own contemporary ecumenical perspective in *Contesting Catholicity: Theology for Other Baptists* (Waco, TX: Baylor University Press, 2015), esp. chap. 3.

2. I will call these bishops "catholic" (universal) though they are also "orthodox" (correct teaching).

3. Of the following three definitions of *Gnostic*, in this textbook, we will use the first. (1) *Gnostic* is often used to refer in general to a number of groups whom Catholic Christians considered heretical, especially in the early Christian centuries, including the Manichees of the time of Augustine (354–430 CE) and the Cathars of the time of Thomas Aquinas (1224–74 CE). (2) Some contemporary biblical scholars want to limit the term *Gnostic* to one particular

group in northern Palestine in the early Christian centuries and use more specific labels for other groups, such as the Marcionites and the Valentinians, who have been formerly included under the general gnostic umbrella. (3) *Gnostic* is sometimes used to label a large variety of religious groups with antimaterial, dualistic views of the universe that have existed for many centuries before and after Christ and still today.

4. I constructed this chart from the writing of Richard Hooker, *The Laws of Ecclesiastical Polity*, bk. 5, chap. 54, para. 10; referred to in *Heresies and How to Avoid Them*, ed. Ben Quash and Michael Ward (Peabody, MA: Hendrickson Publishers, 2007), 3–4.

5. Henri de Lubac, *The Christian Faith: An Essay on the Structure of the Apostles Creed*, trans. Br. Richard Arnandez (San Francisco: Ignatius Press, 1969), 17–57.

6. These translations are found at the Vatican's website, http://www.vatican.va/archive/ccc_css/archive/catechism/credo.htm. The new U.S. Catholic translation is available at: http://www.usccb.org/beliefs-and-teachings/what-we-believe/. A comparison of the original Nicene with the Nicene-Constantinople Creed can be found at: http://en.wikipedia.org/wiki/Nicene_Creed#Comparison_between_Creed_of_325_and_Creed_of_381.

7. These ideas represent Arius's basic thinking, though the actual terms *homoiousion* and *homoousion* were not used until after his death.

8. I list only the christological heresies. To this list could be added Sabbatians, who insist that Christians as well as Jews should celebrate Passover; also the Quartodecimans, who date Easter at the same time as Passover.

9. Berard L. Marthaler, *The Creed: The Apostolic Faith in Contemporary Theology*, 3rd ed. (Mystic, CT: Twenty-Third Publications, 2007), 244–45.

10. Ephesus was not received by the Assyrian Church of the East. There are, in addition, Oriental Orthodox churches in Africa that have historically been considered Monophysite, that is, claiming that in Christ there is only one divine nature. Much ecumenical progress has been made between these churches and Catholic and other Orthodox churches in recent decades through reconsideration of historical sources.

11. Norman P. Tanner, *Decrees of the Ecumenical Councils* (Washington, DC: Georgetown University Press, 1990), 1:28.

12. Anne Hunt, *Trinity: Nexus of the Mysteries of Christian Faith* (Maryknoll, NY: Orbis Books, 2005), 14–17.

13. Marthaler, *The Creed*, 248.

14. Hunt, *The Trinity*, 19–20. Hunt, here, cites Augustine, *Sermon* 52.10.23.

15. Athanasius, *Selected Works and Letters*, http://www.ccel.org/ccel/schaff/npnf204.vii.ii.liv.html.

16. Gregory of Nazianzus, *De Incarnatione Verbi*, 54.16, Epistle 101, http://www.earlychurchtexts.com/public/gregoryofnaz_critique_of_apolliniarianism.htm.

17. Ignatius of Antioch, "Christ the King of Heaven," in *Lives of the Saints with Excepts from Their Writings*, ed. Father Thomas Plassmann (New York: John J. Crawley, 1954).

18. John Zizioulas, *Being in Communion: Studies in Personhood and the Church* (Crestwood, NJ: St, Vladimir's Seminary Press, 1985), 27–39.

19. Catherine Mowry LaCugna, *God for Us: The Trinity and Christian Life* (San Francisco: HarperCollins, 1991), 399.

20. René Girard, *Deceit, Desire, and the Novel: Self and Other in Literary Structure* (Baltimore: The Johns Hopkins University Press, 1965). Cited in *Internet Encyclopedia of Philosophy*, http://www.iep.utm.edu/girard/.

21. René Girard, *Things Hidden since the Foundation of the World* (Stanford, CA: Stanford University Press, 1987). Research for this was undertaken in collaboration with Jean-Michel Oughourlian and Guy Lefort.

22. Nikolaus Wandinger, "Soteriologie," in *Dogmatik Heute: Bestandsaufnahme und Perspektiven*, ed. Thomas Marschler and Thomas Schärtl (Regensburg: Verlag Friedrich Pustet, 2014), 281–319.

23. M. Shawn Copeland, *Enfleshing Freedom: Body, Race, and Being* (Minneapolis: Fortress Press, 2009).

24. Ibid.

25. Jürgen Moltmann, *The Crucified God: The Cross of Christ as the Foundation and Criticism of Christian Theology* (London, SCM Press, 1974); also, *Theology of Hope: On the Ground and the Implications of a Christian Eschatology* (New York: Harper and Row, 1967). See also Peter Althouse, "In Appreciation of Jürgen Moltmann: A Discussion of His Transformational Eschatology," *Pneuma: The Journal of the Society for Pentecostal Studies* 28 (Spring 2006): 21–32.

26. Gordon Zahn, *In Solitary Witness: The Life and Death of Franz Jägerstätter* (Springfield, IL: Templegate Publishers, 1986), 99.

27. Joan Osborne, vocal performance of "One of Us," by Eric Bazilian, recorded in 1995, on *Relish*, Blue Gorilla Records.

Chapter 7

CHURCH DIVISIONS
AND ECUMENISM

In the Gospel of John, after the Last Supper, Jesus prays: "I ask not only on behalf of these, but also on behalf of those who will believe in me through their word, that they may all be one. As you, Father, are in me and I am in you, may they also be in us, so that the world may believe that you have sent me" (John 17:20–21). A few centuries later, the Nicene Creed declared, "We believe in one, holy, catholic, and apostolic Church." What might it mean to say that the Church is "one" when there exist in the United States alone hundreds of Christian denominations?

An outside observer studying the history of Christianity might conclude that the most distinguishing characteristic of Christians is their capacity for dividing from each other. How did all of these divisions come about? What has functioned as the basis for Christian unity in spite of divisions? What is being now done about these divisions? That is the topic for this chapter.

Nearly all Christians identify the faith of their own particular Christian tradition as "apostolic." To be apostolic is to have an authentic link with the faith as preached by the original apostles of Jesus. What provides this link in various Christian traditions?

Claims Concerning Continuity with
the Faith of the Apostles

Some churches claim that their faith communities are the same as those witnessed to in the New Testament. Other churches stress

131

that their doctrines are the same as those taught by the apostles. Yet other churches claim that the life of discipleship and witness found in their churches is the same as that witnessed to by the apostles and the martyrs. Still other churches claim that the bishops in their churches stand in direct succession with the bishops who led the churches in the early centuries. Of course, there are various combinations, emphases, and overlaps in the claims of churches concerning the extent that they trace their apostolicity through the Bible, doctrine, discipleship, and episcopal succession.[1]

CONTEMPORARY CHURCHES' CLAIMS TO APOSTOLICITY	
Basis	Rationale for Claim to Apostolicity
The Bible	Present-day communities are addressed by the words of Christ just the same as the communities in the New Testament
Doctrine	Present church proclamation and doctrine are the same as that given by the apostles
Witness of Discipleship	Present-day Christians follow Christ in their nonviolence, their simple lifestyle, and their willingness to die for their faith
Succession of Bishops	Present-day Christians are united by the same faith and the same Sacraments under the leadership of the bishops who historically succeed the apostles

Catholics and Orthodox

We will begin our study of Christian traditions by focusing on the claims of Catholics and Orthodox with their simultaneous focus on doctrine and on the apostolic succession of bishops. In the early centuries, there was no division between the Catholics and the Orthodox. During the second century, church unity was threatened by the beliefs of Gnostic Christians and other groups considered heretical. How was a Christian to know what the true gospel was and where the true Eucharist was to be found? The catholic-orthodox response was to appoint a bishop to be in charge of teaching, Sacraments, and church governance in each major city or large town where there was a church. The office of the bishop assured church unity in governance, doctrine, and Sacraments.

The authority of the bishop was especially connected with the Eucharist, at which only he or his representative could preside. Eucharistic communities consisted in those who loved each other through Christ and the Holy Spirit. Thus, Catholics and Orthodox believe that doctrine and authority were being stressed not for their own sake but in the service of Christian love. On a larger scale, the bishops themselves formed a network of mutual recognition and support. A new bishop would be consecrated by the laying on of hands by fellow bishops. A Christian who would travel from one local church to another would bring a letter from their bishop affirming that they could receive the Eucharist. By the end of the second century, the office of bishop, or episcopacy, was broadly accepted by most Christians as a gift from God that saved the Church from the Gnostic heretics.[2] Contemporary Catholics and Orthodox share the point of view that the office of bishop, as it expanded church-wide throughout the second century, represents the will of God.

Present-day Catholic and Orthodox (and also Anglican and some Lutheran) churches have maintained historic lines of succession, believing their contemporary bishops to be the legitimate successors of the apostles. These lines of apostolic succession have functioned as the bedrock of Catholic and Orthodox claims to legitimacy.

Prior to Christianity's acceptance, the Roman Empire had been organized into dioceses (large administrative regions) by the emperor Diocletian, a persecutor of Christians. In the fourth century, as the Catholic Church became first tolerated and then the Empire's official religion, the Church itself gradually became organized within these same diocesan structures. Eventually, a bishop became the head of a diocese. Large churches known as basilicas were built along the model of Roman court buildings. A bishop's role took on many aspects of administration.

From the perspective of Catholics and Orthodox, this church with its bishops in historical succession was neither an "established church" nor a "denomination." It was simply "the one Church" that predated its associations with the Roman Empire and which also existed beyond the Empire's boundaries.

Gaining official government approval brought with it a mixed bag of results, some of it negative. As being Christian became officially approved and socially acceptable, some Christians sought a more authentic lifestyle apart from the everyday world. The monastic movement, which had begun in the middle of the third century with monks who lived as hermits in the desert, received increased attention and developed as various types of communities, usually with a "rule" written by a founder. In their origins, these monasteries functioned as a kind of counterculture. Still, most Catholics and Orthodox tend to see some deeply positive aspects to the penetration of Christianity into whole societies and cultures. A key point of difference among Christians of today lies in their view of the relationship between the Church and the human social world.

Although some historians place the date of the "fall" of the Roman Empire in the West in 476 CE with the deposition of the emperor, it is more accurate to see its gradual transformation into the Holy Roman Empire of the Middle Ages. Moving the seat of the Roman Empire from Rome to Byzantium (later Constantinople, and now Istanbul) in the East in 330 CE brought some tension between the emperor and the leading diocese of Rome, in the West. Differences in culture and language were stark. In the West, Latin was the official language; in the East, it was Greek. Romans thought of Greeks as soft; Greeks thought of Romans as brutes. Roman priests were clean-shaven; Greek priests maintained beards. Romans used unleavened bread in the Eucharist; Greeks used leavened bread.

In chapter 6, a difference was noted in the Western and Eastern approaches to the Trinity. Conceptually, the Western Christians stressed one God before three persons; the Eastern Christians would begin reflection with the three persons. A true and lasting doctrinal difference arose in the early sixth century. The Nicene Creed had declared that the Holy Spirit "proceeds from the Father." Churches in the West inserted a new phrase into the Creed: the Holy Spirit "proceeds from the Father and the Son" ("and the Son" = *filioque*). The *filioque* was intended to clarify the equality of the Father and the Son. The East, on the other hand, held that acknowledging that the

Father had a certain priority regarding the processions of the persons did not take away from their equality. In the eyes of the West, the East was functionally subordinating the Son to the Father. In the eyes of the East, leaving out the *filioque* clarified the special role of the Father. Complicating the matter was that the Western church had inserted the *filioque* into the Creed without the approval of the Eastern church.

By this time, the early sixth century, the Bishop of Rome was functioning as the Pope, the head of the Catholic Church. For centuries, Rome had been recognized as having a certain priority as the diocese in which Peter and Paul had both been martyred. Other churches would appeal to Rome as having the final word in the settling of disputes. Eastern churches in the sixth century recognized Rome as among the five highest ranking dioceses ("patriarchates" that also included Constantinople, Antioch, Alexandria, and Jerusalem), and even acknowledged it as holding a primacy of honor among them. The Church of Rome claimed, however, that as the See (official seat) of Peter, the head of the apostles, it had not only a primacy of honor but also a primacy of jurisdiction. In other words, the Pope, as the Bishop of Rome, was the head of the Church and had the authority to tell other bishops what to do.

In 1054, with pressing political and even military issues in the background, a breaking point was reached when representatives of the pope excommunicated the Patriarch of Constantinople, Michael Cerularius, for disobeying a paper order. Cerularius in turn excommunicated the papal representatives. This split between West and East was further sealed when, in 1204, Crusaders, acting on false advice, conquered, sacked, and occupied Constantinople, which they then held for fifty-seven years, until 1261.

Although attempts were made to heal this split, the break proved to be decisive. The Catholic Church, with its center in Rome, occupied the Latin West, and the Orthodox Church, with its Patriarchates, occupied the East. A minority of churches in the East give loyalty to Rome and are known as the Catholic Churches of Eastern Rites, including among many the Byzantine, Melkite, Maronite, and Syro-Malabar Catholic Churches.

Before Martin Luther

Protestants and Catholics have often differed in their assessments of the Catholic Church in the Middle Ages. In the Latin West, the Church was the glue that held the society together. Some have seen in this church a great medieval synthesis that blended faith, reason, culture, politics, and social order to offer a coherent worldview. The Church produced cathedrals, monasteries, and universities. It fostered a culture in which humility and learning were highly valued ideals. This view of the majesty of the Middle Ages, with which I was raised as a child, has its exaggerations, and few people today would hold to it without adding significant qualifications.

Opposite exaggerations have been fostered by those who have seen in the medieval Catholic Church nothing but a corrupt, foul, and superstitious institution that represented the darkest element of the Dark Ages. Few people today would hold this terribly unnuanced view, but remnants of it remain in stereotypical media representations of the Middle Ages as an ignorant and brutal time.

There had been various movements of reform within the Catholic Church throughout the Middle Ages.[3] The Carolingian Renaissance under Charlemagne (768–814) and his successor, Louis the Pious (814–40), was a time in which civil and ecclesial institutions flourished in tandem through the expansion of learning and the reform of liturgical practices. The Gregorian Reform under the leadership of Pope Gregory VII (1073–85), though mostly institutional and legal, had as its goal the restoration of the Church to the purity of the early centuries by more closely regulating moral, sexual, and financial behaviors. The reforms associated with the monastery of Cluny from the tenth through the twelfth centuries brought more discipline to monastic life and more splendor to architecture and liturgy.

On the eve of the Reformation, there could be found plenty of healthy church life and practice, and there could also be found plenty of salient examples of abuses of all that is good and holy.[4] The Church, as the saying goes, is always in need of reform and renewal.[5] This was perhaps true in a particularly pressing way in the early sixteenth century on the brink of the Protestant Reformation. The papacy had lost power and prestige in the previous centuries. For a time, the pope lived in Avignon, France, and at one point, there had been two and then three claimants who had been elected to the chair of Peter, a situation not resolved until 1417. The behavior of fifteenth-century popes, most notably Alexander VI (r. 1492–1503), was scandalous.[6] Some bishops of the time did not even reside in their own dioceses, yet lived luxuriously from revenues collected in their churches. Many priests were relatively uneducated.

In addition, various cultural, social, and political factors at the time combined to bring about enormous changes not only in the Church but in the larger society as well. The printing press along with an abundance of paper contributed to a rise in literacy accompanied by new attitudes toward learning and authority. The Bible became widely available in vernacular languages in translations that challenged conventional church teachings. The Renaissance with its awe-inspiring art and world-shattering perspectives was flourishing throughout Europe. Breakthroughs in classical scholarship were accompanied by a humanism that displaced God and the heavens and made human beings the center of attention. The seeds of nationalist thought were taking root in many places. Then, in 1492, a new world with new peoples was encountered across the Atlantic Ocean.

There had already been a history of organized opposition to the Catholic Church prior to the Protestant Reformation. From the twelfth through the fourteenth centuries, a group of Gnostic-like Christians known as "Cathars" taught that the Catholic Church was the church of Satan. The Cathars, who lived mainly in northern Italy, southern France, and the Rhineland in Germany, maintained their own network of bishops and held councils. Much of the early Inquisition was directed against them, and they were finally eliminated by military force.

Some medieval reform groups focused on apostolic continuity through their witness of discipleship. In the late twelfth century, there began in France a reform movement called the Waldensians after their founder, Peter Waldo (died c. 1205), a rich merchant of Lyon who gave away all his wealth. The Waldensians were also fiercely persecuted, but they still survive today.

In England in the fourteenth century, an Oxford don, John Wycliffe (c. 1330–84), had a vision of an invisible, heavenly church to which only true believers belonged. This heavenly church stood in contrast to the corrupt earthly church. Wycliffe translated the New Testament into English. Wycliff stressed continuity with the apostles through embrace of the Bible. His followers were labelled "Lollards," meaning "Mumblers," by their opponents. In this period, prior to the printing press, the Lollards were unable to circulate their ideas efficiently and the movement died out. In Moravia, now the Czech Republic, Jan Hus (c. 1370–1415) led a similar movement. Hus was promised safe passage to the Council of Constance in 1415 by church officials, but civil officials, allegedly having found him violating the conditions of the agreement by celebrating mass in his room, executed him. His movement, which had strong political backing from Slavic-speaking peoples in the face of occupation by German-speaking peoples, lived on. As with the Waldensians, there are still Hussites to this day.

There were also various reform movements within the Catholic Church, usually in the form of new religious orders. The Franciscans, founded by Francis Bernadone (St. Francis of Assisi, 1182–1226) tried to improve the Church through the embrace of poverty. In contrast to the Waldensians, the Franciscans remained loyal to the pope. Like the Waldensians, however, the Franciscans focused on the Witness of Discipleship. The Dominicans, founded by Dominic de Guzmán (St. Dominic, 1170–1221) tried to improve the Church through intellectual rigor in combatting the Cathar heresy. Various other movements arose among both the clergy and the laity, focusing on prayer and devotions. An ecumenical council, Lateran V, was held in Rome from 1512 through 1517, but it failed to bring about any serious reform.

Martin Luther

The story of the Protestant Reformation begins in 1517 with Martin Luther (1483–1546) formulating ninety-five theses that were critical of the sale of papal indulgences. Indulgences were waivers of punishment due to sin to be applied either to oneself or to a soul in purgatory. It was believed by Catholics that some people who died were neither bad enough to be sent to hell nor good enough to enter immediately into heaven. Purgatory was held by Catholics to be a place where the sinner suffers as in hell except for one crucial difference: they live in hope because they know that eventually they will make it to heaven. In Luther's time, indulgences were being sold in order to raise money for the building of St. Peter's Church in Rome.

Luther did not object to the pope being able to take away from punishment in this life if it had been something imposed by the Church, such as a public penance or excommunication. Luther's theological objections were to (1) granting indulgences intended to take away time to be served in purgatory after the sinner had died, (2) the sale of indulgences for money, and (3) paying more attention to indulgences than to the gospel's call to actual repentance and holiness of life. Early on, Luther had hoped that the pope would agree with his protests against bad practices. Thesis no. 55 stated, "It is certainly the pope's sentiment that if indulgences, which are a very insignificant thing, are celebrated with one bell, one procession, and one ceremony, then the gospel, which is the very greatest thing, should be preached with a hundred bells, a hundred processions, a hundred ceremonies."[7]

Luther's criticisms of Catholic Church teachings and practices expanded rapidly. In 1520–21, he wrote three now-famous treatises that expressed his break with Rome.[8] He taught that Christians are saved by faith alone, not by works, and that all Christians share in the priesthood of Christ. In 1520, a Papal Bull was issued that ordered Luther to recant his heresies; he publicly burned the Papal Bull. In January 1521, he was officially excommunicated.[9] Later that year, he faced trial in the German city of Worms, where he defiantly declared, "Here I stand; I cannot do otherwise"[10] Eventually, Luther would come to teach that the pope was the Antichrist.

Luther was supported by German princes as well as the overall political establishment in northern Germany. He taught a doctrine of two governments (later known as "two kingdoms"), the worldly and the spiritual, both ultimately ruled by God. The Church gives care to the soul and appeals to conscience, but does not rule over the state.

The state attends to the need for order in this world, but has no authority over consciences and souls. The worldly government needs the sword to restrain evildoing.

For Luther and the Reformation in general, literature and music took precedence over the visible and tactile arts. Literature was more like the Word and more directly addressed the spirit than tangible objects that could be interpreted as being "graven images" like those condemned in the Old Testament. The sermon became the great Protestant work of art. Music was thought to transcend the visible, material world in ways that paralleled the relationship between spirit and matter. Luther accepted the classical belief that the planets in their orbits produced a celestial harmony, the music of the spheres, and that music, with its own basis in mathematics and tonal harmonies, allowed for a special kind of participation in God's creation.[11] He promoted the use of music and hymnody in liturgy. Luther is especially associated with the type of hymn known as the chorale, many of which he wrote himself, including the famous "A Mighty Fortress." Lutheran chorales have had a deep impact on German religion, culture, and music through the present day.

In addition to translating the Bible into German, Luther produced many writings, including catechisms. With his bold and daring personality, he was loved and revered by his followers then and still today.

The Radical Reformation

What is known as the Radical Reformation was led by Reformers who pushed for changes that were more far-reaching than those advocated by Luther. These Christians were keenly focused on witness. In 1524–26, the Peasant's War in Germany was led by Thomas Münzer. The peasants had appealed to Scripture and to the principles of Martin Luther. Luther, however, condemned the revolution by the peasants and endorsed their slaughter by the reigning princes. He did not believe that the Bible endorsed the violent overthrow of the civil and political order. In the decades to come, the groups that made up the Radical Reformation would be persecuted and slaughtered by Protestants and Catholics alike.

The Radical Reformers adopted the position that the Church should have no political connections with secular governments. Whereas Luther had basically accepted the teachings of the early ecumenical councils, Radical Reformers came to believe that the Church fell from grace during the reign of Constantine as it blended in with the powers and politics of this world. Anabaptists (who were named such because of their rejection of infant baptism) eventually interpreted Scripture, especially the Sermon on the Mount, as calling for radical nonviolence. Later Anabaptist groups, such as the Hutterites, Mennonites, and Amish, would develop a communal lifestyle separated from the developing modern world.

MAJOR BRANCHES OF THE PROTESTANT REFORMATION			
Branch	**Founding Figure(s)**	**Years founded**	**Country of Origin**
Lutheran	Martin Luther; Philip Melanchthon	1517	Germany
Reformed	Huldrych Zwingli; John Calvin	1518	Switzerland
Radical	Thomas Münzer; Menno Simons	1520s	Germany; Switzerland
Anglican	Henry VIII; Thomas Cranmer	1534	England

Reformed Churches

Reformed churches constitute another major branch of the Protestant Reformation. A movement in Switzerland parallel to that of Luther was led by Huldrych Zwingli (1484–1531) in Zurich starting in 1518. Zwingli and Luther shared many ideas but would part from each other over their different understandings of Christ's presence in the Eucharist. Zwingli went further than Luther in the reform of religious practices. Zwingli believed that the artwork in churches was idolatrous and distracted attention away from true worship. Although he was himself a musician, he found traditional sacred music to be a distraction. He had the organs removed from churches and allowed only congregational singing. Zwingli died in battle in Zurich during an inner-Protestant civil war in 1531.

The figure most associated with the development of the Reformed churches is the French lawyer John Calvin (1509–64). In 1526, Calvin arrived in Switzerland with the mission of structuring the government of the city and church of Geneva according to principles that could be derived from the New Testament. His *Institutes of the Christian Faith* was first published in 1536. Calvin's writings had tremendous influence throughout the Protestant world, and he became the leading intellectual figure in Reformed churches throughout Switzerland, the Netherlands, Scotland, northern France, and Hungary. The Puritan movement in England and then in the American colonies was Calvinist in its inspiration.

When it came to understanding the Sacraments, the Reformed churches occupied a kind of middle ground between Lutheran churches and the Radical Reformation. Regarding the relationship between church and state, though, the Reformed churches were much closer to the Lutheran. Lutheranism itself came to exist in different forms, some closer to the Reformed and some closer—in practice, if not in theology—to the Catholic. In England, the Church of England had its own complex development but came to see itself as the middle way that drew upon the best from the Catholic and Puritan extremes.

The Council of Trent

As noted earlier, many reform movements have existed within the Catholic Church prior to, during, and long after the Protestant Reformation. Although the terminology is debated, some speak of the Catholic "Counter-Reformation," which had its highpoint in the Council of Trent (1545–63). The main business of the Council of Trent was the reform of the Church. The Council issued many new definitions, rules, and regulations to ensure that priests would be properly trained and that Sacraments would be performed according to uniform standards. To use a contemporary term, it would be fair to say that the Council of Trent was mostly about "quality control." The Catholic response to the Protestant Reformation was thus to continue to reform itself, but now with new vigor and a new seriousness. The Society of Jesus (Jesuits), the religious order founded by St. Ignatius Loyola in the years shortly before the Council of Trent, came to be associated with carrying out the reform of the Catholic Church.

The Council of Trent issued directives concerning sacred art, including that it must be true to Scripture, inspire devotion, and not contain inappropriate elements. The council also defined Catholic positions on original sin, rejecting the Protestant view of total depravity. It also rejected the Protestant view on justification by opposing the notion of salvation through faith alone, not through works. The council by no means took opposite positions on these issues, but rather offered some nuanced positions. According to Trent, original sin is indeed devastating, but not total. Human freedom and reason are damaged, but not erased. The first saving grace comes as a gift from God and is not earned; after that, however, the human heart is transformed so that Christians do come to merit grace in a certain qualified and modest way.

The traditional doctrine that one needed to belong to the Catholic Church in order to be saved was also upheld by the Council of Trent, though it clarified that, in addition, one must live a life based on charity and remain in a state of grace. Christians outside the Catholic Church could be saved because of their invincible ignorance if, through no fault of their own, they did not know that the Catholic Church was the one true Church. No one, unless they had a special revelation from God, could be certain that they were saved. The Catholic approach concerning salvation was to live in hope, avoiding the extremes of either presumption or despair.

In contrast to the Council of Trent, Protestants continued to teach that Christians are saved by faith alone. Calvinists were known for their strict doctrine of predestination, emphasizing that the answer to the question of who would be saved had already been determined and was known by God. As the Reformation progressed beyond Luther and Calvin into the later sixteenth century, there emerged a widespread belief that not only did being saved by faith require that one believe that Christ died on the cross for one's sins, but also that coming to this realization and acceptance constituted an experience that gave the believer a deep sense of assurance. Protestants would ask, "Have you been saved?" The expectation was that if you had been saved, you would know it; if you did not know it, it had not happened yet.

John Wesley

Literally, hundreds of different churches have come into being since the time of the Reformation. It would be impossible to mention all or even most of them. The Anglican clergyman John Wesley (1703–91), however, deserves a special mention in any recounting of the development of Christian traditions and churches. Wesley is the founding figure of Methodism. Methodism began as a reform movement within the Church of England in the eighteenth century. Wesley believed that the Church of England was legitimately the established Church of England. He wanted his reform movement not to replace the Church of England but to bring it back to life. He forbade his Methodists to hold their meetings at the same time as Church of England services so that they could attend both. Wesley himself presided at Mass and distributed communion on an average of more than once per week.

Wesley ran the Methodist movement with an almost military rigor. He would arise at four o'clock each morning and then ride on a horse through the country from place to place, giving as many as four sermons per day. In the time between, he would write his journals and sermons. Wesley earned a great deal of wealth through his writings, but he continually gave his money away. He not only preached but also lived by the motto "Earn all you can. Save all you can. Give all you can."

Wesley tried to renew the Church by forming small Christian communities in which members would confess their sins and encourage each other to truly live out the gospel. These groups were divided into classes and bands, with each group having a leader. If a leader judged that a member was not trying their best to live a fully Christian life, then that member would not get a ticket to the quarterly "love feast." The love feast featured penny cake and punch with members showering praise and affirmations on each other into the night.

Wesley's approach was designed to bring about real and lasting conversion. Although most members belonged to the Church of England, there were also a small number of Catholics and Puritans who participated. Wesley had an ecumenical vision: he believed that, if Christians truly lived converted lives, squabbles among the different Christian traditions would eventually fade away.

Wesley did not want Methodists to form their own churches. He did allow for Methodist ordinations in the United States just following the Revolutionary War, but only because he thought that the brand new nation did not yet have an established church, and he hoped that the Methodists might have a strong influence upon whatever established church might eventually arise. In England, Wesley predicted that about one third of the Methodists would break off from the Church of England after his death, but that this group would fade away and the majority would continue as a movement of reform. His prediction was not on target, however. Today the worldwide United Methodist Church and many other churches have their roots in Methodism.

Although Methodists today make up a bit less than 3.5 percent of the world's Christians, the influence of Wesleyan Tradition has been enormous. After centuries of wrangling about doctrine during the Reformation and its aftermath, many Christians were ready for a focus on enthusiastic witness. Methodists were somewhat influential in the First Great Awakening in the United States (through the 1730s and 1740s), and then enormously influential in the Second Great Awakening (mainly from the 1820s through 1840s). The Great Awakenings were periods of rapid and intense growth in religious fervor. This fervor was fueled by traveling preachers and by organizers of large camp revival meetings.

Out of Wesleyan Tradition also grew the Holiness movement in the nineteenth-century United States. Holiness churches focused on bringing their members to a "second blessing" or "entire sanctification," beyond their initial conversion, into a lasting and complete state of grace. Some Holiness churches, such as the Church of the Nazarene, exist today, but they are relatively few in number. From them, however, in the early twentieth century, grew the Pentecostal movement, which now claims six hundred million participants worldwide (counting among them about two hundred million Catholics in the Charismatic renewal). There are many forms of Pentecostal churches, but common practices among them are baptism in the Holy Spirit, speaking in tongues, prophesying, and healing.

Many people tend to think of the high-spirited, spontaneous Pentecostal movement as being somewhat the opposite of the highly organized, tightly regulated Catholic Church. Strong arguments can be made to support this viewpoint, but two things put this tendency at least somewhat in question. First, the large number of Catholics who participate in the Charismatic Renewal suggests that there may be a place where the two styles can meet. Second, the vision of John Wesley also brings the two styles together: he was an Anglican Catholic priest who believed that established Christian churches need to be in communion with other established churches whenever possible, and he was simultaneously an Evangelical reformer whose emphasis on true conversion stands as one of the roots of the Pentecostal movement.

Ecumenical Movements

Even in the 1520s, there were early attempts to heal the split between Reformers and Catholics, but soon the divisions grew bloody, bitter, and beyond short-term repair. The wars that followed were mainly about politics and power, but religion often served as a dividing line among enemies. The Thirty Years War (1618–48), centered mainly in southern Germany and the bordering parts of other lands, stands among the most terrible conflicts in history insofar as it tore apart towns and families. The Peace of Westphalia (1648) consists in a series of treaties that ended the war. The prince or ruler of each region would determine the official religion of that place, but those of other religions were allowed to freely practice in their own way. Religious tolerance became a key political principle of the modern world, but animosity between various Christian traditions has continued to the present day.

In the nineteenth century, the German liberal Protestant theologian Friedrich Schleiermacher (1768–1834) proposed that Catholicism and Protestantism stood in a kind of dialectical relationship, each needing the other for its fulfillment. Johann Adam Möhler (1796–1838), also German, articulated a Catholic position on this question, acknowledging the role of dialectics but arguing that all of the contrary positions to be held in tension with each other belonged within the Catholic Church, not outside. In the United States during the nineteenth century, several Protestant churches, such as the Disciples of Christ, were founded as attempts at some type of ecumenism. All attempts at being "just Christian," however, have ended up being another particular, separate version of Christianity.

Serious attempts at ecumenical progress have been made throughout the twentieth century up to today. The World Council of Churches (WCC), founded in 1948, combined prior movements that had been at work for decades.[12] The WCC has remained a major driving force in ecumenical progress since its inception.

The Second Vatican Council (1962–65) set the Catholic Church on the path of ecumenical progress with its Decree on Ecumenism (*Unitatis Redintegratio*). Prior to the Council, the Catholic Church held to a "theology of return," meaning that the only real solution to the separation of churches would consist in their coming back to Rome. The Vatican II document *Lumen Gentium* taught, in contrast, that "the Church of Christ…subsists in the Catholic Church, though elements of sanctification and truth can be found outside its visible confines" (no. 8). Rather than seeing non-Catholic Christians as heretics and schismatics, the Council looked upon them as separated brothers and sisters who are in partial communion with Catholics. The Council further acknowledged that at the time of the Reformation, there were rights and wrongs on both sides. It recognized that the Holy Spirit has been at work among other Christians in salvific ways.

Vatican II expressed many positions that can be interpreted as reaching out to Orthodox, Protestants, and Free Church Christians.

Many Orthodox have found the Council's stress on local churches as Eucharistic communities appealing. Many Protestants have appreciated how the Council, rather than favoring Tradition over Scripture, spoke of them as the two main expressions of the one revelation of Christ, each needing the other for its interpretation. Many Free Church Christians have been positively struck by the Council's emphasis on freedom of conscience. Although Catholics have hotly debated among themselves just how wide the Council had opened the door to ecumenical progress, no one can question the fact that the door was opened up at least more than a small crack.

The Decree on Ecumenism (*UR*) called for a "spiritual ecumenism" according to which Catholics should grow in conversion, prayer, and knowledge (UR 7–9).

VATICAN II ON ELEMENTS OF SPIRITUAL ECUMENISM		
Conversion	**Prayer**	**Knowledge**
Have a change of heart	For renewing our lives in humility	Acknowledge one's own sinfulness
Forgive others	For moving toward church unity	Learn about separated brothers and sisters
Strive to live holier lives	In common with our separated brothers and sisters	Dialogue with separated brothers and sisters

More Recent Ecumenical Progress

In 1982, the World Council of Churches issued "Baptism, Eucharist, and Ministry," also known as "the Lima document," which laid out a range of points of consensus and remaining differences and invited responses.[13] The responses to the Lima Document have been collected in six volumes.[14] Two further convergence texts have since been issued: *The Nature and Purpose of the Church* (2002) and *The Church: Toward a Common Vision* (2013).[15]

Many significant bilateral and multilateral dialogues have taken place between representatives of various Christian traditions. The dialogues usually focus on a particular teaching or practice. They seek to arrive at mutual understanding, sometimes consensus, and even at times convergence. The published results of these dialogues occupy several thick volumes.

In 1995, Pope John Paul II issued what many consider to be a potentially revolutionary encyclical, *Ut Unum Sint*. He issued this apology:

> The ministry of the Bishop of Rome...the visible sign and guarantor of unity, constitutes a difficulty for most other Christians, whose memory is marked by certain painful recollections. To the extent that we are responsible for these, I join my Predecessor Paul VI in asking forgiveness. (no. 88)

John Paul II went on to ask for advice concerning how he might best carry out his ministry as pope:

> As Bishop of Rome I am fully aware...that Christ ardently desires the full and visible communion of all those Communities in which, by virtue of God's faithfulness, his Spirit dwells. I am convinced that I have a particular responsibility in this regard, above all in acknowledging the ecumenical aspirations of the majority of the Christian Communities and in heeding the request made of me to find a way of exercising the primacy which, while in no way renouncing what is essential to its mission, is nonetheless open to a new situation....
>
> This is an immense task, which we cannot refuse and which I cannot carry out by myself. Could not the real but imperfect communion existing between us persuade Church leaders and their theologians to engage with me in a patient and fraternal dialogue on this subject, a dialogue in which, leaving useless controversies behind, we could listen to one another, keeping before us only the will of Christ for his Church and allowing ourselves to be deeply moved by his plea "that they may all be one...so that the

world may believe that you have sent me" (*Jn* 17:21)? (nos. 95–96)

Ut Unum Sint is a remarkable encyclical that offers ecumenical hope and energy.

A significant agreement was reached between the Lutheran World Federation and the Catholic Church in 2000 in the *Joint Declaration on the Doctrine of Justification*.[16] Both Lutherans and Catholics were able to formulate their own approaches to the doctrine of justification in such a way that, while still disagreeing, they could accept each other's doctrines as no longer being church-dividing. For example, the Council of Trent's affirmation of a positive and necessary role for good works in relation to salvation had been expressed in terms that directly opposed Luther's teaching about justification in Christ through faith and not works. The *Joint Declaration*, in contrast, articulated Catholic and Lutheran teachings in ways that allowed for a mutual understanding and recognition amid different forms of expression:

> According to Catholic understanding, good works, made possible by grace and the working of the Holy Spirit, contribute to growth in grace, so that the righteousness that comes from God is preserved and communion with Christ is deepened. When Catholics affirm the "meritorious" character of good works, they wish to say that, according to the biblical witness, a reward in heaven is promised to these works. Their intention is to emphasize the responsibility of persons for their actions, not to contest the character of those works as gifts, or far less to deny that justification always remains the unmerited gift of grace.
>
> The concept of a preservation of grace and a growth in grace and faith is also held by Lutherans. They do emphasize that righteousness as acceptance by God and sharing in the righteousness of Christ is always complete. At the same time, they state that there can be growth in its effects in Christian living. When they view the good works of Christians as the fruits and signs of justification and not

as one's own "merits," they nevertheless also understand eternal life in accord with the New Testament as unmerited "reward" in the sense of the fulfillment of God's promise to the believer. (nos. 38–39)

In spite of this progress on the doctrine of justification, Lutherans and Catholics have yet to achieve full communion. Many Lutherans retain suspicions about the nature of Catholic belief and practice. Catholics have insisted that differences in ecclesiology, that is, in the theological understanding of the Church, still need to be further resolved. On a positive note, the World Council of Methodists has added its own acceptance of this *Joint Declaration*.

The goal of the ecumenical movement as expressed by the World Council of Churches is "full, visible communion."[17] To achieve full communion does not mean that separate traditions will disappear as they merge into larger units. Churches in full communion recognize in each other valid expressions of the Christian faith. They share Sacraments and ministers. They retain their distinct identity as Christian traditions as they work with each other in carrying out their missions on the local level and beyond.

Some churches have entered into full communion with each other. A large number of Lutheran and Reformed churches in Europe achieved full communion in 1973, and several other major churches have shared in their agreement since then. In 1997–98, the Reformed Church in America, the United Church of Christ, the Evangelical-Lutheran Church in America, and the Presbyterian Church (USA) accepted a full communion agreement. These churches continue to disagree on issues they do not consider to be church-dividing such as the understanding of Christ's presence in the Eucharist and the ordination of lesbian and gay members, although the latter difference affects the extent to which they will share ministers.[18] In recent years, many Anglican, Methodist, Lutheran, Reformed, and other churches have reached local, national, or regional agreements that include the sharing of the Eucharist, and many negotiations are currently in progress.

Frustrations and Hopes

Significant ecumenical efforts continue today, but the strong hopes that fueled the movement in the second half of the twentieth century seemed to have lost steam if not to have entirely run out of gas. Some speak optimistically of an "interim period," while others state flatly that we have entered into an "ecumenical winter." Some point toward the impressive achievements found in the growing agreements of the many ecumenical dialogues and urge patience and trust in the Holy Spirit. Others point to growing disagreements about the ordination of women, lesbian and gay marriage, and a range of sexual and social issues. They express frustration that the dialogues have not resulted in many more agreements and convergences than they have. The convergence of several U.S. Lutheran and Reformed churches mentioned above are a good sign, but these churches were perhaps not so far apart to begin with, and overall, their membership represents less than .01 percent of the Christians in the world. Some fear that a window of opportunity had opened for a time but now appears to have slammed shut.

One helpful approach has been to think of ecumenical progress as an "ecclesial gift exchange" in which all participants bring special elements of their own traditions to the table.[19] One tradition does not have to embrace another tradition's belief or practice as its own in order to appreciate their offerings as a gift. The Pentecostal practice of spontaneously praying in the Spirit can be considered a gift brought to the table, even if it does not become a universally common tradition. The Baptist practice of adult believer's baptism by immersion resulting in discipleship can potentially be recognized by all for what it says about what it means to be a Christian. The Methodist practice of "connection," which bonds various groups and churches together in a real way, can be admired by every Christian. The Lutheran focus on justification by faith alone can be appreciated as a gift for the way in which it focuses on the freely given gift of God's grace. The Reformed churches' care in applying Scripture to church polity as well as to all of life can serve as a model for attentiveness to God's Word. The Anglican path of the middle way can serve as an example of blending elements from across a wide spectrum of views. The Orthodox penchant for living the life of the Holy Spirit in the context of the everyday community witnesses to possibilities for all Christians. The Catholic gift of unity of faith, by which they stick together with the same teachings and the same Sacraments as they are led by a network of bishops in communion with each other, can be recognized as a gift to all the churches, even if the others do not follow this practice.

In recent years, some church leaders and academic theologians have been dialoguing and exchanging papers at gatherings for "receptive ecumenism." To some degree, this approach has been born out of frustration at the disappointing pace of progress achieved through the official bilateral dialogues, but the method of receptive ecumenism has been designed to parallel that process rather than to replace it. The key to receptive ecumenism is for each tradition to take responsibility for learning from other traditions. In other words, rather than having, say, Catholics and Lutherans negotiate in order to find areas of agreement and remaining disagreement, the onus is put on Catholics to become passionately interested in what they can legitimately learn from Lutherans, and vice versa.[20]

The goal of full, visible communion does not require or even encourage that all churches become carbon copies of each other; it requires only that churches can come to recognize the authentic Christian faith in each other. Still, achieving this goal will require some changes within the particular traditions. Many churches, for example, have made efforts to offer the Eucharist more frequently so that their practices can become more recognizable to Catholics, Orthodox, and Anglicans. It could be that the Catholic Church will need to become yet more radically affirming of the individual freedom of conscience of their members than it currently is in order for the authenticity of their faith to become more recognizable to Christians in other churches.

It All Belongs to All of Us

Full visible communion among a wide range of churches appears to be a goal for the somewhat distant future. Christianity does not exist as an abstraction, but exists in the concrete in churches that remain divided from each other. Growing closer together through mutual recognition and appreciation requires the long, hard work of actually getting to know and understand each other. Most progress in ecumenical healing comes through the work of people who remain grounded in their particular faith traditions. Being grounded in a particular faith tradition does not make a person less open to others, and in fact, it can make them more open. The ecumenical movement continues to sail between two extremes. On the one extreme are those who believe that their way is the only way. On the other extreme are those who refuse to accept that differences matter, even when the goal of dealing with differences is to reconstrue them in the most humble, honest, and constructive manner possible.

Remaining grounded in particular faith traditions has not prevented Christians at all points on the spectrum of belief and practice from speaking and acting as if it all belongs to all of us. Contemporary Catholics, for example, might not agree with everything said or done by Luther and Calvin, but for the most part, they accept these figures as having made immensely important contributions to our shared Christian heritage. The fervent Catholic St. Francis of Assisi belongs to all Christians too. Many Catholics and Protestants alike honor the faith and witness of radical Reformers such as Menno Simons, the founding figure of the Mennonites, and John Smyth, the founding figure of the Baptists. Hymns written by Charles Wesley, the brother of John, are sung in many different churches beyond the Methodist. "Amazing Grace," written by the Church of England clergyman John Newton, is among the most recognizable songs in the English language. Christians of the West and of the East benefit greatly from study of each other's traditions.

It is only very recently in Christian history that many Christians would dare to think, "It all belongs to all of us." May the journey toward full, visible communion regain inspiration and move on full speed ahead!

FOR FURTHER REFLECTION

1. In the quote that opens this chapter, Jesus appears to link the unity of the Church with the credibility of Christian witness. In what ways might these two things be connected?

2. Name some of the factors that contributed to the split between the Catholic Church in the Latin West and the Greek-speaking Eastern Orthodox Church. To what extent might some of the factors be labelled historical, cultural, political, religious, or theological?

3. What does it mean to say that "the church is always in need of reform and renewal"? Why is this an important concept? Might this concept be understood differently by different Christians?

4. What factors, historical, cultural, political, religious, and theological, helped to give rise to the Protestant Reformation?

5. Briefly differentiate between Lutheran churches, Reformed churches, Anglican churches, and the churches of the Radical Reformation.

6. What were the teachings and effects of the Council of Trent? How can the Council of Trent be understood as a distinctive moment within a long history of internal Catholic reform?

7. What is the ecumenical movement? What are some of its frustrations? What have been some of its accomplishments?

8. Why is John Wesley a person of significant interest to the ecumenical movement today?

9. Can commitment to a particular Christian faith tradition really go hand in hand with ecumenical progress? Would it be better for Christians simply to leave the old divisions behind?

FOR FURTHER READING

Bellitto, Christopher M. *Renewing Christianity: A History of Church Reform from Day One to Vatican II.* Mahwah, NJ: Paulist Press, 2001.

Burkhart, John. *Apostolicity Then and Now: An Ecumenical Church in a Postmodern World.* Collegeville, MN: Liturgical Press, 2004.

Gros, Jeffrey, FSC, Eamon McManus, and Ann Riggs. *Introduction to Ecumenism.* Mahwah, NJ: Paulist Press, 1998.

Lutheran World Federation and the Catholic Church. *Joint Declaration on the Doctrine of Justification*. 1999. http://www.vatican.va/roman_curia/pontifical_councils/chrstuni/documents/rc_pc_chrstuni_doc_31101999_cath-luth-joint-declaration_en.html.

MacCulloch, Diarmaid. *The Reformation: A History*. New York: Viking Press, 2003.

Murray, Paul D., ed. *Receptive Ecumenism and the Call to Catholic Learning: Exploring a Way for Contemporary Ecumenism*. Oxford: Oxford University Press, 2008.

Second Vatican Council. *Unitatis Redintegratio*. http://www.vatican.va/archive/hist_councils/ii_vatican_council/documents/vat-ii_decree_19641121_unitatis-redintegratio_en.html.

World Council of Churches. *The Church: Toward a Common Vision*. March 6, 2013. http://www.oikoumene.org/en/resources/documents/commissions/faith-and-order/i-unity-the-church-and-its-mission/the-church-towards-a-common-vision.

GLOSSARY

Apostolicity: the character of a church being linked with the faith of the original apostles.

Assurance: for Evangelical Christians, the knowledge that one is saved that follows an experience of conversion to Christ.

Constantinianism: a charge made by churches of the Radical Reformation that the church "fell" from grace when it became mixed up in worldly politics during the reign of the Emperor Constantine in the early fourth century.

Ecclesial gift exchange: a process by which members of various church traditions strive to recognize and accept distinctive elements of each other's traditions as gifts offered to the large Church, even if they do not themselves adopt those particular beliefs or practices.

Ecumenical movement: organized attempts to move separated Christian churches toward the goal of unity.

Faith, not works: the Lutheran and general Protestant positon that Christians are justified by faith alone; they do not merit salvation by their works, even though works remain an important part of Christian Life.

Filioque: "and the Son"; phrase added to the Nicene Creed by Christians of the Latin West that was rejected by Christians of the East.

Full, visible communion: the goal of the ecumenical movement as stated by the World Council of Churches; churches in full communion can share ministers and Sacraments; churches are not to become carbon copies of each other but rather try to understand and accept each other's beliefs and practices.

Justification: being made right before God through the saving work of Jesus Christ.

Predestination: a widespread belief throughout Christian Tradition that God knows and has chosen who has been saved; a doctrine emphasized in a particularly strict fashion by John Calvin and his early followers.

Presumption/Despair: arrogantly assuming that one is saved/ refusing to accept the possibility that one can be saved. Regarding salvation, Catholics have stressed that hope is the mean between the extremes of presumption and despair.

Receptive ecumenism: a contemporary method for ecumenical progress that emphasizes that each tradition put effort into learning from the traditions of others.

Spiritual ecumenism: a practice of conversion, prayer, and learning advocated by the Second Vatican Council.

World Council of Churches: a fellowship of churches that encourages ecumenical progress through mutual understanding and service.

NOTES

1. John Burkhart, *Apostolicity Then and Now: An Ecumenical Church in a Postmodern World* (Collegeville, MN: Liturgical Press), 2004.
2. Francis A. Sullivan, *From Apostles to Bishops: the Development of the Episcopacy in the Early Church* (New York: Newman Press, 2001), esp. 217–36.

3. The information in this paragraph is found in Christopher M. Bellitto, *Renewing Christianity: A History of Church Reform from Day One to Vatican II* (Mahwah, NJ: Paulist Press, 2001), 35–74.

4. On the healthy spiritual life found in many Catholic Churches at the time of the Reformation, see Eamon Duffy, *The Stripping of the Altars: Traditional Religion in England, c.1400–c.1580* (New Haven; London: Yale University Press, 2005). On the ledger sheet of good practices and abuses, see Diarmaid MacCulloch, *The Reformation: A History* (New York: Viking, 2003).

5. In Latin, this is a pithy statement: *Ecclesia semper reformans* ("The Church always reforming.")

6. Many church scandals revolved around power, money, and sex. See Kirstin Downey, *Isabella: The Warrior Queen* (New York: Nan A. Talese/ Doubleday, 2014), 257–75, 394–400.

7. Martin Luther, "The 95 Theses," www.luther.de, http://www.luther.de/en/95thesen.html.

8. The three works are "Address to the Christian Nobility of the German Nation," "The Babylonian Captivity," and "The Freedom of the Christian Man."

9. Martin Luther, "Threat of Banishment and Burning the Papal Bull of Excommunication (1520–1521)," www.luther.de, http://www.luther.de/en/bann.html.

10. *Hier stehe ich; ich kann nicht anders.*

11. James R. Gaines, *Evening in the Palace of Reason: Bach Meets Frederick the Great in the Age of Enlightenment* (New York: HarperColllins, 2005), 48–51.

12. The WCC has 345 member churches that include Protestant, Orthodox, and many other types of churches. The Catholic Church is not an official member for theological reasons, but it does participate actively and has membership in the Faith and Order Commission. There are many churches that are neither members nor participants because of their theological rejection of the ecumenical movement.

13. The "Lima Document" was issued from a meeting in Lima, Peru, on January 15, 1982. For a full download of the document, see http://www.oikoumene.org/en/resources/documents/commissions/faith-and-order/i-unity-the-church-and-its-mission/baptism-eucharist-and-ministry-faith-and-order-paper-no-111-the-lima-text.

14. Max Thurian, ed., *Churches Respond to BEM (Baptism, Eucharist, and Ministry)*, 6 vols. (Geneva: World Council of Churches, 1986).

15. *The Nature and Purpose of the Church* can be found at http://www.oikoumene.org/en/resources/documents/central-committee/2002/the-nature-and-purpose-of-the-church. *The Church: Toward a Common Vision* can be found at http://www.oikoumene.org/en/resources/documents/commissions/

faith-and-order/i-unity-the-church-and-its-mission/the-church-towards-a-common-vision.

16. Lutheran World Federation and the Catholic Church, "Joint Declaration on the Doctrine of Justification," http://www.vatican.va/roman_curia/pontifical_councils/chrstuni/documents/rc_pc_chrstuni_doc_31101999_cath-luth-joint-declaration_en.html.

17. Jeffrey Gros, FSC, "Toward Full Communion: Faith and Order and Catholic Ecumenism," *Theological Studies* 65 (2004): 23–43.

18. "'Full Communion' among Four Reform and Lutheran Denominations," http://www.religioustolerance.org/chr_comm.htm.

19. Margaret O'Gara, "Receiving Gifts in Ecumenical Dialogue," in *Receptive Ecumenism and the Call to Catholic Learning: Exploring a Way for Contemporary Ecumenism*, ed. Paul D. Murray (Oxford: Oxford University Press, 2008), 26–38.

20. Paul D. Murray, "Receptive Ecumenism and Catholic Learning—Establishing the Agenda," in *Receptive Ecumenism*, 5–25.

SACRAMENTS

Chapter 8

SACRAMENTAL CONSCIOUSNESS

We will begin this three-chapter section on the Sacraments with a theme that should by now be familiar. Sacraments cannot be understood apart from Scripture, Tradition, and Christian Life. Imagine telling someone from another planet that when you pour water on someone's head while saying the words of baptism, that person's sins are being washed away as they enter into new life. It might sound rather superstitious, like magic. For that matter, if the ritual of baptism were to be completely abstracted from its context within Scripture, Tradition, and Christian Life, it would have no meaning at all.

There are many people in the contemporary Western world who would likely think that sacramental rituals are superstitious no matter how much explanation is offered of them. Compared with the world of just a few short centuries ago, the world of today is in many ways marked by an absence of the sense of mystery. As described by the philosopher Charles Taylor, we live in "a secular age," a time in which the presuppositions that shape our shared reality are very different from those of former times.[1] Christians who want to preach the gospel often speak of a need to pre-evangelize people by awakening them to a basic sense of mystery and ultimate meaning before introducing a specifically religious message.

Such was not the case at the time of the birth of Christianity. Christian beliefs and practices were first introduced into a world that was fundamentally spiritual. The Greco-Roman world was full of gods, spirits, amulets, and charms. Those in need of advice might visit a soothsayer. Wondrous tales involving miracles could easily find an audience. The rituals of the Roman Empire were to take precedence over all other religious practices. Beyond that, each locality had its own deities whose rituals needed to be performed. And then there were many religious cults that spread far and wide with their own rituals and practices. The Roman cult of Mithras, for example, gathered to ritually slay a bull, cook it, and eat it. This cult was most popular in areas that experienced war, and the participants would pledge loyalty to the provincial ruler or other leader.[2] If this cult were around today, its celebration might appear to be something like a mixture of church-going, attending a political rally, and eating barbecue at a tailgate party. Some cultic practices involved the quest for ecstasy through interaction with a temple prostitute.

Perhaps it is misleading, however, to focus only on sensationalist aspects of polytheistic cultic practices, which Christians pejoratively labeled "pagan" and associated with idolatry. For the most part, ancient cultic practices were not systematically regulated as organized religions. Many cultic practices contained a fair amount of good-natured folk wisdom. The main point here for our purposes is that the Greco-Roman world was full of common beliefs and practices that attest to a sense of living in a mysterious world filled with gods and spirits and lucky charms. Most people valued honor and loyalty. Their lives were guided by proverbs, stories, and songs. They sacrificed to the gods in the hope of being granted favors. As the old Roman proverb goes, "I give in order that you may give."

Both Jews and Christians experienced their faith-based practices as true and reasonable in contrast with the mythology-based, superstitious, and idolatrous practices of others. Both faiths have long traditions that emphasize how reason and faith must ultimately fit together. Jewish faith and practice were distinct from the polytheistic cults in their monotheistic nature, in their rootedness in the long history of a particular people, and in their rejection of the practices of others. Jewish monotheism in the first century was not absolute insofar as it allowed for prophets and religious leaders who embodied the presence of God, and an acknowledgement of the existence of other, lesser gods or manifestations of the divine was a dimension of ancient Jewish faith.[3] What was most distinctive about the Jews was their refusal, in the name of the one God, to worship the Roman gods or any other gods. This refusal at times led to their persecution and death. Christians also refused to worship the Roman gods. Christian worship has deep roots in Jewish liturgical practices.

The fundamental claims of Christianity have been challenged for various reasons throughout its history, but for the most part, it has only been in recent centuries that Christianity has had to contend with a common worldview that is radically skeptical about all religious claims. There is much good to be said about what Taylor calls "a secular world." Modern science, history, and critical thought have made inestimable contributions to contemporary life. Governments that do not favor one religion but rather support a basic pluralism of views appear to work better than either theocracies or totalitarian regimes. Still, as Taylor argues, the presuppositions that structure our shared world are neither unquestionable nor in every case superior to earlier views. The modern, secular world of today has its own particularities, limitations, and difficulties. It places a premium upon empirical reasoning, logic, and consistency. It does not seem to do as well with imagination, paradox, and mystery.

Understanding religious realities such as Sacraments requires neither a rejection of the modern world nor a flight back into the past. For many of us, though, it may require the attainment of what some have called a "sacramental consciousness" or a "sacramental imagination."[4] *Sacramental consciousness* can be defined as "an awareness of the presence and activity of God in and through the things of this world." Christians believe that God can be encountered not only through Sacraments but also in Scripture, nature, human relationships, and the struggle for justice. Catholic and Orthodox versions add an additional focus on the encounter with God through ministry, structured prayer, religious art, church architecture, sacred music, processions, pilgrimages, and various ecclesial activities. Some Christian traditions place more emphasis on the need to avoid idolatry and superstition, yet virtually all Christians can in some way identify with some variation of what we are calling sacramental consciousness.

The Experience of Life's Deeper Dimensions

Before exploring the meaning of a Christian sacramental consciousness, it will be helpful to reflect first simply upon the human experience of life's deeper dimensions. What is time? What is space? What is presence? What does it mean to enter into new life?

There is an early poem by Robert Bly, "Surprised by Evening," which is on one level about the mind and perception. The final stanza reads,

The day shall never end, we think:
We have hair that seems born for the daylight;
But, at last, the quiet waters of the night will rise,
And our skin shall see far off, as it does under water.[5]

The final image is one of drowning, but at the same time, it is a new vision achieved through a total immersion within one's surroundings. We see not only with our eyes but with our entire being. The image of the skin being able to "see" far off under water evokes the thought of the mind being able to see far off when immersed in one's cosmic interconnectedness with all things. Is presence related in some sense to this ability to see in this way? If so, how far off can the mind see?

Presence is a term that has a significant subjective dimension in its meaning. Is a student present in class if asleep? Is a student present if daydreaming? Is one more present to oneself when self-consciously reflecting or when unself-consciously engaged in an absorbing activity? If you are holding the hand of someone who is in a coma, are you present to each other? Is the person in a coma present to you in the same way that you are present to them?

Presence can be used as a relative term. There can be degrees of presence as well as degrees of absence. Suppose Oprah Winfrey were to visit. Oprah is not yet in the room, but she has entered the building in which you have been waiting. The announcement is made that Oprah is "in the building." A wave of excitement runs through the room. It is not just a sense of anticipation that Oprah will be present in the room at any moment. There is also the perception that Oprah is already present in the same building in which you are. This can even extend to cities. If I am in west Dayton and Oprah is in east Dayton, I am conscious of Oprah's being present in my city. There is both a subjective consciousness on my part of this presence, and the objective reality that Oprah is in my city and not somewhere else. And when Oprah is in Washington or even in China, she is present to me in my world in a way that she would not be if she were on the moon or if she had died. Even on the moon, Oprah would be present to me within the same solar system in a way that she would not be if she were in another galaxy. And even if Oprah dies, she will be present to me because she will remain eternally a creature whose existence is sustained by the power and love of the same God who sustains my existence.

Presence is relative to the imaginative frame of reference used to construct one's idea of the space and time that one is occupying. If my frame of reference is my office as I am writing, then I am alone. If my frame of reference is the campus of my university, then there are many people who are immediately present to me. In the film *An American Tail*, Fievel Mouse thinks of how even though he is far away from his parents, "It helps to think we're sleeping underneath the same big sky."[6]

Presence is also something that can be mediated. Are you present to someone when you are communicating by letter? By telegraph? By telephone? By e-mail? Are you present to someone when you are instant messaging? How about if you are communicating through a video telelink?

The presence of one person can be mediated through the presence of another. One person can act as the representative or agent of another. One person can stand in proxy for another. Valid marriages can be contracted when one of the spouses is present only through a proxy.

Presence is also something that can be felt. There are some personalities so charismatic that they light up a room when they enter. There are some people whose very presence can cast a dark gloom on any proceedings. Often such experiences are quite personal. The person whom you can't stand to be around may be the beloved of another. And the presence of one's beloved can make all of the rest of reality fade far into the background. The Flamingos sang of being out of touch with the immediate environment because "I only have eyes for you…Dear."[7] On the other hand, the presence of the beloved can lead to a deeper awareness of the elements of one's surroundings. From *The Music Man* (or from the Beatles, if you prefer), we remember that even though bells rang in the hills, "I never heard them at all / Till there was you."[8]

These songs capture elements of experience associated with the depth-dimensions of reality. The person who is in love sees reality in a transformed way. It is as though the lover has uncovered a secret, and this discovery is the key that opens up the deeper recesses of reality. The secret is not a piece of intellectual information, but a whole way of being and perceiving. Louis Armstrong's familiar "What a Wonderful World" paints a picture of reality perceived through love's eyes. He sees "friends shaking hands saying how do you do / They're really saying I love you."[9]

Presence can be mediated through story and ritual. In chapter 5, we explored the power of narrative in shaping the world in which we live. Imagine that you are in Gettysburg, Pennsylvania. You come across the battlefield on which General Pickett ordered his fateful charge during which thousands of his soldiers died in one day. This field may look like a hundred other fields that one can see in that geographical region. You, however, know the story. You have studied the history. You have heard the narrative. Perhaps you have seen the battle reenacted during a tour of the battlefield, in a film such as *Gettysburg*, or in a documentary. You know that this is a special, even a sacred place. Is it here where General Pickett's soldiers made that charge? Your blood runs cold and you tremble.

Imagine that someone who had gotten off the highway to stop for lunch has become lost for a moment and drives within sight of the field in which you stand. To that person, this field is just like any other field. It is you who knows the secret through narrative and through ritual reenactment. It is you who are able to perceive the specialness, the deeper reality of this place. It is you who senses the presence of the many brave people who sacrificed their lives in this tragic event. Knowledge of the past is connected with the experience of the present and with hope for the future.

Sacramental Consciousness and Augustine

A Christian with a sacramental consciousness experiences the world as created by God, redeemed by Christ, and sanctified by the Holy Spirit. Christians of different traditions differ concerning the degree to which they affirm an overlap between what is explicitly Christian and a basic human experience of the sacred. Some stress more the connectedness. Others stress more the contrast.

Today, one often hears about the vastness of the cosmos, the number of stars, and of how relatively small the earth is and how tiny and speck-like each human being. And then we are told of how humble we should feel in relation to such vastness. Augustine would agree about the importance of humility, but his approach to the measure of each person in relation to the material universe is virtually the opposite. Early in his life, when Augustine was a Manichee, he would contemplate the reality of God. He would look out at the visible universe and think about how it is that God could be present to all that is. At that time, he thought that God must be something like light particles, something that could penetrate space that is otherwise occupied in the way that light can penetrate air.

As mentioned previously in chapter 6 in connection with the doctrine of the Trinity, Augustine learned from reading the Neoplatonists to turn within in order to contemplate the workings of his own mind.[10] In human consciousness, Augustine found something greater and deeper than the material universe. The human mind is able to conceive of the universe in a way that the universe itself cannot. The human mind can perceive, imagine, understand, judge, remember, anticipate, and decide. With its powers of memory and imagination, the human mind binds together the past, present, and future. There is nothing in the material universe that can be seen with the eyes that is greater than the power of the human mind. Although the reality of God is far beyond the human mind, still God is more like a mind that both transcends and is present within the material universe than like light particles that permeate space. Augustine judged that each human person, having a mind and soul, is more like God than the entire material universe and is, in that sense, greater than any other created thing. Through the practice of meditation, Augustine claimed that he had encountered God as the light above his mind, the light that draws him toward truth and that allows him to know truth.

As a Christian, Augustine came to believe that there was an even better way to encounter God than through meditative self-examination as practiced by Neoplatonist philosophers. The best available access to God, a path easily open to everyone, is through following Christ. One did not have to be an elite philosopher to accept and live out the simple message of Christianity. Yet Augustine continued to explore the mystery of God through reflection on God's creation of the human mind and its capacities for linking past, present, and future as well as for linking the material and spiritual worlds. For Augustine, there is much more than meets the eye.

Augustine thought that there were just two kinds of people in the world.[11] There are those who see the world only as an arena in which to pursue their own desires, and those who see the world in connection with the will of God. The first group lives in the earthly city. The second group lives in the City of God. Inhabitants of both cities are mixed together in this world and are not to be sorted out until the end of time. The residents of the earthly city have a severely limited and misdirected appreciation of beauty and pleasure; only those who occupy the City of God live with a true sense of the beauty of what has been made by the all-good and all-loving Creator. After his own experience of conversion, Augustine cultivated a sense of gratitude toward and praise for God who had delivered him from the misdirection of his earthly ambitions and his carnal habits. He had an ongoing awareness of the providence and action of God not only in creation and in the lives of others but also and especially in his own life.

All things are good, thought Augustine, when they are contemplated or pursued in the light of God's will. No human thought or deed is good if it is pursued as an end in itself, apart from God. In his *Confessions*, when examining his conscience, Augustine dramatizes the pull he experienced in the context of everyday life between, on the one hand, living with a conscious awareness of the presence and activity of God and, on the other hand, a forgetfulness of God:

When a hound in pursuit of a hare is part of a show at the circus I will not watch, but when it happens in the country and I chance to be passing, the chase may distract me from some deep thought and attract me to itself. It is not the swerving of my horse's body that alters my course, but the inclination of my own heart; and unless you [God] promptly show me my weakness and command me to use the spectacle as a means of lifting my mind to you by some suitable reflection, or else to disregard the whole thing and pass on, I stand foolishly gaping....True, I pass from watching them to praising you, wonderful creator and dispenser of all that is, but it is not in that frame of mind that I begin to watch. To get up without delay is one thing, not to fall in the first place is another.[12]

Augustine's own struggle to maintain his awareness of the presence and activity of God in and through the things of this world may sound somewhat extreme to modern ears. Yet being aware of the presence and activity of God in and through the things of this world constitutes the very definition of sacramental consciousness.

Sacramental Consciousness and the Catholic Imagination

As Augustine illustrates, sacramental consciousness carries over to the experience of the everyday. The Christian narrative and ritual express an experience of a world that is created, redeemed, and sanctified by God. Priest-sociologist-novelist Andrew Greeley offers a particularly Catholic perspective on this topic:

Catholics live in an enchanted world, a world of statues and holy water, stained glass and votive candles, saints and religious medals, rosary beads and holy pictures. But these Catholic paraphernalia are mere hints of a deeper and more pervasive religious sensibility which inclines Catholics to see the Holy lurking in creation. As Catholics, we find our houses and our world haunted by a sense that the objects, events, and persons of daily life are revelations of grace....This special Catholic imagination can appropriately be called sacramental. It sees created reality as a "sacrament," that is, a revelation of the presence of God. The workings of this imagination are most obvious in the Church's seven sacraments, but the seven are both a result and a reinforcement of a much broader Catholic view of reality. And Reality.[13]

Chapters 9 and 10 will pay more attention to the differences among various Christian traditions regarding Sacraments and sacramental consciousness. The rest of this chapter will continue to offer a Catholic perspective.

Sacramental consciousness stands in tension with any approach to reality that reduces everything to the plain and observable facts of the present moment. Once a colleague and I stood before a large Renaissance painting of the Communion of Saints. In the center sat Mary holding her child, Jesus. To the left were Peter and Paul. To the right were St. Lawrence of the third century and three Dominican saints of the thirteenth century. My colleague remarked that the artist had no sense of history in that the painting included figures from three widely separated centuries. I responded that this artist had been completely aware of what he was doing, for the Communion of Saints occupies a realm beyond time and space in which people are united to each other by the love of God. One of the main points of the painting is to illustrate how the community experienced among those who love Christ transcends not only time and space but even death. In many paintings of the saints, one of the figures will look out toward the viewing audience and extend a hand, inviting the viewers to experience themselves as present within the sacred conversation.

Catholic sacramental consciousness can readily be found in art related to church architecture and liturgy. Baptism signifies entry into the community that embodies the new life in the Spirit. In many churches, the baptismal font stands near the physical point of entry into the church. In Florence, the magnificent octagonal Baptistery of

St. John stands outside and across from the entry into the *Duomo* (Cathedral). The three sets of doors to the baptistery display bronze reliefs that depict scenes from the Old Testament symbolizing sin, redemption, and restoration, which are complemented by scenes representing the life of John the Baptist, who is considered to symbolically embody the link between the Old and New Testaments. The one who is baptized can now exit through the east doors and enter the *Duomo*, signifying entry into new life and the Communion of Saints. For the Communion of Saints brings together those in the present world with those who have gone before them in death, all being joined together by the love of God.

The Eucharist is celebrated within the context of the Mass. The Church is the space in which the Mass is celebrated. As explained in chapter 4, the Catholic Mass constitutes, on one level, a symbolic and dramatic reliving of the Last Supper and, on another level, a symbolic and dramatic reliving of the life, death, and resurrection of Jesus. It involves a multidimensional type of remembering known by its Greek name, *anamnesis*. *Anamnesis* is a form of remembering that allows those remembering to enter into the drama and thus to experience the events being remembered. The setting for this drama is cosmic. Through prayer and the reading of Scripture, the participants bring to mind their presence in a universe that is created, redeemed, and sanctified by God. Already in this sense, everyone who has ever lived, all the saints, the angels, and the triune God are present among those assembled. They all stand within God's universe, a universe that includes everybody and everything.

Of course, the word *presence* is being used analogically here, that is, with various shades of meaning that may overlap, yet differ. There is the real presence of Christ through his body and blood under the appearance of bread and wine, which the communicants partake. A reading of the text of Eucharistic Prayer I of the Roman Canon[14] indicates that other particular groups and individual people are brought to mind during the consecration. Prior to the prayer of consecration, there is mention of the holy catholic Church; the pope and the bishop of the diocese by name; all who hold and teach the catholic faith; those named in special intention; all gathered for the present worship; and Mary, Joseph, apostles, martyrs, and various saints, many by name. After the prayer of consecration, there is mention of Abel, Abraham, and Melchisedech; those who have died, naming some by special intention; and again the apostles, martyrs, and all the saints are mentioned, with some being named. The Father and the Holy Spirit are also explicitly mentioned. I do not find any explicit mention of angels in Eucharistic Prayer I, but they are mentioned in other parts of the Mass. All can be counted as present. This is perhaps one reason why many Catholic churches are so big: even if there are only a few living persons attending a particular Mass, the room is still crowded.

A sacramental consciousness is always at the same time an eschatological consciousness. It joins together the *already* and the *not yet*. It moves beyond the most immediate confines of time and space. It is willing to make distinctions, but it is much more interested in making connections and seeing interrelationships. To see in the eucharistic assembly a joining together with the heavenly hosts should not make one forget that sinners inhabit the pilgrim church in its earthly journey.

The Church
as Sacrament

Vatican II's *Lumen Gentium* said that "the Church is in Christ like a sacrament or as a sign and instrument both of a very closely knit union with God and of the unity of the whole human race" (no. 1). Although the council did not use the phrase "sacramental consciousness," this type of awareness underlies the notion of the Church as Sacrament. Comparing the Church to a Sacrament was part of an overall attempt to move beyond any misunderstandings of the Church as impersonal by reducing it to its institutional elements. The Church is here understood as Christians in their union with God and in their relation to all human beings. As Sacrament, the Church makes visible the presence and activity of Jesus Christ, who is himself the one who makes visible the presence and activity of God. For

Christian revelation does not consist simply in units of information, but is, first of all, friendship with God through Christ.

Many sacramental dimensions of the Church were explored throughout *Lumen Gentium*. The mystery of the Church is made visible in the people of God. The holiness of the Church is lived out visibly by the clergy, laity, and those in religious orders. The heavenly church is made visible in this world through the pilgrim church on its journey. The Church is the Communion of Saints, which includes, at the same time, the heavenly and pilgrim churches.

In each particular church, or diocese, the entirety of the Church is made present. Each particular church includes not only the people and their bishop, but also the bishop's connections with the other bishops and their churches, as well as the pope. And this is not even to mention the connections with God, the angels, and the saints. Each particular church can be thought of as a communion, or network of relationships. The Church universal is, in this regard, a communion of communions.

Sacramental Consciousness in a U.S. Hispanic Perspective

Catholic theologian Roberto Goizueta contrasts the communitarian experience of Hispanics with the individualism that characterizes the U.S. dominant culture. He argues that individualist presuppositions will prevent understanding of what is happening in a sacramental experience. In the dominant culture of the United States, the individual is experienced as the basic unit of social reality. Participation in various communities, while important, is secondary and ideally voluntary. For the U.S. Hispanic, in contrast, personhood is experienced as fundamentally relational. The community precedes the individual person. The individual person is important, but always within the context of the community. One has no identity that can be completely separated from the groups within which one belongs.

Goizueta describes how in Hispanic culture, one person is experienced on an everyday level as the mediator of other persons.[15]

If you encounter me, you also encounter my mother, father, sisters, brothers, cousins, godparents, teachers, friends, and a whole host of other people. In reality, one person contains and presents a myriad of other people. To say that anyone who is a friend of mine is also a friend of my family is to be taken in absolutely the most literal of ways.

Goizueta connects this communitarian experience with an exploration of the meaning of religious practices. He examines what it means for an elderly Hispanic woman in San Antonio on Holy Thursday to kiss the feet of Jesus on the crucifix. He explains that this woman is already related with Jesus because she lives in a community in which Jesus and Mary are every day present members:

> For this elderly woman, Jesus and Mary are truly present *here*. These religious statues or figures are not mere representations of a reality completely external to them, rather they are the concrete embodiment, in time and space, of Jesus and Mary. These are, in short, sacramental images: natural, particular entities that mediate, embody, and reveal a supernatural, universal, absolute reality.[16]

This woman kissing the feet of Jesus on a crucifix is really relating with Jesus.

Goizueta claims that a person whose individualist presuppositions are exclusively shaped by the dominant culture cannot grasp that a person kissing the feet of Jesus on a wooden crucifix is really kissing the feet of Jesus. This person is kissing a piece of wood, and to think that she is really doing anything more can only indicate ignorance and superstition. What we are calling a sacramental consciousness will perceive the relational interchange between the woman and Jesus as the primary reality taking place. That a piece of wood sculpted into a particular shape is being used is obvious but relatively unimportant. What is most important and most real is that the woman is relating with Jesus. Jesus is one who has experienced suffering and who understands her suffering.

Sacramental Consciousness in
an African American Perspective

Theologian M. Shawn Copeland (also discussed in chapter 6) writes about how the biases that foster racism can be countered by concepts and practices fueled by a Catholic imagination.[17] Copeland finds the counterpoint to racism to be human solidarity, and the Christian vision of solidarity to be expressed as the Body of Christ. "Body of Christ" refers to many related things: it is the body of the man Jesus; the body that was tortured and crucified; the body of the risen Christ; the body that is received along with the blood in the Eucharist; the mystical Body of Christ as made up by the members of the church with Christ as their head. Copeland calls for a living out of the meaning of the Body of Christ both in liturgy and in everyday life.

Solidarity, says Copeland, begins in *anamnesis*. As mentioned above, *anamnesis* is the type of remembering by which the participants in a ritual recall God's saving work and symbolically participate in the events being remembered. The Body of Christ that is the church is formed through the sharing in the body of Christ that is the Eucharist. It is the church as the Body of Christ that must live out in everyday life a solidarity that will combat racism.

Copeland urges that *anamnesis* plays a role in how people in the United States today remember the victims of slavery and of lynching. She is treating U.S. history as an ongoing drama in which all people of the United States participate. Her goal is not to alienate the powerful or to make people feel guilty, but rather to transform the national imagination so that the dignity of all people can be recognized and honored. She draws upon the work of Lutheran theologian Jürgen Moltmann to connect the torture and crucifixion of Christ with the torture and murder of all of the victims of history. Through the manner of his own passion and death, Christ made this identification. Copeland urges her readers to see in the wounds of slaves the wounds of Christ, and to see in the lynching of African American men the cross on which Christ hung.

The wounds of Christ, explains Copeland, are not things about which we simply forget. Artistic representations of the risen Christ include his wounds as signs of his glory. They represent the suffering he bore out of love for humankind. They represent the sins humans have committed and that Christ took upon himself. The wounds of slaves who were tortured and killed as well as those of men who were lynched should be seen in connection with the wounds of Christ. They are the wounds of those who bore the suffering brought on by the sins of others. The slaves and lynched are those whose bodies were offered up in the struggles upon which the United States of today is built. The memory of these people and their dignity should be honored today.

This *anamnesis* of the suffering and death of African American slaves and of the victims of lynching functions to transform our imaginations of who we are in the present. All of us should remember with respect and gratitude the suffering of those who came before us. The Body of Christ includes people of all races and ethnicities. Copeland envisions that a eucharistic solidarity of the Body of Christ in the here and now of everyday life be lived out as a counter to racist attitudes and practices. Such a vision of the presence and activity of God in and through the things of this world represents a sacramental consciousness *par excellence*.

In the next chapter, we will examine three Sacraments of initiation into Christian Life: baptism, confirmation, and Eucharist.

FOR FURTHER REFLECTION

1. What does it mean to say that we live in a secular age? What are some benefits? Are there any losses?

2. Have you ever had an experience that you felt put you in touch with deeper dimensions of meaning than you might ordinarily experience?

3. Can you give your own examples of situations when the notion of whether or not someone is "present" is complicated?

4. For Augustine, how is an awareness of the presence and activity of God linked with the capacities of the human mind?

5. What besides a lack of historical sense might explain an artist's depiction of characters from different centuries in the same painting?

6. How can the concept of presence be applied in an analogical fashion to speak of various modes of presence at a Catholic Mass?

7. What is the point of thinking of the Church as being like a Sacrament?

8. Why does Roberto Goizueta think that it is hard for an individualist to understand that an elderly Hispanic woman kissing the feet on a crucifix is really kissing the feet of Jesus?

9. How does M. Shawn Copeland reflect a sacramental consciousness in her theological vision for how to combat racist attitudes and practices?

FOR FURTHER READING

Eggemeier, Matthew. *A Sacramental-Prophetic Vision: Christian Spirituality in a Suffering World*. Collegeville, MN: Liturgical Press, 2014.

Goizueta, Roberto S. *Caminemos con Jesús: Toward a Hispanic/Latino Theology of Accompaniment*. Maryknoll, NY: Orbis Books, 1995.

Greeley, Andrew. *The Catholic Imagination*. Berkeley: University of California Press, 2000.

Shea, John. *Stories of God: An Unauthorized Biography*. Chicago: Thomas More Press, 1978.

Tracy, David. *The Analogical Imagination: Christian Theology and the Culture of Pluralism*. New York: Crossroad, 1981.

Wadell, Paul J. *Becoming Friends: Worship, Justice, and the Practice of Christian Friendship*. Grand Rapids, MI: Brazos Press, 2002.

GLOSSARY

Analogical: refers to words and concepts that are applied with a broad range of overlapping yet distinct meanings; also refers to an imagination that tends to make positive comparisons and connections.

Anamnesis: type of remembering in ritual that allows participants to symbolically participate in the meaning of the event being remembered.

Baptism: the Sacrament that washes away original sin and gives entry into new life; the Sacrament of entry into the church.

Body of Christ: a name for the Church understood as its members being united with Christ as their head; also, what is received in the Eucharist along with the blood of Christ; also the body of Jesus that hung on the cross; also the body of the risen Christ.

Catholic imagination: a type of sacramental consciousness that includes a focus on sacred objects as well as the presence of God in everyday life.

Communion of Saints: the Church as including both the heavenly church and the earthly church.

Earthly church: the Church as made up of presently living persons; also the pilgrim church.

Eucharist: the Sacrament of the real presence of Christ; the body and blood of Christ under the appearances of bread and wine.

Heavenly church: the Church as made up of those who are in heaven.

Monotheism: belief in one God; contrasted with polytheism, which is belief in many gods.

People of God: the Church understood as composed of the people in history who make it up, with reference to their relation with God.

Pilgrim church: the Church understood as being on a journey through this world, with a focus on its incompleteness; also see Earthly church.

Sacramental consciousness: awareness of the presence and activity of God in and through the things of this world.

Solidarity: a lived awareness of the interconnectedness of all human beings; can also apply to connectedness within particular groups; can also be extended beyond the human-life world.

NOTES

1. Charles Taylor, *A Secular Age* (Cambridge, MA: Harvard University Press, 2007).

2. Reinhold Merkelbach, "Mithraism," in *Encyclopedia Britannica*, http://www.britannica.com/EBchecked/topic/386080/Mithraism.

3. Traditional assumptions concerning the absoluteness of biblical monotheism were challenged in a groundbreaking article by Peter Hayman in "Monotheism—A Misused Word in Jewish Studies?" *Journal of Jewish Studies* 42 (Spring 1991): 1–15. Hayman's position is now taken by many biblical scholars to have set the direction of what is now the standard approach to this question.

4. These terms are used by a number of authors. For "sacramental consciousness," see John Shea, *Stories of God: An Unauthorized Biography* (Chicago: Thomas More Press, 1978). For "sacramental imagination," see Mary Catherine Hilkert, *Naming Grace: Preaching and the Sacramental Imagination* (New York: Continuum, 1978). Related terms are "the analogical imagination" and the "Catholic imagination." For these, see David Tracy, *The Analogical Imagination: Christian Theology and the Culture of Pluralism* (New York: Crossroad, 1981), esp. chapter 10. See also Andrew Greeley, *The Catholic Imagination* (Berkeley: University of California Press, 2000); Andrew Greeley and Mary Greeley Durkin, *How to Save the Catholic Church* (New York: Viking, 1984); Terrence W. Tilley, *Inventing Catholic Tradition* (Maryknoll, NY: Orbis Books, 2000), 125–34.

5. Robert Bly, "Surprised by Evening," in *Silence in the Snowy Fields* (Middletown, CT: Wesleyan University Press, 1953), 15.

6. Phillip Glasser and Betsy Cathcart, vocal performance of "Somewhere Out There," by Cynthia Weil, James Horner, and Barry Mann, released November 21, 1986, on *An American Tail: Music from the Motion Picture Soundtrack*, MCA Records.

7. The Flamingos, vocal performance of "I Only have Eyes for You," by Harry Warren and Al Dubin, released in 1959, on *Flamingo Serenade*, End Records. For lyrics, see http://www.angelfire.com/va/srisons/eyesforyou.html.

8. Barbara Cook, vocal performance of "Till There Was You," written by Meredith Wilson. © 1950, 1954, and 1957 Franck Music Corporation, USA. Renewed 1978, 1982 Frank Music Corporation and Meredith Wilson Music.

SACRAMENTS

Published and administered by MPL Communications Limited. All Rights Reserved. International Copyright Secured.

9. Louis Armstrong, vocal performance of "What a Wonderful World," by George David Weiss and Bob Thiele, recorded August 16, 1967, on *What a Wonderful World*, ABC 10982, HMV. For lyrics, see http://www.links2love.com/love_lyrics_128.htm.

10. This paragraph and the following rely mainly on Augustine, *Confessions*, bk. 7.

11. The points in this paragraph constitute basic themes from Augustine, *The City of God*.

12. Augustine, *The Confessions*, trans. Maria Boulding, OSB (Hyde Park, NY: New City Press, 2001), 214 (bk. 10, no. 57).

13. Greeley, *The Catholic Imagination*, 1–2.

14. Eucharistic Prayer I can be found under "Mass of the 1970 Missal," at *The Catholic Liturgical Library* website, http://www.catholicliturgy.com/index.cfm/fuseaction/text/index/4/subindex/67/contentindex/22/start/9.

15. Roberto S. Goizueta, *Caminemos con Jesús: Toward a Hispanic/Latino Theology of Accompaniment* (Maryknoll, NY: Orbis, 1995), 48–65.

16. Ibid., 48.

17. M. Shawn Copeland, *Enfleshing Freedom: Body, Race, and Being* (Minneapolis: Fortress Press, 2009).

Chapter 9

SACRAMENTS OF INITIATION: BAPTISM, CONFIRMATION, EUCHARIST

As discussed in chapter 8, sacramental consciousness is an awareness of the presence and activity of God in and through the things of this world. In chapter 5, we examined how Christian revelation is grounded in a loving friendship between God and human beings. Christians experience God's love in many ways, but most of all as expressed through the life, death, and resurrection of Christ and the sending of the Holy Spirit. The Sacraments are rituals in which the love of God, the sacrifice of Christ, and the ongoing presence of the Holy Spirit are made available to Christians in the course of their lives.

Virtually all Christians recognize baptism and Eucharist as clearly having been mandated by Christ in the New Testament. Contemporary Orthodox Christians speak of their rites as "mysteries." Traditionally, they have counted many more than seven rituals as mysteries, though in ecumenical dialogues, they have been willing to affirm the seven Sacraments as having a special ranking. Anglicans call baptism and Eucharist "Sacraments of the Gospel" and the other five "sacramental rites." Lutherans, Reformed, and Methodist Christians recognize two Sacraments, baptism and Eucharist, as being instituted by Christ. Some Lutherans also call penance (reconciliation) a Sacrament. Baptists prefer the term "ordinances" to "Sacraments" in order to emphasize what has been ordained by Christ. They limit baptism to believing adults and practice some form of the Lord's Supper. Pentecostal practice varies widely, but all have baptism and some form of Eucharist, and some recognize seven Sacraments.

Catholics teach that there are seven Sacraments instituted by Christ: baptism, confirmation, Eucharist, reconciliation, anointing of the sick, holy orders, and marriage. The claim that Christ instituted all seven of these Sacraments, if taken to mean that he did so directly and intentionally, is not historically provable by recourse to Scripture alone. Catholics acknowledge that the seven Sacraments emerged gradually over the centuries under the guidance of the Holy Spirit. In a traditional Catholic mode of thinking, to say that the Holy Spirit guided a development is at the same time to infer that this development is in accordance with the intentions of Christ.

In this textbook, we will follow the basic Catholic pattern of seven Sacraments with some significant attention to ecumenical concerns. After a brief discussion of the historical development of the seven Sacraments, this chapter will focus on the three Sacraments of initiation: baptism, confirmation, and Eucharist.

Seven Sacraments

Many ritual practices developed throughout the early Christian centuries. The belief that there are exactly seven Sacraments appears to have emerged in the early middle ages with the help of a certain kind of medieval sacramental consciousness regarding numbers, in this case the number seven.[1] In the first six books of the Old Testament alone can be found seven days of Creation, a Sabbath every seventh day, seven years of plenty and seven years of famine in Egypt, seven days of eating unleavened bread, a sevenfold wrath, seven elders, seven altars, seven priests carrying seven trumpets, and so on. In the New Testament Book of Revelation, one finds seven churches, seven golden lampstands, seven stars, seven spirits of God, seven flaming torches, seven seals, a lamb with seven horns and seven eyes, seven angels with seven trumpets, seven thunders, and a great red dragon with seven heads and seven diadems on his heads.

Most relevant to the topic of Sacraments is the fact that in Galatians 5:22, Paul names seven fruits of the Holy Spirit. Within the medieval mindset, it was not difficult to see a connection between the number of fruits of the Spirit and the number of Sacraments that God eventually provided for the church. From within this perspective, if indeed the Holy Spirit guided the unfolding of the seven Sacraments, then it follows also that the Sacraments had been instituted by Christ, since the Holy Spirit would not guide the development of anything that did not represent Christ's intentions. To these ways of thinking, we must add the firm belief that the unity of the Church required a great deal of similarity of belief and practice among all Christians. Church authorities often made virtually absolute claims about the reflection of the will of God in church practices. How things are is how God must have wanted things to be, they often said.

Such a medieval mentality, making use of a mystical approach to numbers, does not fit comfortably with modern ways of thinking. Traditionally, many conservative Protestants have rejected this mentality in favor of a view based on "scripture-alone."[2] Many liberal Protestants have replaced the medieval mentality with a more critical view of history. Some Protestants and most Catholics try to appropriate elements of the medieval mentality even as they have moved beyond it into a new historical context. Many contemporary Catholics acknowledge the importance of questions that emerge from modern historical-critical viewpoints. For example, most Catholics today will acknowledge the unlikelihood that Jesus in his lifetime consciously envisioned the development of exactly seven Sacraments. Still, contemporary Catholic theologians honor the seven Sacraments as having emerged within the Tradition, even as they also acknowledge some degree of historical contingency. In other words, although they are careful not to overstate either scriptural or historical justifications for the exact number, they appreciate the emergence of the seven Sacraments as something fitting or appropriate and, as such, even beautiful.

The five ritual traditions that, along with baptism and Eucharist, constitute the seven Sacraments have long roots in Christianity prior to the middle ages. Practices of affirming, forgiveness, healing, ministry, and marriage have been connected with Christian faith from the earliest times. Arriving at the number seven involved the inclusion of some rituals and the exclusion of others rather than a process of invention from scratch. Three of the five—holy orders, confirmation, and anointing of the sick—involve anointing with chrism (consecrated oil). In the Old Testament, there were three types of people who would be anointed: priests, prophets, and kings. Christ was interpreted as being in himself priest, prophet, and king. Being a Christian meant sharing in this threefold office of Christ.

The ordination of priests and bishops, later called holy orders, emerged as an important practice in the second and third centuries when the Church had to consolidate and strengthen its structures of authority in response to the threat of Gnosticism. Ordination of bishops and priests was closely linked with presiding at the Eucharist.

Confirmation, the Sacrament of strengthening one's faith, emerged very gradually as a Sacrament of initiation, along with baptism and Eucharist. In the third to fifth centuries, baptism and Eucharist were received together at Easter in a way that involved a series of anointings. Often, if a priest had administered these Sacraments of initiation, a second anointing was reserved for the bishop. The exact lines of historical development are not clear, but the eventual development of confirmation appears to be connected with two things: the practice of this second anointing by a bishop as well as the practical need for a Sacrament of strengthening for those who had been baptized as infants.

The anointing of the sick has some significant basis in the New Testament, especially Mark 6:13, in which Jesus instructs the disciples to anoint the sick with oil, and James 5:14–16, in which the sick are to ask for priests to pray over them and anoint them with oil. Gradually, the Sacrament came to be associated with the last rites, which were to be received only in cases when death appeared to be imminent. For this reason, for many centuries it was called extreme unction. In more recent years, the anointing of the sick has been administered not only in danger of death but in response to any serious illness.

The remaining two Sacraments—reconciliation and marriage—have as their "matter" not an anointing with chrism from without but rather the verbal expression of the recipient's inner intentions. These

Sacraments have traditionally been noted for the way in which they build upon natural patterns that exist in human relationships.

Reconciliation as a Sacrament has roots in the New Testament as well as in early Christian penitential practices. In the second and third centuries, disputes arose concerning whether and how Christians were to be readmitted to communion after they had denied their faith by submitting to the laws requiring the worship of the Roman gods. To this sin, known as "apostasy," were added other serious sins such as murder and adultery. Some Christians argued forcefully that such sinners should not be readmitted. The practice that the bishops supported was that those who had committed such serious sins could be readmitted by the bishop—one time only—after a significant period of public penance. Starting about the sixth century, Celtic missionaries from the British Isles carried with them to continental Europe new practices of individual penance as a ritual that could be received as many times as a person would fall into sin.[3] Variations of this practice would eventually become common throughout the Church. In 1215, the Fifth Lateran Council required confession at least once a year if a person had committed a serious sin.

Marriage received much attention and care from Christian leaders and writers throughout the first millennium. Augustine said that "sacrament" is one of the qualities of marriage insofar as its unity signified the eternal unity of Christians (although this is quite different from formally labeling marriage a Sacrament). There is some evidence that Christian marriage rituals developed earlier (seventh century) in the East than they did in the West. Marriage was not officially included by theologians as a Sacrament until the twelfth century. In the West, there was no prescribed Christian ritual for marriage until after the Council of Trent. Prior to Trent, marriages were usually contracted according to local customs.

Traditional Catholic Focus on the Objectivity of Sacramental Grace

The seven Sacraments should be both related to and distinguished from the sense of sacramentality that accompanies any sacred object or activity. Traditional Catholic theology has insisted upon a clear distinction between the seven Sacraments and other ways of encountering Christ, such as in loving human relationships, extraordinary acts of kindness, and the faces of the poor. Still, the manner in which the seven Sacraments are connected with all ways of encountering the love of God remains extremely important. Sacraments put Christians in touch with the deeper dimensions of the meaning of their lives, the dimensions of loving, belonging, affirming, connecting, healing, forgiving, committing, and of mediating God's presence. These links with the deeper dimension of reality involve an interplay between the Sacraments and various elements of our human experience. This interplay will be a point of focus in our study of each individual Sacrament.

In the *Summa Theologiae*, Thomas Aquinas several times quoted a phrase that he identified simply as a traditional saying: "sacraments effect what they signify." There is a lot of meaning packed into this brief statement. A Sacrament is an effective sign. On the one hand, a Sacrament is a sign of a reality that is happening. For example, baptism signifies the washing away of sin and entry into the Christian community. On the other hand, baptism causes this reality to happen.

It is important to hold both of these dimensions together. If a Sacrament is thought to be a cause apart from realities that are happening, it is like a magic trick. If, however, a Sacrament is a mere celebration of things that are otherwise already happening, then the Sacrament itself is not a cause of anything. Using a dialectical mode of thinking, Aquinas attempted to simultaneously protect the objective dimensions of Sacraments as instrumental causes, which carry forward and apply the grace that comes through Christ, and the subjective dimensions of Sacraments as personal interchanges between God and humans.

Over the centuries, the main complaint of Reformers about Catholic sacramental understanding and practice was that it stressed the objective dimensions too much. Martin Luther, for example, thought that the sacramental system of the Catholic Church did more to interfere with the Christian's personal relationship with God than to facilitate it. Reacting against Protestant rejections of the notion of sacramental causality, Catholics made causality their main point of emphasis, at times in an exaggerated manner. By the early twentieth century, Catholic sacramental understanding and practice, with its heavy focus on the objective reality of God's grace as mediated through the properly performed ritual, stood in need of development. Even many Catholics had come to think that the standard practices had become too focused on formalities and too distant from the human experience of God's grace.

For example, an adult who would be baptized in the mid-twentieth century in the United States would often be given a child's catechism and told to know the answers to certain questions. A priest would interview the person, including quizzing them on a few basic matters. The baptism would often take place on a Sunday afternoon, after the last Mass in a side chapel, with only the priest, the person being baptized, and the sponsor (often a spouse) present.

Three Sacraments of Initiation:
Baptism, Confirmation, and Eucharist

In the decades leading up to Vatican II, a liturgical movement arose that aimed to resituate the Sacraments within the context of Scripture, Tradition, and the experience of Christian community. One of the results of the liturgical movement in the Catholic Church was a new Rite of Christian Initiation for Adults, issued in 1972. This new rite restored an ancient ritual pattern from the fourth and fifth centuries by which adults who became Christians would be engaged in a lengthy and substantial process of initiation, one which could last between one and three years. This process would involve teachers and sponsors and, over the course of the liturgical year, different stages of initiation celebrated in the midst of weekly liturgies. The catechumens, those seeking baptism, would be dismissed from the congregation after the Liturgy of the Word (the readings and the homily) but before the Liturgy of the Eucharist (the consecration of the bread and wine and its reception as the body and blood of Christ) in order to receive instruction on the readings. When Easter arrived, during the course of the Easter Vigil, the catechumens would be baptized, anointed, and then receive the Eucharist. In the weeks after Easter, the newly initiated would enter a final period of instruction about the deeper meaning of the sacramental mysteries that they had now experienced.

AIMS OF THE RESTORED CATECHUMENATE
Restore traditional practices from the early Christian centuries
Emphasize interconnectedness of the three Sacraments of initiation
Highlight the participation of the church community
Link sacramental initiation with the social process of initiation
Link these Sacraments with Scripture, Tradition, and Christian Life
Clarify the relationship between these Sacraments and natural processes of growth and development
Draw the primary theological meaning of baptism from adult baptism

The contemporary restoration of the adult catechumenate of the early centuries achieved several objectives. It brought the three Sacraments of baptism, confirmation, and Eucharist together in such a way as to emphasize their interconnectedness as Sacraments of initiation into a relationship with God through Christ and the Holy Spirit. Also, it highlighted the participation of the church community in these Sacraments through the active roles of sponsors and teachers and through the connections with Sunday liturgies and the Easter Vigil. The involvement of the whole community linked the formal elements of the Sacraments with the social process of initiation through the building of relationships. The liturgical connections helped to highlight the relationship between these Sacraments and the biblical narrative of salvation. The appropriation of ancient practices helped to stress a deep continuity with earlier Christian Tradition. Moreover, the restored catechumenate clarified the relationship between these Sacraments and natural human processes of growth and development. As Paul VI expressed it:

> The sharing in the divine nature which is granted to men through the grace of Christ has a certain likeness to the origin, development, and nourishing of natural life. The

faithful are born anew by baptism, strengthened by the sacrament of confirmation, and finally are sustained by the food of eternal life in the Eucharist.[4]

Finally, the restored catechumenate made clear that, even if the majority of those who receive baptism are infants, the theological meaning of baptism must be drawn from what it means for an adult to be baptized.

The Rite of Christian Initiation for Adults is often called the "RCIA" to the dismay of many liturgists who think that the abbreviation might make it sound more like the "Roman Central Intelligence Agency." An alternative is to call it simply the "catechumenate," though this term has its own technical difficulties since many participants in the process have already been baptized and are simply entering into full communion with the Catholic Church. The catechumenate has functioned as a tool for renewal in many Catholic parishes over the last several decades. The regular meetings lead to the formation of a faith community that involves various modes of learning and support, including the sharing of stories. Those who participate as sponsors often testify that they have benefitted from the process as much as the candidates whom they sponsor. The formation of a catechumenal faith community at the heart of a parish often has ripple effects that reverberate throughout the parish and beyond.

By now it should be clear that the new Rite of Christian Initiation for Adults brought together the Sacraments of baptism, confirmation, and Eucharist for those not previously baptized to enter the Catholic Church. We will now further consider each of these Sacraments individually.

Baptism

Although there are notable exceptions, most Christians recognize and accept the baptism of those who belong to other faith traditions and do not rebaptize a person who converts to another tradition.

BAPTISM IS LINKED WITH:
Conversion in faith
Being saved through Christ
Entry into the life, death, and resurrection of Christ
The washing away of sin
Entry into the new life of grace: faith, hope, and charity
Entry into the Christian community
Reception of the Holy Spirit
The coming of God's kingdom
The ability to receive the other Sacraments, especially the Eucharist

Baptism both signifies and causes entry into the community of those who are explicitly saved through Christ. It is linked with a conversion of mind and heart. It entails the washing away of sin and entry into the new life of grace. It means entering into Christ's life, death, and resurrection as the point of access to the love of God. Baptized persons participate in the divine life through faith, hope, and charity as they receive the Holy Spirit. Baptism is a sign of the coming of the kingdom of God. It finds fulfillment in the Eucharist.

The Acts of the Apostles recounts how forty days after his resurrection, Jesus ascended into heaven, telling the disciples that they will be baptized with the Holy Spirit. On the fiftieth day (Pentecost), the Holy Spirit descends upon the disciples:

> And suddenly from heaven there came a sound like the rush of a violent wind, and it filled the entire house where they were sitting. Divided tongues, as of fire, appeared among them, and a tongue rested on each of them. All of them were filled with the Holy Spirit and began to speak in other languages, as the Spirit gave them ability. (Acts 2:2–4)

The disciples then go out to preach the gospel and to call people to conversion. Through baptism, they would enter into a community of new life centered on the breaking of bread (Eucharist):

So those who welcomed his message were baptized, and that day about three thousand persons were added. They devoted themselves to the apostles' teaching and fellowship, to the breaking of bread and the prayers.

Awe came upon everyone, because many wonders and signs were being done by the apostles. All who believed were together and had all things in common; they would sell their possessions and goods and distribute the proceeds to all, as any had need. Day by day, as they spent much time together in the temple, they broke bread at home and ate their food with glad and generous hearts, praising God and having the goodwill of all the people. And day by day the Lord added to their number those who were being saved. (Acts 2:41–47)

An Ideal Meaning of *Church*

Understanding baptism requires reflection upon the many legitimate meanings and uses of the word *church*. Theologians often use different images from Scripture and Tradition to highlight these various meanings. Some meanings bring out the ideal of the Church as holy and spotless. The Church is thus the mystical Body of Christ, or the Communion of Saints. Other images bring out the incompleteness of the Church as it is still on its earthly journey. In this regard, the Church is the people of God or the pilgrim church.

Baptism is understood theologically, first, in relation to the Church in its ideal sense. It is the Church as Christ founded it and as he made it, holy. The holiness of the Church is a gift given to it by Christ. Those who are baptized share in the Church's holiness. Their sins are washed away. They experience a new birth into the life of grace.

Vatican II's *Lumen Gentium* emphasized, though, that ultimately there are not two churches but one Church made up of various elements:

the society structured with hierarchical organs and the Mystical Body of Christ, are not to be considered as two realities, nor are the visible assembly and the spiritual community, nor the earthly church and the Church enriched with heavenly things; rather they form one complex reality which coalesces from a divine and a human element. (no. 8)

Sacraments are full of ideal meanings, and rightly so, as they express various dimensions of a loving interchange between God and human beings. One cannot understand what Christians believe about baptism without speaking about sins being washed away as one enters a holy church. Those who are baptized, though, are being made part of a Church that is at the same time both the mystical Body of Christ and the pilgrim church, both holy and still on a journey.

Baptism and Eternal Salvation

Christians have traditionally believed that baptism opens up the doors to eternal salvation. They have differed concerning how baptism is to be administered, on the relationship between personal conversion and the ritual Sacrament, and on whether or not infants should be baptized. They have also differed on the status of non-Christians and on the possibility of salvation for those who have not explicitly accepted Christ. Much, though not all, of the traditional Christian witness concerning the salvation of non-Christians has been negative until recent decades.

Thomas Aquinas taught that someone who died for the faith as a martyr without having received baptism of water had instead received baptism of blood. He also taught that one who died while preparing to be baptized had received baptism of desire. Theologians have long debated whether baptism of desire might have a much wider range of application, perhaps even including people of good will who had never heard of Christ.

Vatican II's *Gaudium et Spes*, having explained that salvation comes through Christ and the Spirit, stated,

All this holds true not only for Christians, but for all men of good will in whose hearts grace works in an unseen way. For, since Christ died for all men, and since the ultimate vocation of man is in fact one, and divine, we ought

194

to believe that the Holy Spirit in a manner known only to God offers to every man the possibility of being associated with this paschal mystery. (no. 22)

More recent official Catholic documents have stressed a conservative version of this teaching by emphasizing the importance of Christ and the Church in the attainment of salvation for all. Catholic priest and theologian Jacques Dupuis (1923–2004) was reprimanded by the Congregation for the Doctrine of the Faith for going too far by characterizing non-Christian religions as complementary paths to salvation.[5] Neither side in the dispute denied the possibility, even the likelihood, of the salvation of non-Christians. What was being contested was the degree to which it is necessary to emphasize that salvation ultimately comes through Christ and that Christians therefore still need to preach the gospel for the salvation of the world.

Such questions of emphasis regarding the salvation of non-Christians loom very large in our contemporary pluralistic world.

Confirmation

Confirmation is a Sacrament of strengthening one's faith. It is administered by anointing with consecrated oil (chrism). In Eastern churches, chrismation is a part of every baptism, whether performed by a priest or by a bishop. In the Latin West, baptism was followed by chrismation, but a second chrismation was reserved to the bishop. This second chrismation by a bishop emphasized, symbolically, the link between the one being baptized and the entire Catholic Church. By about the ninth century, Catholics in the West came to regard confirmation as a distinct Sacrament.

With theological hindsight, Catholic theologians linked confirmation with the ancient second anointing by the bishop. These theologians referred to a passage from Acts of the Apostles:

Now when the apostles at Jerusalem heard that Samaria had accepted the word of God, they sent Peter and John to them. The two went down and prayed for them that they might receive the Holy Spirit (for as yet the Spirit had not come upon any of them; they had only been baptized in the name of the Lord Jesus). Then Peter and John laid their hands on them, and they received the Holy Spirit (Acts 8:14–17).

These theologians also referred to the story of Pentecost in the Acts of the Apostles and saw in confirmation a deepening of the reception of the Holy Spirit that takes place at baptism. In other words, they read in the story of Pentecost both the reception of the Holy Spirit that comes with baptism as well as the further strengthening of faith that comes through the Holy Spirit at confirmation.

Confirmation for Youth

When a previously unbaptized adult is received into the Catholic Church during the Easter Vigil, confirmation is received as the second of the three Sacraments of initiation. Most Christians, however, are baptized as infants. Confirmation is received years later. It is often thought of as a Sacrament of Christian maturity. Actual practices vary from diocese to diocese or region to region. Catholic teaching specifies only that the recipient must have reached the age of discretion. Some Catholics argue that confirmation should precede first communion, and so the recipient should be seven or eight. Other Catholics think that the Sacrament should correspond to a traditional age of maturity, thirteen or fourteen. Yet other Catholics think that confirmation should be linked with a young adult's conscious decision of a life direction suitable at eighteen or nineteen. Still others think that the age of confirmation should be completely individualized, with some most needing it at fourteen, others at eighteen, and perhaps others at thirty or forty.

The historical development of confirmation as a Sacrament distinct from baptism is linked with the practice of infant baptism. As we saw in a quote above, Paul VI directly linked confirmation with the natural process of human maturity. Debates about the right time are legitimate, and regional differences in practice could represent a healthy variety rather than a problem. A danger arises, however, in that the contemporary tendency to overvalue personal choice can, in some cases, reflect me-centered values rather than good theological or pastoral concerns. If a traditional danger in Catholic sacramental theology has been to overstress the objective side to the detriment of subjective human experience, many discussions about confirmation have reflected the opposite danger by appearing to want to make it be more about personal choice than about receiving the grace of God.[6]

Pentecostals and Baptism in the Holy Spirit

Pentecostals practice "baptism in the Holy Spirit," which is in some ways parallel to confirmation, but which more dramatically and immediately issues in the reception of spiritual gifts, such as speaking in tongues, prophesying, and healing. It is considered to be something distinct from and in addition to water baptism.

Charismatic Catholics, who have been deeply influenced by the Pentecostal movement, also practice baptism in the Holy Spirit. They are careful, however, to distinguish this practice from confirmation. They teach that baptism in the Spirit is not a Sacrament, but rather a practice that helps bring the effects of the Sacraments more fully to life.

Precisely what some Catholics find in the Pentecostal influence is a faith made more fully alive. Some Pentecostals who convert to Catholicism say that they want to escape the drama and the intense focus on their personal experience. Perhaps it is the case that the Holy Spirit can be found working across a broad spectrum of approaches to faith.

Eucharist

Catholics believe that the Eucharist is the source and summit of Christian Life. It is the Sacrament of Christ's presence by which Christians partake of Christ's body and blood. Christians of various denominations stress different aspects of the meaning of the Lord's Supper. For Catholics, it both is a meal and a sacrifice. It is a celebration of the Paschal Mystery, that is, of the passion, death, and resurrection of Christ. It is a coming together of Christ and his Church.

In the earlier quote taken from Paul VI, the Eucharist can be compared with nourishment. As food and drink are necessary for sustaining natural life, so is partaking of the body and blood of Christ necessary for sustaining spiritual life. Unlike baptism and confirmation, which can be received only once, the Eucharist can be received frequently, even daily.

We have already explored, in chapters 4 and 8, how participation in the Eucharist allows Christians to experience symbolically not only the Last Supper but also the life, death, and resurrection of Christ. Through participation in the Mass, Christians make this experience their own. We have also spoken of how in each local Eucharistic assembly, the entire Church is present, including references to the bishops of other local churches, to those who have died and are now with God, to all the angels and saints, and to the Father, Son, and Holy Spirit. As expressed in Vatican II's *Lumen Gentium*:

> Our union with the church in heaven is put into effect in its noblest manner especially in the sacred Liturgy, wherein the power of the Holy Spirit acts upon us through sacramental signs. Then, with combined rejoicing we celebrate together the praise of the divine majesty; then all those from every tribe and tongue and people and nation who have been redeemed by the blood of Christ and gathered together into one Church, with one song of praise magnify the one and triune God. Celebrating the Eucharistic sacrifice therefore, we are most closely united to the church in heaven in communion with and venerating the memory first of all of the glorious ever-Virgin Mary, of Blessed Joseph and the blessed apostles and martyrs and of all the saints.

The Eucharist thus brings together the pilgrim church on earth with the church in heaven, one Communion of Saints united by the love of God through Christ and the Holy Spirit.

New Directions for the Eucharist

Catholics believe that, in the deepest senses, the Eucharist is exactly the same Sacrament before Vatican II as after. Still, there are many notable differences in the style of the Mass. Before Vatican II, the Mass was said entirely in Latin with the exception of the Kyrie, which was said in Greek, and the Gospel and homily, spoken in the vernacular (the language of the particular place). Hymns were also often sung in the vernacular, though Latin hymns were not unusual. The altar was placed against the back wall, and the priest had his back to the people. Laypeople said their responses in Latin, and they did not enter the sanctuary behind the communion rail. A great focus was placed upon the moment when the priest, acting in the person of Christ, spoke the words of consecration. When distributing the consecrated bread, the priest placed the communion host directly on the tongue of each recipient. Many laypeople did not pay much direct attention during Mass, sometimes lost in their own thoughts or prayers. It is not too much to say that, for most Catholics, attending Mass was mostly a duty performed out of a sense of obligation. When I was a child, I remember adults preferring to attend whichever Mass was said by the priest who took the shortest time. This was especially true for the noon Mass on Sundays when a football game was scheduled for television at 1:00 pm.

Although improvements in the style of the Mass were clearly needed, many of the things I mentioned can be defended within their own time. In line with the general tendency to stress the objective dimension of the Sacraments, there was a deep sense of the sacred at a Catholic Mass. By entering the church, one was clearly moving into a sacred space, a space in which God was experienced as being present in a special way. The use of Latin meant that wherever one was in the world, one could attend a Mass that was the same as everywhere else. What some referred to as the "smells and bells" (from incense and the ringing of bells at the moment of the consecration) added to a profound sense of being connected with a historical tradition that was being passed down and lived out across many centuries. Even the lack of immediate attention and participation by the congregation could be interpreted positively as a way of emphasizing that God's grace works on many levels, beyond mere conscious awareness.

CHANGES IN THE MASS INTRODUCED AFTER VATICAN II
Emphasis on fully conscious and active participation
Entire Mass celebrated in the vernacular
Altar pulled away from back wall of the sanctuary so the priest faces the people
Serious attention given to the Liturgy of the Word
An ecumenical lectionary
Eucharist distributed in both kinds
Eucharistic host placed in the recipient's hand
Lay ministers who read and who distribute communion
Ordained deacons—many married—who read the Gospel and give the homily
Two *epicleses*—two moments of invoking the transforming power of the Holy Spirit

The Second Vatican Council and its aftermath brought many changes in the Mass, many of which had ecumenical implications. The Vatican II document *Sacrosanctum Concilium* called for "fully conscious and active participation in liturgical celebrations" (no. 14). The entire Mass would now be celebrated in the language of the people. The altar was pulled away from the back wall of the sanctuary so that the priest could face the people, emphasizing the priest's membership in the community in which he plays a leading role.

The Liturgy of the Word, which consists in readings from Scripture as well as the priest's homily, was given renewed importance, liturgically and theologically. What some now call "breaking open the Word" was recognized as an important complement to "the breaking of the Bread" in making present the reality of Christ. In cooperation with other Christians, a new lectionary of readings for the Mass closely aligned the weekly texts to be used in the churches of various Christian traditions. Assisting the priest in the reading of the Gospel and the giving of the homily were now permanent deacons, often married men, sacramentally ordained to the service of the Church. Symbolizing a new inclusive sense of the Church, laypeople could now deliver all the readings except for the Gospel and could also distribute the Eucharist as lay ministers. Placing the host in the hand of the recipient functioned as a way of emphasizing the full participation of all present in the celebration of the Mass. In other words, the host was no longer simply delivered, but required the cooperation of the person receiving it.

One of the most important changes in Catholic sacramental theology and practice is represented by the addition of a second *epiclesis* to some of the Eucharistic prayers in the revision made after the Council. The *epiclesis* is the invocation of the Holy Spirit. In the traditional Catholic Mass of the Latin Rite, there had been one invocation of the Holy Spirit to transform the gifts of bread and wine into the body and blood of Christ. This one *epiclesis* had corresponded with the intense focus, given in the Mass, to the moment when the priest pronounces the words of consecration. In some of the revised Eucharistic prayers, a second invocation of the Holy Spirit was added, requesting that, through the Eucharist, the Holy Spirit would transform the congregation into the Body and blood of Christ. That is, the congregation, by receiving the body and blood of Christ in the Eucharist, would be made into the Body and blood of Christ. Christians are used to hearing both that the Eucharist is the body of Christ and that the Church is the Body of Christ. The revised Eucharistic prayers bring these realities together, giving a renewed emphasis to the role of the congregation in the context of the Mass and in the mission that they carry forth into the world.

In this chapter, we have discussed the history and meaning of the Sacraments with a special focus on the Sacraments of initiation. In the following chapter, we will examine the remaining four of the seven Catholic Sacraments: marriage, holy orders, reconciliation, and anointing of the sick.

FOR FURTHER REFLECTION

1. Why has there been disagreement among Christians about the number of Sacraments?

2. How did the Catholic Church come to recognize seven Sacraments?

3. Why do many Christians accept only baptism and Eucharist as Sacraments?

4. Why do Baptists prefer the term *ordinances* to *Sacraments*?

5. What does it mean to say that "Sacraments effect what they signify"?

6. What is meant by the claim that Sacraments put Christians in touch with the deeper dimensions of the meaning of their lives?

7. In what ways is a discussion of objectivity and subjectivity important for assessing different points of emphasis in understanding Sacraments?

8. Why do some Christians want to talk about sacramental causality? Why have other Christians rejected such talk?

9. For what reasons did the Catholic Church, in 1972, issue a new Rite of Christian Initiation for Adults?

10. How is baptism connected to ideal meanings of the word *church*?

11. Why have there been disagreements concerning the proper age for receiving confirmation? What is your opinion?

12. What was the significance of adding a second *epiclesis* to some of the Eucharist Prayers issued by the Catholic Church after Vatican II?

FOR FURTHER READING

Caldecott, Stratford. *The Seven Sacraments: Entering the Mysteries of God.* New York: Crossroad Publishing, 2006.

Gabrielli, Timothy R. *Confirmation: How a Sacrament of God's Grace Became All about Us.* Collegeville, MN: Liturgical Press, 2013.

Johnson, Maxwell E. *The Rites of Christian Initiation: Their Evolution and Interpretation*. Revised and Expanded Edition. Collegeville, MN: Liturgical Press, 1997.

Mick, Lawrence E. *Understanding the Sacraments Today*. Revised Edition. Collegeville, MN: Liturgical Press, 1997.

Morrill, Bruce T. *Encountering Christ in the Eucharist: The Paschal Mystery in People, Word, and Sacrament*. Mahwah, NJ: Paulist Press, 2012.

Osborne, Kenan B. *Christian Sacraments in a Postmodern World: A Theology for the Third Millennium*. Mahwah, NJ: Paulist Press, 1999.

Vorgrimler, Herbert. *Sacramental Theology*. Translated by Linda M. Maloney. Collegeville, MN: Liturgical Press, 1992.

GLOSSARY

Baptism in the Holy Spirit: a practice of Pentecostals and Charismatic Catholics signifying an awakening of the gifts that they believe should accompany baptism.

Baptism of blood: a way of expressing how those who die as martyrs without having received the water of baptism are considered to be full members of the Church.

Baptism of desire: a way of expressing how those who die while preparing for baptism are considered to be full members of the Church.

Charismatic Renewal: groups of Catholics who belong to small faith communities influenced by the Pentecostal Movement. There is a focus on the gifts of the Holy Spirit manifested in speaking in tongues, prophesying, and healing.

Confirmation: the Sacrament of strengthening one's faith; received by adults along with baptism and Eucharist as a Sacrament of initiation; often received as a "Sacrament of maturity" years later for those who had been baptized as infants.

Consecration: the part of the Mass during which the priest speaks the words that cause and signify the changing of the bread and wine into the body and blood of Christ.

Epiclesis: an invocation of the Holy Spirit. In some Eucharistic prayers, the Holy Spirit is first invoked to bring about the change of the bread and wine into the body and blood of Christ; a second *epiclesis* calls upon the Holy Spirit to transform those who receive the Eucharist into the Body of Christ.

Grace: God's love; often used to talk about God's love in the ways that it impacts human beings.

Kyrie: Greek for "Lord"; a prayer in the Mass that calls upon the Lord's mercy.

Lectionary: a book of readings from Scripture arranged in a three-year cycle according to the liturgical calendar as they are to be read at Mass.

Liturgy of the Eucharist: the second of two major parts of the Mass, during which the bread and wine are consecrated and received, also known as "the breaking of the bread."

Liturgy of the Word: the first of two major parts of the Mass centered on Scripture readings and the homily, also known as "breaking open the Word."

Objectivity of sacramental grace: the grace of a Sacrament as caused by the communication of what Christ merited through his passion and death.

Ordinances: the term that Baptists and other free church Christians prefer to *Sacraments* in order to emphasize that baptism and Eucharist are clearly ordained by Christ in the New Testament.

Pentecostalism: a rapidly growing Christian Tradition that focuses on the gifts of the Holy Spirit manifested in speaking in tongues, prophesying, and healing.

Rite of Christian Initiation for Adults (RCIA): a Catholic rite issued in 1972 that restores sacramental practices of the fourth and fifth centuries by linking together baptism, confirmation, and Eucharist.

Sacrament: Christian rituals by which the invisible love of God is made visible; for Catholics, the Sacraments are seven rituals by which the love of God, the sacrifice of Christ, and the ongoing presence of the Spirit are made available to Christians in the course of their lives.

Sacramental causality: an approach to understanding and analyzing Sacraments, traditionally favored by Catholics, which highlights how Sacraments bring about the very things of which they are a sign.

Sacraments of initiation: baptism, confirmation, and Eucharist considered in combination as marking the entry of the person into the Church.

Subjective dimensions of grace: the elements of God's love connected with human experience and spiritual growth as celebrated in the Sacraments.

NOTES

1. An illuminating account of the development of the Sacraments is found in Stratford Caldecott, *The Seven Sacraments: Entering the Mysteries of God* (New York: Crossroad Publishing, 2006).

2. Catholics have also offered scriptural justifications for each of the seven Sacraments, but this evidence also depended upon a reading of Scripture within the context of Tradition that does not work for those who look to "scripture-alone."

3. See Thomas Cahill, *How the Irish Saved Civilization: The Untold Story of Ireland's Heroic Role from the Fall of Rome to the Rise of Medieval Europe* (New York: Doubleday, 1995).

4. Paul VI, "Apostolic Constitution on the Sacrament of Confirmation" (*Divinae Consortium Naturae*, 1972), in *The Rites of the Catholic Church as Revised by the Second Vatican Council* (New York: Pueblo Publishing, 1976), 290.

5. For a discussion of Dupuis's case, see Francis A. Sullivan, "Ways of Salvation?" *America* 9 (April 2001): 28–31.

6. For an insightful study of the confirmation debate, see Timothy R. Gabrielli, *Confirmation: How a Sacrament of God's Grace Became All about Us* (Collegeville, MN: Liturgical Press, 2013).

Chapter 10

SACRAMENTS OF COMMITMENT AND HEALING

In the previous chapter, we explored the three Sacraments of initiation: baptism, confirmation, and Eucharist. In this chapter, we will examine what Catholics accept as the remaining four Sacraments: holy orders, marriage, reconciliation,[1] and the anointing of the sick.

This book is intended to be both Catholic and ecumenical in a real way. Historically, Catholics and most Protestants have had contrasting theological understandings of the Sacraments. Much of the difference concerns sacramental causality. Catholics have emphasized that a Sacrament is both a cause and a sign. For Thomas Aquinas, for example, baptism is a sign that a person is entering the Church and that their sins are being washed away. At the same time, receiving the Sacrament of baptism causes one's entry into the church and the washing away of sin. The ritual and the reality that the ritual signifies work in tandem.[2] In contrast, most Protestants have rejected the language of causation when applied to the Sacraments. For them, baptism celebrates a conversion to Christ that has already taken place before the ritual celebration.

This chapter will focus on the meaning of holy orders, marriage, reconciliation, and anointing of the sick, with a particular stress on their institutional and social dimensions. Holy orders is not just a Sacrament administered to an individual, but it is also something connected with the institutional structure of the Church. Marriage is not only between two people but is also connected with the family, which is the building block of a healthy society. Reconciliation and anointing of the sick are administered to individuals, but the things that they signify also speak deeply to communal and social realities.

Holy Orders

Holy Orders and Church Structure

In the Catholic Church, holy orders is the Sacrament of ordained ministry. The Catholic understanding of the Sacrament of holy orders is linked with other Catholic beliefs about the structure of the Church and the manner in which the Church safeguards the authority given to it by Christ. In the early Christian centuries, it was necessary to strengthen the institutional structure of the Church to guard against the threat of Gnostics and other heretics. There were deep concerns about who represented the true Christian faith and who did not. One specific concern was the question of who would be admitted to the Eucharist as presided over by a validly ordained minister. Holy orders causes and signifies the ability of the person being ordained either to preside over or to assist in special ways in the Eucharistic celebration.

Virtually all Christian traditions today claim in some way to be in continuity with the faith as preached by the apostles. For Catholics, Orthodox, Anglicans, and some Lutherans, ordination is directly linked to apostolic succession and the office of the bishop.[3] Many Lutheran churches claim apostolic succession through the office of the priest. These concepts inform beliefs about Tradition and the structure of the Church. As discussed in chapter 7, other churches make different claims concerning their ties to the true Christian faith as preached by the apostles. Some stress that their communal life is identical to the life of the Christian communities in the Bible. Others emphasize that their doctrines line up with the teaching of the apostles. Still others focus on their Christian witness as evidence of connection to the apostolic faith.

Many Christians who do not recognize the apostolic succession of bishops do recognize something sacramental about the service of ordained ministers. They do not understand holy orders as a Sacrament or a sacramental rite, however, because they reject the sacramental system and the sacramental theology of the established churches. In ecumenical dialogues, these Christians ask for recognition of their own claims to being apostolic.

Martin Luther stressed the priesthood of all believers. He retained the tradition of ordaining men who are capable and trained for positions of ministerial leadership, but he otherwise de-emphasized distinctions between clergy and laypeople. For Luther, to be ordained as a minister was mainly to take on a different function, not to become part of a higher spiritual class of human beings. In contrast, Catholic theology of the time claimed that ordination brought about a real change in the person of the priest, not merely a change in function.

Catholics have tried recently to find a middle position on this question. Contemporary Catholic theology still holds that the Sacrament of holy orders involves a real change, not simply a change in function. The change, however, is not something that simply happens to the ordained minister as an individual, but is rather a change in that person's relationship to others in the liturgical ordering of the Church. [4] Deacons, priests, and bishops are thought to hold a special place or office in the liturgical ordering of the Church that cannot be reduced to a function.

Bishop, Priest, Deacon

What makes holy orders a Sacrament for Catholics is how it operates as a special channel of the working of God's grace through Christ and the Holy Spirit. *Grace* is a word used to name God's love. In relation to Sacraments, grace is God's love as it has an impact upon our lives. It is through God's grace that Christians are saved and given further aid in living the spiritual life.

There are three degrees of ordained ministry: deacon, priest, and bishop. Some deacons are permanent deacons because they will not become priests. The permanent diaconate is open to men who are married. Otherwise, being a deacon is a stage in becoming a priest. Deacons are ordained to serve in the church. The services they perform are varied and numerous. They visit the sick and the bereaved, give counsel to those in need of direction, provide aid for the hungry, and so on. They also assist in the Mass by reading the Gospel and giving the homily.

Priests preside at Mass and administer reconciliation and anointing of the sick. A priest (or now sometimes a deacon) usually baptizes, although in cases of necessity, anyone can baptize. In the Sacrament of marriage, the spouses themselves are the ministers, and the priest (or now sometimes a deacon) serves as the Church's official witness. As in the case of deacons, a priest ministers in various ways.

Catholic priests and bishops are required to be celibate.[5] The bishop is most often the head of a diocese, which is a particular church, usually defined as a geographical area. As the head of a diocese, it is the role of the bishop to teach, govern, and sanctify. The bishop is thus in charge of doctrine, authority, and the Sacraments, respectively. There are also other roles that bishops perform, such as being an auxiliary (helping bishop) in a diocese or working in a Vatican curial office. The bishop is said to receive the fullness of the Sacrament of orders. The bishop is the proper presider at the Eucharist. From an administrative standpoint, a priest acts as the bishop's representative.[6] The bishop is also the proper minister of confirmation and holy orders.

Vatican II placed a strong emphasis upon the office of the bishop for several reasons. To emphasize the bishops was also to highlight how the apostolic leadership of the Church has been passed down through the centuries. It also helped to place the authority of the pope within a balancing context so as to give a less top-heavy picture of how the Church operates. Furthermore, bolstering the power of the bishops helped to emphasize how the Church universal, with its center in Rome, is made up of many local dioceses spread throughout the world. The bishop not only represents the Church universal to his local church, but also represents his local church to the Church universal. Each particular diocese or local church is understood as a communion among all of its members, with the bishop as their sign of unity. In this context, *communion* refers to a community of people who are bonded to each other through the love of Christ and of the Holy Spirit. As explained previously in chapter 8, the Church universal is understood as a communion of communions.

Lay Ecclesial Ministers

Many tensions surround the Catholic understanding of ministry and church structure today. Vatican II tried to maintain the distinctions between priests (fathers), vowed religious (brothers and sisters), and laity while at the same time emphasizing a basic commonality among them within the one people of God. The Council did not go so far as Luther in declaring the priesthood of all believers, but it did speak of a common priesthood of the faithful in which all the baptized share. It spoke further, however, of an essential distinction between the common priesthood of the faithful and the ordained priesthood. The Council taught that it is the special task of the lay faithful to live lives of Christian witness in the world, whereas priests and vowed religious are called to work within the Church structures.

Since the time of the Council, this distinction has become more nuanced as many variations have been recognized and permitted. In Europe and in the United States, the number of priests and religious has dropped dramatically. Many priests and vowed religious work "in the world." Many laypeople now work within the Church as lay ecclesial ministers. These changes in the picture of ministry, both within the Church and without, have proceeded at a rapid pace. Much of this shift has been positive, but there are still many tensions being worked out.

These tensions can run particularly high when the lay ecclesial minister is a woman. In many Christian traditions today, women are ordained as minsters, although there also remain many traditions in which women are not ordained.[7] Catholics are among those who do not ordain women as priests.[8] Official Catholic documents make strong claims about reserving ordination to men only, even though they admit that their supporting arguments are mainly speculative. They argue that it seems as though Jesus intended to hand on a particular leadership role to the twelve apostles mentioned several places in the Gospels.[9] This group of twelve is made up of men only. There is a two-thousand-year tradition of priestly ordination being limited to men. Church leaders have argued that they lack the authority to overturn such a long-standing tradition that may represent the intentions of Jesus. Why would Jesus limit this leadership role to men only? Perhaps, they argue, he intended the Eucharist to symbolize the relationship between Christ (the bridegroom) and his Church (the bride). In such a case, it would be appropriate for the one who plays the role of Jesus in the Mass to be a man.

As noted, the official documents admit that these arguments are speculative. They also claim, however, that arguments to the contrary are at least equally speculative. The burden of proof, they say, remains on those who argue for a change, and at this time of history, no proof is thought to be possible. In *Ordinatio Sacerdotalis* (1994), John Paul II forcefully declared,

> Although the teaching that priestly ordination is to be reserved to men alone has been preserved by the constant and universal Tradition of the Church and firmly taught by the Magisterium in its more recent documents, at the present time in some places it is nonetheless considered still open to debate, or the Church's judgment that women are not to be admitted to ordination is considered to have a merely disciplinary force.
>
> Wherefore, in order that all doubt may be removed regarding a matter of great importance, a matter which pertains to the Church's divine constitution itself, in virtue of my ministry of confirming the brethren (cf. Luke 22:32) I declare that the Church has no authority whatsoever to confer priestly ordination on women and that this judgment is to be definitively held by all the Church's faithful. (no. 4)

Many Catholic theologians have pointed out that even with this strong language, John Paul II avoided phrasing that would have been necessary for his statement to be officially considered infallible.[10] There can be no doubt, however, that he intended to bring to a close a contentious conversation that he feared could potentially rip the Church apart.

Those who disagree with official teaching on women's ordination usually argue that questions of cultural differences and historical interpretations loom large here. Is the Church of today really bound to practices that were perhaps more appropriate in New Testament times? Is it possible that the Holy Spirit, who has often guided the Church into new territory, might offer Church leaders authority to make more changes than they themselves realize? Pope Francis has recently been calling for more discussion of the role of women in the Church. Despite his effort, many women in Europe and North America express worry that Pope Francis, with his Latin American assumptions about gender roles, might be less equipped to address women's issues than he is to tackle questions about global justice and climate change. The role of women in the Catholic Church remains an issue of enormous difficulty—though perhaps also opportunity—today.

Marriage

In the Christian imagination, marriage is connected with God. Throughout the Old Testament, the covenant between God and Israel is often spoken in terms of a marriage, and Israel's unfaithfulness to that covenant is labelled adultery. The New Testament uses marital imagery in several places, with Jesus as the bridegroom and the Church as the bride of Christ. Not all Christians call marriage a Sacrament. For all Christians, though, marriage is a sacramental type of reality. Focusing on the sacramental dimensions of marriage is to see it as a special channel of God's grace. Catholics believe that receiving the Sacrament of marriage both causes and signifies a covenantal relationship that ideally lasts as long as both people live.

Love and Marriage

There is a long history of marriage as a natural, human institution connected with civil laws. Some commentators claim that marriage has often been connected with family and social arrangements more than with the concept of romantic love. There may be some truth in this claim, but it is not the whole story. Historically, marriage has been linked with love, even if the word *romantic* might not always fit. Those who defend arranged marriages say that in contemporary society, couples fall in love, get married, and then spend the rest of their lives trying to hold it all together. In traditional societies, couples have arrangements made, get married, and then spend the rest of their lives growing together in love. Love, faithfulness in sexual intimacy, and care for children belong to marriage.

The importance of romantic love can be exaggerated to the point of distortion. In a work in the 1930s, Denis de Rougement studied Western mythology, literature, and opera and concluded that romantic love is more often associated not with marriage but with adultery. De Rougemont thought that a naïve stress on romantic love within marriage might do more to weaken the institution than to strengthen it. Today, we live in a world in which many young people wonder if love is something that can last. Can one really hope that it is possible for two people to fall in love and remain in love for the rest of their lives?

Marriage is a Sacrament that is bigger than both of the spouses. Married love exists in a deeper context than just being something magical between two people. Their commitment to each other is more important than anything they happen to feel about each other on any particular day. Yes, they love each other, and yes, the feelings are there, but they do not wake up in the morning in love with each other every day. There are days and even periods when maybe they would like to strangle each other.

In a sacramental world, feeling like you want to strangle each other does not mean that you do not love each other. As the saying goes, love is more what you do than a state you are in. It is important that the saying is "more…than" rather than "instead of." Yes, you are in love, but there are days when being in love is based more on commitment and trust than on hearing bells ring. Unrealistic expectations about what it means to be in love on a day-to-day basis can be a major cause of trouble in a marriage.

I do not intend strong cautions about the difficulties of married life to take away from realistic expectations that marital relationships can be and, in many cases, are enjoyable and gratifying in consistent and deep ways. Many married couples who struggle to balance one or two careers with one child or more find both while it is happening and in retrospect that there is nothing that could match it in terms of meaning and personal fulfillment. In a Catholic perspective, marriage is a Sacrament of God's love being lived out in a real way. But it is not an everlasting cloud of romantic love. And it is not always easy. As Pope Francis put it: "Marriage is an act of faith between a man and woman who are both fragile and limited, but courageous enough to follow Christ and seek to love each other as he loves them."[11]

Marriage and Inclusion I: Many Types of Families

Many Christians believe strongly that the family is the basic building block of a healthy society. Not too many decades ago, a family was understood ideally in a normative manner as consisting of two parents and their children. A widow and her children could be just as acceptable, though she was thought of as sadly missing something through no fault of her own. Families with adopted children were praised.

In U.S. society today, divorce along with various economic and cultural changes has played a major role in reshaping the social order. Single-parent families and various types of blended families have become a big part of the statistical norm.[12] In some urban areas, the number of children born to single mothers is larger than the number of children born to married parents. Some women choose to be artificially inseminated in order to have and raise a child on their own.

The present-day culture wars in the United States and in other places draw sides between those who emphasize a traditional ideal of families in spite of current statistics and those who argue there are simply many different types of families and these families need to be fully embraced on their own terms. Some people go so far as to see traditional norms as oppressive and to think that the highest value needs to be placed upon personal choice of lifestyle.

In my judgment, Christians need to find a way to transcend the either-or extremes of the culture wars. On the one hand, Christian Tradition contains many strong encouragements in support of marriage as it has been traditionally understood. For example, all people are called to honor their father and their mother. They are further called not to commit adultery. On the other hand, there are several instances in Scripture where Jesus calls his followers beyond natural family loyalties to affirm first God's will and to find community with others who do likewise. The following scene is related in the Gospel of Mark:

> Then his [Jesus'] mother and his brothers came; and standing outside, they sent to him and called him. A crowd was sitting around him; and they said to him, "Your mother and your brothers and sisters are outside, asking for you." And he replied, "Who are my mother and my brothers?" And looking at those who sat around him, he said, "Here are my mother and my brothers! Whoever does the will of God is my brother and sister and mother." (Mark 3:31–35; see also Matt 12:46–50; Luke 8:19–21)

It is important to fully embrace various types of families in various types of arrangements. All human beings share a basic dignity, and all families are made up of persons who share in that basic dignity.

Still, Christians should not give up on the ideal that it is generally always by far the best situation when a child is born to two parents who can nurture and protect him or her. Every child should have a father and a mother whom they can honor. Healthy marriages provide the appropriate context for bearing and raising children. Catholic social teaching holds that the family is the basic unit of a healthy society.

Balancing the two ideals of a child born to two parents and fully embracing various types of families may be a difficult thing to do. I believe, however, that present-day Christians are called to find a way to do it. Holding in tension two points that are true, yet which can appear to be contradictory could help move us beyond the culture wars.

Marriage and Inclusion II: LGBT

Same-sex attraction and expression and its relationship to marriage present another major issue of tension between Tradition and inclusion. A simple, commonsense reading of the six or so places where the Bible mentions this topic can easily support the belief that same-sex relations are morally wrong. Likewise, on a commonsense level, one finds historical consistency in Catholic teaching that same-sex behavior is wrong not only because of what the Bible says, but also because it is against natural law. A natural law approach is based on the belief that the will of God can be discerned within basic patterns in nature. Many things found in Scripture can also be arrived at through reason; therefore one does not need special revelation to conclude that God designed human beings and the process of procreation in such a way that it is natural for a man and a woman to have sex that, in principle, is open to the begetting of children. In this view, other forms of sexual expression are "unnatural." Supporters of this natural law approach claim further that the overall testimony found in the beliefs and practices of various cultures lends support to this position.

Suppose, however, one is a modern thinker, whether religious or not, and inclined to challenge traditional approaches. Some biblical scholars argue that the passages cited in Scripture addressing this topic really have little connection or application to the phenomenon of homosexuality as we experience it today. Some historians and cultural anthropologists claim that what people interpret as homosexuality has been culturally constructed in radically different ways in different times and places. The natural law approach appears to many people to be based upon a one-size-fits-all assumption that does not take into account the statistical reality of the significant number of people who experience same-sex only attraction. Contemporary medicine and psychology accept same-sex orientation as a descriptive category, not as an illness or a disorder. Is it possible that God's intentions for all people cannot be fully discerned by focusing on the design of human genital parts? Can the fruitfulness of marriage be appreciated as much in terms of loving relationships as in the procreation of children?

Now add to these factors a reigning secular worldview that places a priority upon individual rights. Within such a framework, how can the right to marry be denied to anyone?[13] Now add a strong focus on social inclusion. Within a modern view of things, it is hard not to see in the LGBT community a group that historically has experienced social exclusion and even oppression.

Many Christians, while acknowledging that modern individualism and ideologies of inclusion have their limitations, still see something deeply Christian within a basic call for equal rights as well as a radical commitment to be as inclusive as possible. The arguments on either side of this issue can seem to those who hold them to be obvious and irrefutable. Some churches have experienced threats of schism (institutional division) over the ordination of gay and lesbian ministers and even bishops.[14] Those who are attempting somehow to work in the middle find some values on both sides that all must continue to acknowledge.

I have no quick and easy answers to offer to the questions raised here.

Marriage and Christian Division

Divisions among Christians are more like divorces than like contractual splits in business. Many of the particular Christian traditions today are experiencing an intense level of disagreement and sometimes division within themselves. These disagreements often center on issues of sexual identity and behavior. Other disagreements reflect political stances regarding economic classes and the proper role of government in achieving social well-being. Being a Baptist, a Methodist, a Lutheran, or a Catholic today does not appear to predetermine whether one's stance is gay-friendly or gay-cautious, pro-high taxes or pro-low taxes, in favor of radical change to save the environment or in favor of dismissing such claims as a myth or a hoax. What can make things more confusing is that people on either side of these pressing issues tend to interpret their faith traditions as unequivocally supporting their own side.

When divisions occur among Christians, those who had been bonded together in Christ's love are in many ways being torn apart. Deep hurts and what appear to be irreconcilable differences lurk in the background. In addition to mutual understanding, what is needed is forgiveness and healing. Forgiveness and healing bring us to consider the two remaining Sacraments.

Reconciliation and Anointing of the Sick

Reconciliation is the Sacrament that signifies and causes the forgiveness of sins. Anointing of the sick signifies and causes spiritual and sometimes physical healing. Forgiveness and healing speak to the deepest dimensions of human relationships. Anyone who believes in God can recognize that any offense against another human being is also an offense against God. Spiritual healing within or between individuals or groups takes place within the context of a relationship with God.

Reconciliation

In the Gospel of Matthew, Jesus spoke of the importance of forgiveness in an interchange with Peter:

> Then Peter came and said to him, "Lord, if another member of the church sins against me, how often should I forgive? As many as seven times?" Jesus said to him, "Not seven times, but, I tell you, seventy-seven times. (Matt 18:21–22)

Other translations say "seventy times seven." In either case, seven was a symbolic number, and whether the translation says "seventy-seven" or "seventy times seven," the meaning is as many times as is necessary.

When Catholics receive the Sacrament of reconciliation, they confess their sins to a priest, express sorrow, and are given absolution. They are also given a penance to perform, usually prayers, a reading, or some task related to what they had done wrong. Reconciliation is now sometimes celebrated in a communal setting, but each person still confesses their sins privately to a priest. Communal prayers precede and follow the individual confessions.

Anointing of the Sick

Anointing of the sick is a Sacrament administered by a priest to anyone who is suffering from a serious ailment or illness or who may be facing an upcoming operation. Many churches offer this Sacrament on a monthly basis after a particular Mass. It is often given by a bedside or in a hospital room. Ideally, family, friends, and fellow parishioners are present. In some cases, it is given at an accident scene. Before Vatican II, anointing of the sick had been called extreme unction and was only given as the last rites in cases when death appeared imminent. Imminent death remains a major occasion for the Sacrament of anointing of the sick, but it is now administered much more frequently and in relatively less dangerous circumstances.

In contrast, in the United States and Europe, the frequency of Catholics receiving reconciliation has declined dramatically. The decrease in reconciliation is mainly linked with cultural shifts in both society and in the Church regarding attitudes toward authority and the perceived relationship between laypeople and the clergy. These shifts in Catholic sacramental practice may also reflect a shift in perceptions about the relative balance between forgiveness and healing. The traditional Catholic stress on our being sinners in need of forgiveness has been complemented by a greater sense that we are also sick people who need to be healed.

Jesus was a healer. In several cases, Jesus links healing with forgiveness. Each of the three Synoptic Gospels relates a version of the following event:

> And just then some people were carrying a paralyzed man lying on a bed. When Jesus saw their faith, he said to the paralytic, "Take heart, son; your sins are forgiven." Then some of the scribes said to themselves, "This man is blaspheming." But Jesus, perceiving their thoughts, said, "Why do you think evil in your hearts? For which is easier, to say, 'Your sins are forgiven,' or to say, 'Stand up and walk'? But so that you may know that the Son of Man has authority on earth to forgive sins"—he then said to the paralytic— "Stand up, take your bed and go to your home." And he stood up and went to his home. When the crowds saw it, they were filled with awe, and they glorified God, who had given such authority to human beings. (Matt 9:2–8; see also Mark 2:1–12 and Luke 5:17–26)

In the Gospels, healing is often connected with the exorcism of evil spirits. In this way, healing involves both the curing of a disease or condition and the opening of a person to overcome their spiritual blindness or deafness to the good news of the coming of God's kingdom.

St. Augustine held that people sin because they are sick, but they are still to be held responsible. Whether or not he was correct in his opinion, there are some questions regarding guilt and sickness that seem impossible to definitively sort out. In a well-known case in 2015, a jury came back with a judgment concerning a young man, diagnosed with schizophrenia, who had used automatic weapons to slaughter people in a movie theater in Aurora, Colorado. Was he a criminal who needed to be punished, or a sick man who needed institutional treatment? The selected jury consisted of people who approve of the death penalty. The jury rejected the man's plea of insanity and instead found him guilty. To some degree, however, the jury thought that this young man was both a criminal and a sick person. Even though he was found guilty of a mass murder, he was spared the death penalty. He received twelve life sentences, plus 3318 years in prison.

Reconciliation in the Aftermath of Apartheid in South Africa

Reconciliation, whether between individuals, in families, or in larger contexts, can be complicated. Forgiveness can be hard, even in some cases not fully possible. Healing, at least if it is to be complete, requires forgiveness. We have seen with holy orders and marriage that Sacraments and what they signify are about more than just individuals. Sacramental realities have institutional and social effects. Reflecting on the long, hard process of reconciliation in South Africa can help to get a sense of how forgiveness and healing can have a major social impact.

Apartheid was a system of racial segregation implanted in South Africa between 1948 and 1994. Protests by rebel forces had been violent and brutal. The government reactions to protests were also violent and brutal. Simply eliminating apartheid did not seem to be enough to move the society forward. The reality of the injustices that had been committed needed to be brought out into the open and confronted by all.

In 1995, the Truth and Reconciliation Commission (TRC) was founded. It began hearings in 1996 that lasted through 1998. These hearings brought together the victims of violence and injustice and allowed them to confront the perpetrators. Perpetrators were usually granted immunity from prosecution in order to facilitate a process intended to bring about truthful witness that could possibly lead to forgiveness and reconciliation. Overall the work of the TRC has been judged by most observers to have been reasonably successful. Even when forgiveness could not be fully achieved, going through the process usually seemed to help.

The TRC had its critics, though, who thought that it favored the perpetrators, especially in its granting of immunity. Many social problems remain in South Africa. No one could claim that the TRC succeeded in bringing about a general reconciliation between the black and white communities.

In the present century, many TRC-like processes have been worked through in South Africa as well as many other countries and regions, such as Northern Ireland, Rwanda, Guatemala, East Timor, Australia, and South Korea. These processes try to address a large range of issues, "such as facing the past, memory, confession, repentance, remorse, reparation, restoration and justice."[15]

Need for Empathy

Forgiveness and reconciliation call people to relate to each other on a spiritual plane. I once gave a brief report to the Jena Center for Reconciliation Studies[16] about my own work on overcoming intellectual differences among Christians. I focused on how positions that appear to be conflicting may, in some cases, be discovered to reflect differences in styles of attaining understanding and expressing knowledge. The director of the Jena Center, Martin Leiner, remarked that my intellectual work was all well and good, even necessary, but that in the actual work of reconciliation, he found there was one factor even more significant: it was most important that, when groups with a history of conflicts meet to reconcile, there must be present in each group some members who are especially empathetic. Empathy can be defined as the ability to think and feel from within the viewpoint of another. Insofar as love can be defined as a way of relating in a self-transcending manner, one might say that empathy is a kind of capacity to love. Leiner found that a group process of reconciliation was more likely to be successful if structured in such a way as to empower the more empathetic members to take leadership roles.

Forgiveness and Healing in the Ecumenical Movement

Few things can rile a person more than the suggestion that they need to apologize.

If what I have said about church divisions being more like divorces than corporate break-ups is true, then ecumenical reconciliation may require something like a TRC to bring out acknowledgment of guilt, forgiveness, and true mutual recognition and appreciation. Vatican II's *Unitatis Redintegratio* acknowledged that when historical separations of church communities have occurred, "often enough, men of both sides were to blame" (no. 3). Starting in the late 1990s, in preparation for the coming millennium, Pope John Paul II made a series of apologies for wrongs that had been committed in the name of the Church. These apologies included but went far beyond wrongs against fellow Christians. They encompassed Jews, Muslims, Galileo, women, various ethnic groups, native peoples, African slaves, and later, victims of sex abuse.

In regard to other Christians, John Paul II apologized to the Orthodox for the capture of Constantinople in 1204; to victims of the Inquisition; to Protestants for the Catholic part in the religious wars that took place following the Inquisition; and he apologized specifically for the execution of Jan Hus at the Council of Constance in 1415.

As discussed in chapter 7, the current goal of the ecumenical movement, full visible communion, does not call for a corporate merger of the various Christian traditions, but rather for mutual understanding that will lead to mutual recognition and sacramental sharing. Particular Christian traditions are expected to maintain their identity and integrity. Catholics will still have seven Sacraments, no more and no less. Other Christian traditions will have different theological understandings and practices, though hopefully full communion will include some significant movement toward each other. When it comes to matters of Christian ecumenism, what we call "mutual understanding" must involve both forgiveness and healing. To be forgiven is a wonderful thing. Becoming able to forgive is at least as wonderful.

Sacraments in their core are about friendship with God and with others through God, and their impact goes far beyond the life of any one individual. The Sacraments of holy orders, marriage, reconciliation, and anointing of the sick signify (and, Catholics believe, cause) core interactions within the context of human relationships with each other and with God. Holy orders involves a commitment to loving service of others within the context of the Church. Marriage is a lifelong love commitment with a partner that includes an openness to having children. Reconciliation is about repairing the damaged love in one's relationship with God and with others. Anointing of the sick brings the love of God to bear on illness in order to bring about spiritual and sometimes physical healing. These Sacraments and what they signify affect not only the spiritual lives of individuals but also communities and whole societies.

FOR FURTHER REFLECTION

1. Explain a basic difference between Catholic sacramental theology and the sacramental theology of many Protestants.

2. For churches that maintain apostolic succession through the office of the bishop, how is holy orders (ordination) related to the structure of the church?

3. What might "the priesthood of all believers" mean in churches in which some individuals are ordained as priests?

4. How do different views of apostolicity relate to different views of the meaning of ordination?

5. How is marriage sacramental?

6. What might represent a naïve view of the role of romantic love in marriage? What might represent a more realistic view? Is it possible in this case to be realistic and optimistic at the same time?

7. Is it possible to affirm both traditional views of marriage and relatively inclusive views about families at the same time? Why or why not?

8. Why is there so much disagreement among Christians today concerning the morality of same-sex relationships?

9. Is it true that ecumenical divisions are more like divorces than like corporate break-ups?

10. How are forgiveness and healing sacramental? How are they linked with each other?

11. How can one distinguish between a criminal who is at fault and a mentally sick person who needs medical attention?

12. Why was something more needed in South Africa than simply the ending of apartheid?

13. Have you ever been offended when someone suggested that you should apologize?

14. Why is empathy so important in the process of reconciliation?

15. Why is reconciliation often so difficult?

FOR FURTHER READING

Accattoli, Luigi. *When a Pope Asks Forgiveness*. Translated by Jordan Aumann. New York: Alba House, 1998.

SACRAMENTS

Bernardin, Joseph Cardinal. *The Gift of Peace: Personal Reflections*. Chicago: Loyola Press, 1997.

Cahill, Lisa Sowle. *Family: A Christian Social Perspective*. Minneapolis, MN: Augsburg Fortress, 2000.

Chauvet, Louis-Marie. *The Sacraments: The Word of God at the Mercy of the Body*. Translated by Madeleine Beaumont. Collegeville, MN: Liturgical Press, 2001.

Ilibagiza, Immaculée, Steve Erwin. *Left to Tell: Discovering God amidst the Rwandan Holocaust*. Carlsbad, CA: Hay House, 2007.

Kane, Thomas A. *Healing God's People: Theological and Pastoral Approaches; A Reconciliation Reader*. Mahwah, NJ: Paulist Press, 2013.

Keller, Paul Jerome. *101 Questions & Answers on the Sacraments of Healing: Penance and Anointing of the Sick*. Mahwah, NJ: Paulist Press, 2010.

Rougemont, Denis de. *Love in the Western World*. Translated by Montgomery Belgion. Revised edition. New York: Pantheon Books, 1956.

Rubio, Julie Hanlon. *A Christian Theology of Marriage and Family*. Mahwah, NJ: Paulist Press, 2003.

———. *Family Ethics: Practices for Christians*. Washington, DC: Georgetown University Press, 2010.

Schreiter, Robert J. *The Ministry of Reconciliation: Spirituality & Strategies*. Maryknoll, NY: Orbis Books, 1998.

Stasiak, Kurt. *From Sinners to Saints: A Guide to Understanding the Sacrament of Reconciliation*. Mahwah, NJ: Paulist Press, 2014.

Wood, Susan K., ed. *Ordering the Baptismal Priesthood: Theologies of Lay and Ordained Ministry*. Collegeville, MN: Liturgical Press, 2003.

Wood, Susan K. *Sacramental Orders*. Collegeville, MN: Liturgical Press, 2000.

GLOSSARY

Anointing of the sick: a Catholic Sacrament administered to those who are seriously ill for the purpose of spiritual and sometimes even physical healing.

Apartheid: a system of racial segregation implanted in South Africa between 1948 and 1994.

Apostolic succession: the belief that the authority to teach, govern, and sanctify in the church has been handed down historically from the apostles to bishops.

Celibacy: the state of abstaining from marriage and sexual relations.

Curia: administrative offices in Vatican City that carry out various ministries on behalf of the pope.

Deacon, priest, bishop: the threefold order of ministry in the Catholic Church.

Empathy: the ability to think and feel from within the viewpoint of another.

Forgiveness: what results when a person who has been offended lets go of feelings of anger, resentment, and plans for retribution.

Healing: the physical or spiritual process of mending of illness or conditions of suffering.

Holy orders: a Catholic Sacrament of ordination into the threefold ministry of Deacon, Priest, and Bishop.

Lay ecclesial minister: a person who ministers within the church as a layperson, one without ordination or religious vows.

Marriage: a lifelong love commitment with a partner that includes an openness to having children.

Natural law: laws or moral norms that can be determined through human reasoning without the need for special revelation.

Papal apologies: apologies made by recent Catholic popes concerning historical wrongs committed by Catholics in the name of the church.

Permanent deacon: a person ordained to the priesthood without the expectation of becoming a priest; most permanent deacons are married men.

Priesthood of all believers: a biblical concept associated with Martin Luther that stresses how all Christians share in the one priesthood of Christ.

Reconciliation: a Catholic Sacrament administered by a priest through which sins are forgiven; formally called the Sacrament of penance and reconciliation.

Truth and Reconciliation Commission (TRC): a government appointed group in South Africa that granted immunity to perpetrators before holding court-like proceedings intended to bring about reconciliation between the perpetrators of injustices and their victims.

NOTES

1. The formal name found in official documents for what Catholics usually call the Sacrament of "reconciliation" is the Sacrament of "penance and reconciliation." Penance refers to sorrow for one's sins as well as to prayers or other tasks performed to express sorrow; reconciliation refers to the repair of relationships that had been in some way broken.

2. In recent years, the French sacramental theologian Louis-Marie Chauvet, without rejecting the language of causality, has tried to shift the emphasis more toward the language of gift and relationship. See *The Sacraments: The Word of God at the Mercy of the Body*, trans. Madeleine Beaumont (Collegeville, MN: Liturgical Press, 2001).

3. Francis Sullivan demonstrates how a Church-wide episcopacy (office of bishop) emerged about the middle of the second century in response to the Gnostic threat. This development was accepted by Christians as a gift from God designed to give unity to the Church in the face of the heresies that threatened to tear it apart.

4. See Susan K. Wood, ed., *Ordering the Baptismal Priesthood: Theologies of Lay and Ordained Ministry* (Collegeville, MN: Liturgical Press, 2003).

5. There are some Catholic priests who are married, usually men who had been ordained in a different Christian Tradition and who retained their priesthood when they became Catholic. Among the Orthodox, priests are not celibate unless they are also monks. Orthodox bishops are celibate, always being selected from among the monks.

6. In another liturgical sense, the priest who celebrates the Eucharist acts in his own right in the person of Christ (*in persona Christi*).

7. A 2014 PEW study of which major religions and denominations ordain women can be found at http://www.pewresearch.org/fact-tank/2014/09/09/the-divide-over-ordaining-women/.

8. Some Catholics argue that women should be ordained as deacons and that there is historical precedence for this. See Gary Macy, William T. Ditewig, and Phyllis Zagano, *Women Deacons: Past, Present, Future* (Mahwah, NJ: Paulist Press, 2012). The ordination of women as deacons is a distinct issue relative to the question of the ordination of women as priests.

9. The three main official Catholic documents that address the question of the ordination of women are *Inter Insignores* (1976) http://www.vatican.va/

roman_curia/congregations/cfaith/documents/rc_con_cfaith_doc_19761015_inter-insigniores_en.html; *Mulieris Dignitatem* (1988) http://w2.vatican.va/content/john-paul-ii/en/apost_letters/1988/documents/hf_jp-ii_apl_19880815_mulieris-dignitatem.html; and *Ordinatio Sacerdotalis* (1994) http://w2.vatican.va/content/john-paul-ii/en/apost_letters/1994/documents/hf_jp-ii_apl_19940522_ordinatio-sacerdotalis.html.

10. Catholic teaching holds that under certain circumstances, the pope is able to declare a doctrine concerning faith or morals without error.

11. Quoted from "Pope Francis: Marriage Is Brave Promise to Love Like Jesus, Not Showy Ceremony," *National Catholic Reporter*, 6 May 2015, http://ncronline.org/blogs/francis-chronicles/pope-francis-marriage-brave-promise-love-jesus-not-showy-ceremony.

12. Statistics from the Pew Research Center can be found at http://www.pewresearch.org/fact-tank/2014/12/22/less-than-half-of-u-s-kids-today-live-in-a-traditional-family/; statistics from the Center for Disease Control and Prevention can be found at http://www.cdc.gov/nchs/fastats/unmarried-childbearing.htm.

13. In July 2015, the United States Supreme Court affirmed a right to same-sex marriage by a 5-4 vote.

14. The most famous case involved the ordination to bishop of a gay man, Gene Robinson, in the Episcopal Church in the United States in 2003. The Anglican Church worldwide has avoided schism, but deep disagreements remain. Other Christian traditions facing threats to unity include United Methodists, Presbyterians, and Mennonites.

15. Christoffel H. Thesnaar, "Seeking Feasible Reconciliation: A Transdisciplinary Contextual Approach to Reconciliation," AOSIS Publishing, 2014, http://www.hts.org.za/index.php/HTS/article/view/1364/4466.

16. The website for the Jena Center for Reconciliation Studies is http://www.jcrs.uni-jena.de/.

CHRISTIAN LIFE

Chapter 11

LOVE AS THE GREATEST COMMANDMENT

This section of three chapters will focus on Christian Life. The following two chapters will focus on specific forms of Christian moral teaching. In this chapter, we will address foundational questions related to Christian Life, such as the call to holiness, the importance of love, and the problem of inauthenticity. Love is the deepest touchstone of the Christian faith, but it is also a concept that is often misused.

Love and the Universal Call to Holiness

Christian Life, which includes morality, is not just about rules and virtuous achievements. Morality needs to be grounded in something deeper, in a spiritual relationship with God that carries over to one's relationship with others.

Vatican II's *Lumen Gentium* issued a call to holiness for all Christians. Holiness is linked with Christian discipleship, the following of Christ. The mark of the Christian disciple is love: "It is the love of God and the love of one's neighbor which points out the true disciple of Christ" (*Lumen Gentium* 42). Christian love is expressed in terms of a relationship with the triune God. To love is to follow Christ. To follow Christ is to seek and do the will of the Father by listening to and carrying out the promptings of the Holy Spirit.

Holiness↔Christian Discipleship↔Love↔Seeking/Doing the Will of God↔Holy Spirit

For Catholics, the Council's emphasis on the universal call to holiness needs to be understood within the historical context of a tradition that for centuries had stressed a huge distinction between, on the one hand, lay Christians and, on the other hand, those called to enter the ordained priesthood or vowed religious life.

In the years before Vatican II, young Catholics were taught that there were three types of vocation: (1) priesthood or religious life, (2) married life, and (3) single life. Having a particular interest in God or holiness would usually be interpreted as a call to become a priest or a religious. On the positive side, this distinction helped to increase the numbers of priests and religious and to strengthen the Catholic Church as an institution. In the United States during the first half of the twentieth century, Catholics thought of the church mainly as a hierarchical institution bound up with a sense of the sacred. The institution, with its organization and power, accomplished many things that supported lay Catholics in the midst of a sometimes hostile culture. The church as institution provided a network of parishes, schools, hospitals, orphanages, and various social services.

There was also a positive side to the notion that vocation has most fundamentally to do with one's state in life, not with one's work or career. This vision allowed married lay Catholics to see their roles as mothers and fathers as being more important than their job and the social status (or lack of) attached to it.

On the negative side of the strong distinction between clergy/ religious and laypeople was the implication that laypeople had no special call to lead holy lives. There was a general tendency to think of clergy as shepherds and religious as examples for the laity, whose main religious task seemed to be to keep the commandments in order to not fall into a state of sin. It was the priests and the religious who were called to lead holy lives.

Vatican II stressed that all Christians are called to holiness, and that the special call of laypeople is to live out their faith in the world, particularly in the contexts of family, work, and society. Clear distinctions between clergy, religious, and laypeople were retained, but these distinctions were contextualized within a Church understood as the entire people of God. All members share in the threefold ministry of Christ as priest, prophet, and king. Drawing upon various efforts begun prior to the Council, Vatican II made the concept of Church more lay-inclusive.

Lay Christian witness to the Gospel is sometimes done using explicit words but more often something implicit through the testimony of how Christians live their lives. The complex and ever-changing situation of the world calls for Christians to become "artisans of a new humanity" (*Gaudium et Spes* 30), those who can creatively blend new discoveries and developments with the wisdom of the Christian Tradition. This call for lay Christians to transform the world through their work and social action complements well the traditional stress on the lay vocation as oriented either toward marriage and the family or toward single life.

The call to holiness is the call to live life on a spiritual basis by answering the command to put first the love of God and neighbor. Vatican II tried to overcome the clericalism that puts priests and religious on high pedestals while viewing the laity as nothing more than sheep needing to be shepherded. The Council had no intention, however, to demote priests and religious by denying their exceptional calls to be leaders and examples of holiness. What the Council wanted was to promote laypeople to share in the call to holiness with their own special task of transforming the world through their activities in the family, in work, and in the larger social sphere.

Love in Scripture

The scriptural testimony to love is overwhelming. Israel's covenant with God is often described in terms of a marital love relationship. When asked which commandment is the greatest, Jesus responds, "'You shall love the Lord your God with all your heart, and with all your soul, and with all your mind.' This is the greatest and first commandment. And a second is like it: 'You shall love your neighbor as yourself.' On these two commandments hang all the law and the prophets" (Matt 22:36–40). In the Sermon on the Mount, Jesus exhorts his audience: "Love your enemies and pray for those who persecute you, so that you may be children of your Father in heaven; for he makes his sun rise on the evil and on the good, and sends rain on the righteous and on the unrighteous" (Matt 5:44–45). In his talk with the disciples after the Last Supper, Jesus says, "This is my commandment, that you love one another as I have loved you. No one has greater love than this, to lay down one's life for one's friends" (John 15:12–13). Paul writes, "If I speak in the tongues of mortals and of angels, but do not have love, I am a noisy gong or a clanging cymbal" (1 Cor 13:1). In the Johannine writings, we find that "God is love" (1 John 4:16), and that "God so loved the world that he gave his only Son, so that everyone who believes in him may not perish but may have eternal life" (John 3:16).

Bernard Lonergan:
Authenticity, Hypocrisy, and Conversion

There is a deep concern in the contemporary world about authenticity. Authenticity can be defined initially as a mark of individuals or communities that are doing their best in their ongoing struggle to be who they truly are. Authenticity is something to which people of all faiths and worldviews aspire.

The opposite of authenticity is hypocrisy. Hypocrisy describes an individual or community that professes something but does not really live it out. No one aspires to be a hypocrite.

Authenticity is linked with love in at least two ways. First, love lives in the deepest part of the heart and thus requires authenticity as an urgent concern. Second, love may be the most abused concept in the world, one that seems to come easily to the lips of anyone who would want to mislead and manipulate others with twisted meanings. Sadly, talk about love is often inauthentic. As the advertisement says, "Love is what makes a Subaru a Subaru."

Authenticity is more than simple honesty or total consistency because we are all aware of how easy it is to come up short, even when we are trying our best. No one is perfect, and so being less than perfect does not necessarily mean that one is inauthentic. One can profess something without perfectly living it out and still not be a hypocrite. The true hypocrite would be someone who is not really trying to live out that to which they claim to be committed.

Both individuals and communities can be authentic or inauthentic. One's struggle to become who one truly is can be greatly hampered or even become next to impossible if the communities in which one lives on a daily basis are themselves full of mistrust, deceit, and injustice. An inauthentic community can poison the individuals who live within it. On the other hand, a small number of inauthentic individuals can poison the moral atmosphere of an entire community.

Bias

Love draws us outside of ourselves to live authentically in a world that includes not just ourselves and those who are in the groups to which we belong. Jesuit philosopher and theologian Bernard Lonergan (1904–84) offered a critical analysis of how individuals and communities are held back from mature growth by biases. Biases distort our understanding, our values, and our ability to love. They hold us back from authenticity.

Lonergan discussed four types of bias: dramatic bias, general bias (also called commonsense bias), individual bias, and group bias. Dramatic bias is often rooted in psychological problems caused by problems in childhood development. Often the best way to address dramatic bias is through psychoanalysis or group therapy.

LONERGAN'S FOUR TYPES OF BIAS	
Type of Bias	**Meaning of the Bias**
Dramatic bias	I really should see a psychoanalyst
General (or Commonsense) bias	I reject all plans to address social problems as based on theoretical nonsense
Individual bias	The world revolves around me
Group bias	The world revolves around us

In contrast to dramatic bias, the other three types of bias have to do more with how an individual or a group relates to other individuals and groups. The structures that facilitate these biases are thus both individual and social. They reflect errors that are more intellectually than emotionally based. Commonsense bias rejects any kind of solution to problems that is based upon theoretical analysis. For the most part, people with a commonsense bias see morality only in terms of individual choices about lifestyles and rules and do not think that an analysis of social conditions points toward anything more than conditions about which we should be sad. They think that the conditions themselves represent simply the way things are. They do not recognize social conditions as problems that call for large-scale creative solutions. They think all that is needed is to lecture problematic individuals to get their act together.

Individual bias is manifested by those who see everything only in terms of themselves. Their main interest in life is their own comfort and satisfaction. Self-interest is the key determiner of their values and decisions. They lack any higher social vision.

Group bias is basically like individual bias but applied to groups. Groups can be families, clubs, neighborhoods, classes, ethnicities, or races. People in the group see everything only in terms of their own viewpoints and interests.

Bias, Sin, and Conversion

Seen in a theological perspective, bias can be identified as a type of sin. One way of thinking about sin is as choosing not to love. Bias is thus an obstacle to love.

Where lies the path toward authenticity? This question itself leads to hotly contested answers. One modern secular trend has been in the support of the individual who must freely determine him- or herself over against the influence of conventional society. Yet other secular voices have pointed toward individualism itself as among the deepest of all contemporary distortions. Any solution must simultaneously engage both individuals and larger social groups together in the quest for authentic communication and social action.

Lonergan finds the solution to bias is conversion. *Conversion* does not here primarily mean changing group allegiance, although that is a common and legitimate meaning of the term. Lonergan, however, uses the term to describe a process of growth that can take place without a person or a community necessarily shifting from one worldview to another.

LONERGAN'S THREE TYPES OF CONVERSION	
Religious conversion	Falling in love with God
Moral conversion	Basing decisions not simply on personal satisfactions but according to higher values
Intellectual conversion	Being able to distinguish between different types of truth claims and to hold in tension points that might otherwise appear to be in opposition

Conversion is ultimately the pathway to love. Lonergan identified three types of conversion: religious, moral, and intellectual. Religious conversion is a falling in love with God. It results in a state of being in which God is a conscious factor in all of one's personal relationships. Religious conversion runs counter to every type of bias, though it needs to work in conjunction with the other types of conversion.

Religious conversion leads to moral conversion, by which one's choices are based not simply on self-satisfaction but on higher values. Moral conversion fights most directly against the individual and group biases that prevent individuals and communities from attaining the higher viewpoint that can radically include the viewpoints and well-being of others.

Intellectual conversion is usually the result of a self-examination of the activities of one's own mind as it comes to know things. The intellectually converted person can often hold together different types of ideas that might otherwise appear to be contradictory. For example, some religious ideas reflect a kind of symbolic consciousness that can seem to conflict with more scientific formulations of things. For the intellectually converted person, the truth that God created human beings as something distinct and special is not incompatible with the truth that humans evolved through a complicated process that took millions of years. The intellectually converted person can sort things out by recognizing different expressions of knowledge as reflecting different modes of knowing.

Intellectual conversion can help in overcoming every kind of bias, but it is especially useful for countering the commonsense bias that refuses the theoretical insights and critical analysis that can break one out of one's narrow, protected world.

Racism as Bias

In chapters 6 and 8, we drew upon the work of M. Shawn Copeland for concrete examples, respectively, of the meaning of the incarnation and of sacramental consciousness. In *Enfleshing Freedom*, Copeland draws specifically on the work of Lonergan in order to apply the categories of bias and conversion to the subject of racism.[1] Racism is related to a dramatic bias by which many white people fear black people as they project unto them every bad trait that they refuse to accept within themselves. Racism is also related to a group bias by which many white people perceive black people as inherently inferior, which motivates them to erect and maintain political, social, economic, and cultural barriers. Racism is further related to a commonsense bias by which many white people reject any scientific, historical, or social analysis that challenges their presumptions about the inferiority of black people, which breeds resentment toward any type of social efforts to level the playing field.

Copeland is trying to address everyone, whatever their race or ethnicity, when she names the path that can lead people beyond racism as conversion. Religious conversion, by which one falls in love with God, opens one up to loving people of all races and ethnicities. Copeland is not calling for a generic love of humankind, but a concrete love that acknowledges and embraces differences. Moral conversion draws people beyond the individual and group biases that allow them to base their decisions solely on the self-interest of their own racial or ethnic group to a higher vision based on moral and social values. Intellectual conversion calls people beyond the commonsense biases that uncritically accept racist distortions concerning the history, capacity, and ultimate value of others.

The title of Copeland's book, *Enfleshing Freedom*, expresses her major theme: embodiment. Embodiment functions for Copeland in a way that parallels Lonergan's use of authenticity. To embody Christian faith is to live it out authentically.[2] Too many Christians live with a "dis-embodied" faith—a faith that exists in some abstract, spiritual realm but does not carry over into how one lives one's life. As human beings, Christians are subject to the human tendency to compartmentalize their thoughts and actions. How is it that some people can think of themselves as Christian, even devoutly Christian, but have little to no sense of concern about addressing social problems? Copeland applies the concept of embodiment most directly to her subject of racism. Overcoming racism calls for an embodied faith. As Christ took on human flesh, so the faith of a Christian needs to take on flesh as something truly lived out in the world. Racism can be contested by a faith that recognizes it as sin, as a form of idolatry. It can be contested by liturgies that celebrate the Body of Christ as truly inclusive of all races, genders, and nationalities. And it can be contested by living out the inclusivity celebrated in the Eucharist by practicing solidarity as the Body of Christ within the world.

Much of the racist thinking and acting that Copeland describes from U.S. history has been done by white Christians. Her use of Lonergan to address these atrocities gives an example of how one can begin to sort out the good from the bad in one's own religious tradition. Not everything in one's own religious tradition is good. Catholics can point to horrible things such as the centuries-long persecution of Jews and the more recent cover-up of sexual abuse of minors. These are examples of Christian faith and Tradition being lived out in an inauthentic manner. Drawing upon Lonergan, these atrocities can be named as manifestations of bias and a lack of conversion. They exist within the history of one's religious tradition, but they have misdirected the pilgrim church away from the goal of its journey toward the kingdom of God.

Christian faith is not something that exists in an abstract way apart from communities that live it out. Knowing about the dark side of one's own tradition can help one to live one's faith discerningly and humbly, with a willingness to examine both oneself and one's tradition with a critical eye toward remaining biases. The appropriation of Christian Tradition must always be done within the context of a faith community and in accordance with the authentic pursuit of religious, moral, and intellectual conversion. According to Lonergan, such is the path that Christians must take to overcome biases, the personal and social distortions that prevent us from loving fully and authentically.

Nietzsche: Christians Are Hypocrites

In order to explore further the ways in which what is claimed to be love can sometimes degenerate into inauthenticity and hypocrisy, we will examine some criticisms of Christianity made by the nineteenth-century German philosopher Friedrich Nietzsche (1844–1900). Nietzsche claimed that Christian talk about love is fundamentally hypocritical. He charged Christians with being people who talk a lot about self-sacrifice and love of enemies but who, in the end, simply try to fulfill their own basic instinctual desires just like everyone else. Nietzsche thought that calling themselves Christians had no real impact on their lives beyond turning them into hypocrites.

In *The Antichrist*, Nietzsche painted a sympathetic picture of Jesus as something of a hero.[3] For Nietzsche, Jesus himself was a person of the highest character who bravely lived according to his chosen principles. Nietzsche briefly acknowledged in passing that in every age, there may be a few who manage to live as Jesus lived. On the whole, however, Nietzsche judged that Christianity took shape as the opposite of what Jesus was all about. He observed that, instead of forgiving their enemies, the apostles blamed the Jewish leaders for Jesus' death. In a spirit of revenge, and to overcome their loss, they concocted the story of the resurrection. According to Nietzsche, even worse was Paul, who practically ignored the life and teachings of Jesus in order to invent Christianity as a kind of eternal life insurance policy, promising heaven to those who give Christian leaders power and control.

Nietzsche held that it is natural for human beings to strive to fulfill their instinctual desires, or *eros*. *Eros* is traditionally included among the various forms of love along with *philia* (brotherly love or friendship) and *agape* (a transcendent, divine type of love that sacrifices for the other). *Eros* often refers exclusively to sexual desire, but for Nietzsche it included that but was also much more. Nietzsche equated *eros* with a will to power, which he also called a will to life.[4]

He thought that in ancient societies, the aristocrats or nobles lived passionately and honorably in fulfillment of their *eros*. In Nietzsche's somewhat romantic imagination, nobles were people of strength and character who lived their lives in a way that was beyond conventional ideas of good and evil. Good was whatever they said was good. Nobles told the truth, not out of fear or obedience, but because they were proud of being strong people who did not have to lie. Nietzsche thought that the values of the nobles represented a "master-morality" according to which those who were strong set the rules and others respected their inherent superiority.[5]

Eros and its fulfillment were for Nietzsche the best things that human beings had going. His claim against Christianity was that it tried to poison *eros*.[6] This is like saying that Christianity tried to kill love. Nietzsche saw this attempt to poison *eros* as connected with what he called a "slave morality," introduced to the world by Christianity as a counter to the "master-morality" of the nobles.[7] He described a slave morality as what emerges when weak people get together and construct a morality that will give them advantages that they cannot otherwise achieve. According to Nietzsche, all proper values are thereby turned upside-down: weakness becomes a key value; strength and achievement are criticized; the rich are evil and the poor are good; to be good is to conform to society's rules; everyone should be equally weak and pathetic; it is better to be humble than to strive to fulfill one's natural desires; and human instincts are bad and surrendering oneself is good.[8]

For Nietzsche, Jesus himself was the champion of nonviolence and of a simple lifestyle. He followed his principles by returning love in response to the evils showered upon him. Christianity, however, is practically the opposite of what Jesus was about, arising out of resentment and valuing weakness and humility in place of strength and pride. Nietzsche judged that the Christians of his time followed neither Jesus nor Christianity. Being Christian made no difference in how they acted in that they mostly followed their own instincts and desires in search of worldly success and respect. Nietzsche thought that Christians are hypocrites because, in contrast to the nobles who fulfilled their will to power as a point of pride, Christians condemn outwardly the kind of motivations that really drive them inwardly.

Benedict: Christian Love Is Authentic

Pope Benedict XVI, now pope emeritus, issued an encyclical letter in 2005, the first year of his papacy. Titled "God is Love," the encyclical expresses Benedict's vision of what is most essential in Christianity.[9] Benedict directly addresses Nietzsche by name in this encyclical. The key point in Benedict's response is his counterclaim that Christianity really values *eros*. Benedict thinks that Christianity does not want to poison *eros* because *eros* is an important dimension of human love. Christianity also realizes, however, that *eros* can often be pointed in the wrong direction. It is not enough simply to pursue fulfillment of one's natural instincts. *Eros* needs guidance.

There are also other types of love, such as *philia*, which is the love of friendship. Most relevant in Benedict's discussion, however, is *agape*, which is a divine-like love exemplified best in Jesus' self-sacrifice on the cross. In contrast with Nietzsche, Benedict thinks of Jesus first of all as the Word made flesh. *Agape* is a self-transcending love expressed by truly valuing the beloved in a way that goes beyond one's own self-interest.

Benedict teaches that Christianity wants *eros* to find its fulfillment in *agape*. In the encounter with divine love, *eros* is not destroyed but rather transformed. *Agape* redirects *eros* toward a higher end. Benedict uses the example of the love between a woman and a man. Sexual desire is not bad, but it can easily be misdirected. People often look for love in all the wrong places, frequently with terrible consequences. Young people, for example, can develop bonds of sexual intimacy that far surpass their present ability for long-term commitment. They can be deeply hurt by a breakup or else feel pressured to remain in a long-term relationship that is not right for them. Even worse, they can experience sex as something that lacks the type of intimacy it is meant for, thus devaluing the meaning of sex in a way that they might carry on into the rest of their lives.

Ultimately, says Benedict, sexual desire is directed toward marriage as its proper fulfillment. Within marriage, sexual expression takes place within a context of mutual commitment that reaches, in many ways, far beyond simple self-interest. Yet sexual desire remains an important dimension of marital love. *Agape* by itself is not enough, just as *eros* by itself is not enough. Human love is in need of both together.

Benedict responds further to Nietzsche by rebutting the charge that Christians claim to act out of love but really just seek their own fulfillment like everyone else. Nietzsche makes the specific accusation that Jesus was a man of action but that Christianity is just about belief. It is worth noting that Nietzsche's critique on this point may have had more weight in connection with nineteenth-century European Christianity than with the Christianity of today.

Benedict's response to Nietzsche on this point reflects one of the main themes of this textbook. In Christianity, belief and action work together. Benedict actually uses three categories: faith (belief), worship, and service (action). Along with faith and worship, service is an integral dimension of Christianity. Faith, worship, and service combine in a single package. One should not reduce Christianity to just one or two of these three elements. Each needs the support of the other for Christianity to be whole.[10]

Benedict demonstrates that service (action) has been an important dimension of Christianity throughout its history. He traces Christian service from the Acts of the Apostles until contemporary times. Among many examples, Benedict discusses how Julian the Apostate, when he tried to banish Christianity from the Roman Empire and restore pagan practices, retained one element, that of Christian service to those in need. Christian service has been carried out through the centuries in institutions such as schools, hospitals, orphanages, and other social service organizations. In this way, Benedict refutes Nietzsche's charge that Christianity is really about belief rather than action. On the contrary, Benedict demonstrates that throughout Christian history, one can find strikingly specific examples of how belief has been translated into activities of charitable service.

Nietzsche had implied that the more you give yourself to God, the less there is left of you. Benedict draws upon Augustine to explore the paradox that the more you give yourself over to God, the more you become who you really were all along. Within this Christian spiritual perspective, the self that we hold on to apart from God is a false self. We think that we want certain things, but our misdirected *eros* mostly just gets us into trouble. In contrast, however, the more we align our own will with the will of God, the more we find that God's will actually becomes our will. What God, who loves us, wants for us, is what we really wanted for ourselves all along even though we did not know it. In this perspective, what Christians value is not weakness but rather the strength to help those in need. Humility is not to be equated with weakness, as Nietzsche implies, but is rather a sign of the strength that comes through the grace of God. This point represents another example of how God's love transforms and fulfills our *eros* rather than destroying it. This thinking underlies my favorite quote from Augustine: "Love God, and do what you will."

As Benedict envisions the meaning of Christianity, Christians are not hypocrites. Perhaps some are, but not the great majority. God is love, and the highest expression of God's love is found in Christ's death on the cross. Christians live out their love of God in faith, worship, and service. Some Christians have lived extraordinarily holy lives. Christian love is a forgiving love, so not being perfect does not necessarily make you a hypocrite—just a person in need of forgiveness. Christian love lived out in service is also expressed in faith and in worship.

A Further Point from Pope Saint John Paul II

John Paul II did not directly address Nietzsche's criticisms of Christianity in his writings. I draw upon John Paul II's 1981 encyclical, *Laborem Exercens*, however, in order to fashion a response to one of Nietzsche's criticisms of Christianity that was not directly addressed by Pope Benedict. Benedict's response to Nietzsche focused mainly on *eros* as related to sexual love, whereas Nietzsche equated *eros* more generally with what he called "the will to power." Nietzsche's will to power is not limited to sexual desire but includes a wide range of human aspirations, including the motivations that drive people in their work.

What is the meaning of human work? What is the meaning of social success? Surely it must be acknowledged this is an area where *eros* can indeed be misdirected. Too many people are driven in their career ambitions by purely selfish motivations. Too many people measure their own human value and that of others according to standards of wealth and social status.

If Nietzsche were right about Christianity, Christian teaching, in its intention to poison *eros*, would advise people not to pursue careers or to be concerned about social success or making a good living. Christians would thus be hypocrites because they profess Christian teaching but still pursue conventionally defined social success. John Paul II, however, takes an approach that seeks not to kill *eros* but to point it in the right direction. John Paul II discusses four purposes of work. First, one needs to make a living. Second, one should seek work that is self-fulfilling in relation to one's particular interests and aptitudes. So far, John Paul II is affirming the need to fulfill basic human instincts. But then he adds a third purpose: everyone is called to make a contribution to the larger society. This requirement begins to carry each person into the realm of self-transcendence.

JOHN PAUL II'S FOUR PURPOSES OF WORK
Make a living
Express oneself in self-fulfilling ways
Contribute to society
Enter into the pattern of Christ's death and resurrection

Finally, John Paul II recommends that Christians link their work with the deeply spiritual purpose of entering into Christ's death and resurrection. Labor, no matter what type, always has a dimension that is painful. Even those people who say they love their work experience it often as toil and trouble. They seem to love even more when the moment for leisure arrives. John Paul II explains that Christians can interpret their work as entailing the embrace of the cross. They experience also, though, that embracing the cross leads eventually to the new life of the resurrection.

It is not wrong to pursue a career. Perhaps there are some Christians who are called to renounce all inclinations toward career building and socially approved success, but such a call, like the call to take religious vows of poverty, chastity, and obedience, would be considered exceptional. For the majority of Christians, a career and the way in which they pursue it is a major part of their call to holiness. The pursuit of their vocation entails the fulfillment of their natural instincts as shaped and honed by their encounter with the love of God. Christians do not reject their natural instincts, but rather they try to point them in the right direction.

In this chapter, we have focused on some fundamental questions about holiness, love, conversion, and authenticity. The next chapters will examine several forms of Christian moral and social teaching.

FOR FURTHER REFLECTION

1. What is meant by "the universal call to holiness"?

2. What evidence could one cite in order to make the case that Christianity is really all about love?

3. What are some potential problems and pitfalls in discussing the topic of love?

4. What is authenticity? Why is authenticity a matter of particular concern in our time?

5. How can we possibly know if the way we think now will not soon become subject to some radical revision? How can we possibly become our true selves?

6. Give an example or two for each of the types of bias discussed by Lonergan.

7. What does Lonergan mean by conversion? What are the three types of conversion? How does Lonergan link conversion with authenticity?

8. Try to summarize briefly the main points of Nietzsche's critique of Christianity. What do you think is his best argument? What do you think is his weakest argument?

9. Try to summarize briefly the main points of Pope Benedict's response to Nietzsche's critique. Do you find his response convincing? Why or why not?

10. How can John Paul II's points about the meaning of work be used to formulate a response to Nietzsche's claim that Christianity tried to poison *eros*?

11. What difference should being a Christian make in the life of a Christian?

FOR FURTHER READING

Benedict XVI, Pope. *Deus Caritas Est* (God is Love). http://w2.vatican.va/content/benedict-xvi/en/encyclicals/documents/hf_ben-xvi_enc_20051225_deus-caritas-est.html.

Lonergan, Bernard. *Insight: A Study of Human Understanding.* Toronto: University of Toronto Press, 1992.

———. *Method in Theology.* New York: Herder and Herder, 1972.

Nietzsche, Friedrich. *The Antichrist.* Translated By H. L. Mencken. New York: Alfred A. Knopf, 1920.

———. *Beyond Good and Evil.* Translated by Helen Zimmern. New York: Boni and Liveright, Inc., 1917.

———. *The Genealogy of Morals.* Translated by Horace Samuel. New York: MacMillan, 1911.

United States Conference of Catholic Bishops, *Co-Workers in the Vineyard of the Lord: A Resource for Guiding the Development of Lay Ecclesial Ministry.* 2005. http://www.usccb.org/upload/co-workers-vineyard-lay-ecclesial-ministry-2005.pdf.

Vatican Council II. "The Universal Call to Holiness in the Church." Chap. 5 in *Lumen Gentium* (November 21, 1964). http://www.vatican.va/archive/hist_councils/ii_vatican_council/documents/vat-ii_const_19641121_lumen-gentium_en.html.

GLOSSARY

Agape: a type of love expressed as true concern for the other; a divine type of love; a love that includes a willingness to sacrifice and to suffer.

Authenticity: a state of integration that goes beyond mere honesty toward an ability to challenge the distortions in oneself and in one's surroundings in order to be in the deepest manner who one really is.

Bias: an emotional or intellectual defect that traps a person and holds them back from needed insights and correct judgments.

Conversion: the attainment of a new horizon that allows one to overcome biases; growth in religious, moral, or intellectual maturity.

Discipleship: following Christ, no matter what the cost.

Eros: a type of love expressed as basic instinctual human desire; sometimes used specifically to name sexual desire, but also used to refer to the full range of human desire.

Inclusion: Recognizing and respecting all peoples as among those who truly count and who can fully participate in all social realities.

Master-morality: What Nietzsche calls the values of the noble class who are able to name for themselves that which is to be considered good.

Philia: a type of love expressed as friendship.

Slave-morality: What Nietzsche calls the values of the weak who construct social rules to their own advantage and thus turn what is natural upside-down.

Universal call to holiness: the teaching that each Christian is called to live authentically in a way that makes a difference.

Will to power: For Nietzsche, this term is another name for *eros*. It is the natural inclination for people to follow their instincts and to achieve whatever is within their capacity.

NOTES

1. M. Shawn Copeland, *Enfleshing Freedom: Body, Race, and Being* (Minneapolis: Fortress Press, 2010).

2. Ibid., chap. 5.

3. Friedrich Nietzsche, *The Antichrist*, trans. H. L. Mencken (New York: Alfred A. Knopf, 1920). In my classes, I use passage nos. 35–43, pp. 106–43.

4. Friedrich Nietzsche, *Beyond Good and Evil*, trans. Helen Zimmern (New York: Boni and Liveright, Inc., 1917), IX, 257–61, esp. 259.

5. Ibid.

6. Ibid., IV, 168.

7. Ibid., IX, 257–61.

8. Ibid., IX, 257–261; also *The Genealogy of Morals*, trans. Horace Samuel (New York: MacMillan, 1911), First Essay, nos. 10–14.

9. *Deus Caritas Est*, http://w2.vatican.va/content/benedict-xvi/en/encyclicals/documents/hf_ben-xvi_enc_20051225_deus-caritas-est.html.

10. In this textbook, I regularly speak of four elements of Christianity rather than three. Benedict XVI uses the one category of faith to include what I distinguish as Scripture and Tradition. My additional categories of Sacraments and Christian Life line up fairly well with Benedict's categories of worship and service.

Chapter 12

COMMANDMENTS, VIRTUES, PACIFIST ACTIVISM

This chapter will focus on three major approaches to Christian morality today. I label these approaches: (1) The Ten Commandments, (2) virtue ethics, and (3) pacifist activism. These three approaches are not mutually exclusive. All three are important for Christian morality, though different Christians might integrate these approaches in various proportions and rankings.

The Ten Commandments

The Ten Commandments (also the Decalogue), which appear in Exodus as well as in Deuteronomy,[1] were used by medieval Christian theologians as a way of cataloguing the moral teachings of the Church. Martin Luther used the Ten Commandments in a practical and popular way in his catechisms, an approach that was also adopted in Catholic catechisms. (Catechisms are like basic handbooks of religious instruction.) For many centuries, the Ten Commandments functioned as the usual way that most Christians were taught about morality. They were creatively used as categories under which could be listed a large variety of moral obligations and sins. As with all revelation known through Scripture and Tradition, the Ten Commandments need to be respected as representing the Word of God, yet at the same time, being expressed and configured in human language and concepts.

THE TEN COMMANDMENTS[2]
1. I am the LORD your God: you shall not have strange gods before me.
2. You shall not take the name of the LORD your God in vain.
3. Remember to keep holy the LORD's Day.
4. Honor your father and your mother.
5. You shall not kill.
6. You shall not commit adultery.
7. You shall not steal.
8. You shall not bear false witness against your neighbor.
9. You shall not covet your neighbor's wife.
10. You shall not covet your neighbor's goods.

From a faith perspective, the Ten Commandments represent God's law as given to Moses and as reaffirmed in the New Testament by Christ. Knowing what the Ten Commandments meant in their own time, how they have been understood throughout various periods of history, and what they mean for Christians today requires study, interpretation, and discernment. For example, the seventh commandment reads, "You shall not steal." Stealing has obvious connections with individual crimes of taking what is not one's own, whether that be food, or possessions, or money. For the Old Testament prophets, stealing included also a social meaning. For the rich to maintain a separate lifestyle apart from and with no concern for the poor was a type of stealing.[3] In the New Testament, Jesus issued serious warnings to the rich. Several of the Church fathers in the early Christian centuries equated indiscriminate land ownership with stealing from the poor. As was discussed in a previous chapter, Bartolomé de las Casas interpreted owning slaves as a type of stealing, for the owner is taking the fruits of their labor without returning compensation.

Martin Luther, in his *Large Catechism*, interpreted the seventh commandment as addressing a wide range of issues including the dealings of those who make the marketplace unfair and who burden the poor. Luther also saw in the seventh commandment a positive appeal to perform material good works for one's neighbors.[4] Overall,

Luther treated the commandments within the context of Christian faith and one's relationship with God.

Various catechisms throughout recent centuries list for each of the Ten Commandments what is expected and what is forbidden. For example, the *Baltimore Catechism* addresses the fifth commandment, "You shall not kill," in this way:

> By the fifth commandment we are commanded to take proper care of our own spiritual and bodily well-being and that of our neighbor.
>
> The fifth commandment forbids murder and suicide, and also fighting, anger, hatred, revenge, drunkenness, reckless driving, and bad example.[5]

That the fifth commandment forbids, among other things, "reckless driving" is not drawn directly from the Bible but is obviously a concrete application for our own times. Perhaps a future edition will include texting while driving.

For the sixth commandment, the *Baltimore Catechism*, which had been used widely for many decades in the U.S. Catholic context, includes not only what is commanded and what is forbidden, but also gives advice about preserving the virtue of chastity:

> By the sixth commandment we are commanded to be pure and modest in our behavior.
>
> The sixth commandment forbids all impurity and immodesty in words, looks, and actions, whether alone or with others.
>
> The chief dangers to the virtue of chastity are: idleness, sinful curiosity, bad companions, drinking, immodest dress, and indecent books, plays, and motion pictures.
>
> The chief means of preserving the virtue of chastity are to avoid carefully all unnecessary dangers, to seek God's help through prayer, frequent confession, Holy Communion, and assistance at Holy Mass, and to have a special devotion to the Blessed Virgin.[6]

The Catechism of the Catholic Church, written as a resource for the entire Catholic Church, treats the commandments yet more extensively and in depth than the *Baltimore Catechism*.[7] Sins against the sixth commandment include, among other things, lust, masturbation, pornography, incest, fornication, prostitution, and rape. This *Catechism* also tries to emphasize in a positive manner the role of chastity in Christian Life, the importance of marital love, and the gift of having children.

The Ten Commandments remains an important tool for Christians to communicate the basic moral teachings of their faith. As stated previously, however, Christian morality is about more than the rules. It is even more about our relationship with God and with others. Focusing on the rules requires a complementary focus on how forgiving and being forgiven constitute key elements of Christian faith and practice. It also requires discerning what one is called to do in a positive manner, often by working with others in groups and larger organizations.

In today's world, knowing exactly what the rules are and how they apply is not always so simple. Such complexities, however, should not lead one in the direction of an anything-goes moral relativism. On an everyday level, in spite of the complexities, it remains important for Christians to keep the commandments, and to know that when they break the commandments, they sin against God, others, and themselves, at times with far-reaching consequences.

As important as this approach to morality through the commandments is, by itself it can tend to be negative and moralistic. Christian salvation is not primarily to be thought of as an award handed out to those who were able to break the fewest rules. The law is there for our benefit, to give us guidance. As Jesus put it, "The sabbath was made for humankind, and not humankind for the sabbath" (Mark 2:27).

Virtue Ethics

Virtue ethics has arisen in contemporary Christian moral theology as a counter-balance to the limitations of traditional rule-based approaches. This important school of thought places its main emphasis upon personal formation and the building of character within the context of a Christian community. This approach draws much upon the treatment of virtue in Thomas Aquinas's *Summa Theologiae*.[8] Aquinas himself drew deeply upon Aristotle in his discussion of natural virtue, and also somewhat upon Plato for supernatural virtue. The Greeks did not make a distinction between natural and supernatural virtue. They spoke simply of virtue.

Aristotle on the Virtues

The key question in the history of world philosophy has been about happiness. What will make human beings happy? Aristotle thought that the answer was neither wealth, pleasure, nor social recognition.[9] The happy person is the person of virtue. A virtue is a good habit, and a vice is a bad habit. Good habits, or virtues, are developed through formation, training, and education. A virtuous person is a person of good character.

A virtue is always the mean between two extremes. A mean is not the same as a midpoint, and so a virtue is always closer to one extreme than to the other. Take the example of courage, which is the mean between cowardliness and rash-mindedness (or foolhardiness). Courage is not at all like cowardliness, yet neither is it the exact opposite. Courage is closer to rash-mindedness, but at the same time, quite distinct from it. In a battle, a coward runs away while the fool rushes ahead and is likely to be killed. The person of courage neither automatically runs away nor foolishly rushes into battle, but rather makes the proper judgment of the situation. The person of courage might, in some cases, retreat, in other cases, put his or her own life at risk, and in other cases, carefully and with relative safety carry out a particular mission.

There is no clear formula for how the courageous person will act. The courageous person has the training and formation to be able to make the proper judgment and to act upon that judgment in each particular case. Aristotle explicitly named the extremes between which a number of virtues constituted the mean, as illustrated in this chart:[10]

ARISTOTLE ON VIRTUE AS A MEAN BETWEEN TWO EXTREMES			
Feeling/Action	Deficiency	Mean	Excess
anger	unirascible	good-tempered	irascible
fear/confidence	cowardly	courageous	rash/foolhardy
some pleasures	insensible	temperate	self-indulgent
giving/taking money	ungenerous	generous	wasteful
giving/taking money	stingy	magnificent	tasteless/vulgar
truth	self-deprecating	truthful	boastful
giving amusement	boorish	witty	buffoonish
honor/dishonor	humble, timid	having proper pride	vain

Not everything can be made into a virtue that represents a mean between extremes. Aristotle used the examples of theft, murder, and adultery. Is it a virtue to be moderate about murder, engaging in it neither too often nor too infrequently? Aristotle said that murder cannot be virtuous because it is in itself already a defect, representing an extreme.

Aquinas on the Natural Virtues

Aquinas drew upon Aristotle when he placed all of the many virtues within one of four basic categories: prudence, justice, fortitude, and temperance. One might name dozens of virtues, but in the end, each virtue will be either a variation of or closely related to one of these four.

THE FOUR CARDINAL (OR NATURAL) VIRTUES	
Prudence	Justice
Fortitude (Courage)	Temperance

Aquinas called these "natural virtues" in order to distinguish them from "supernatural virtues." Prudence and justice are intellectual virtues in that they impact the mind; fortitude and temperance are moral virtues because they impact the appetite. Prudence is another name for practical reason. It is considered chief among the virtues because without it none of the other virtues can really work. If one lacks prudence, no matter what one's good intentions, whatever one tries to do will be carried out in an ineffective way.

There are different types of justice. Individual justice is carried out among persons on an everyday basis. Legal justice is carried out in contracts and in business and is enforced by the courts. Distributive justice, also called social or economic justice, concerns the fair distribution of wealth within the larger society. Many people and groups can have an impact on distributive justice, but usually it is enforced (or not enforced) by those with political power.[11]

Fortitude is also called moral courage. It can include courage on the battlefield, but more often refers to the kind of courage that it takes to make good moral choices and to stand up to peer pressure or fight against distorted social values. Fortitude is associated with anger in that one must be motivated to correct what is wrong. Anger is not a vice. It is possible to have too much anger and thus to be in need of personal growth or even counseling. It is also quite possible, however, to lack the appropriate anger that a situation might call for and instead be indifferent to the injustices that surround one. Examples could range from looking the other way from physical abuse taking place in a neighbor's apartment to ignoring industrial abuse of the environment.

Temperance refers to moderation in satisfying basic physical appetites most often in regard to eating, drinking, and sexual behaviors. Eating too much is a vice, but so is eating too little. Drinking too much wine is a vice, but so is refusing to celebrate properly. As Aquinas put it, "The vice opposed to drunkenness is unnamed; and yet if a man were knowingly to abstain from wine to the extent of molesting nature grievously, he would not be free from sin."[12] When it came to sexual desire, Aquinas distinguished it from lust, which he called an excess. He recognized, though, that sexual desire is basically good in that it is ordered toward the preservation of the human race: "Wherefore just as the use of food can be without sin, if it be taken in due manner and order, as required for the welfare of the body, so also the use of venereal [sexual] acts can be without sin, provided they be performed in due manner and order, in keeping with the end of human procreation."[13]

Aquinas on the Supernatural Virtues

Aquinas thought that natural virtues lead to a kind of natural happiness in this life, a point that could be known through human reason. He also believed, however, that Christian revelation communicates certain things that human beings otherwise could not figure out simply by their own reasoning. One of the most distinctive elements of Christian revelation is the knowledge that human beings are called not simply to a natural earthly happiness but to enjoy eternal, supernatural happiness with God. Whereas natural virtues lead human beings toward their natural end, supernatural virtues lead human beings to their supernatural end.

The supernatural virtues are faith, hope, and charity (love).[14] Aquinas taught that, through these supernatural virtues, human beings are able to participate in eternal life, the very life of God.[15] In Catholic Tradition, faith is identified as a kind of intellectual virtue that enables the mind to trust God and so to believe God's revelation that has been handed down through Scripture and Tradition. Hope and charity shape the spiritual appetites, enabling people to trust that God's justice and mercy will have the final word and to base their lives on love.

SUPERNATURAL VIRTUES		
Faith	Hope	Love

Faith, hope, and love are gifts from God that transform people so that they live their lives in a spiritually fruitful way. They are able to share in the divine life, even as they continue their life's journey on earth. The supernatural virtues are not acquired but are rather freely given to human beings by God. This is an important point for Aquinas insofar as a Christian must be humble and give the glory to God. No one can claim merit for the gift of love as it is first freely given.

Luther and other Reformers who would follow Aquinas 250 years later declared that Christians are saved by faith and not by works. It has often been observed that what Luther meant by the word *faith* contained what Catholics mean by faith, hope, and charity. In contrast, Aquinas thought that in a certain qualified way, one can talk about merit in relation to the growth of faith, hope, and love and to the good works that flow from these virtues. The practice of love does result in the growth and deepening of that love. Aquinas was careful, though, to say that the merit that humans earn and the divine reward that they receive are in no way in proportion to each other. To use a modern example, God's rewarding us with eternal life for our good deeds would be a little like parents giving their child a Jaguar for having received all passing grades on a report card. The student did do something to earn the car, but maybe not really. On the one hand, Aquinas wanted to acknowledge that there is such a thing as merit in order to honor certain passages in Scripture that seem to suggest that there is. On the other hand, the way Aquinas spells it out makes it clear that no one can really earn heaven as some kind of just reward. God's grace in every way remains always a wonderful gift.

Aquinas calls faith, hope, and love "infused virtues" because they are received as gifts. These virtues come to a person from outside of themselves and not as a reward that has been earned. Still, they are not received magically. In various places in Aquinas's writing, it is clear that he thinks that infused virtues are usually received through participation in the Sacraments and in the life of the Church.

There is an interesting, almost mirror-image relationship between natural virtues and supernatural virtues. Supernatural virtues are not acquired, but once they are received, they can be further developed. Natural virtues are acquired, but once one receives the supernatural virtues, then virtues that correspond to the old natural virtues can be in one as gifts that flow from one's faith, hope, and charity. Such gifts are called infused natural virtues.

Aquinas does not give clear examples of infused natural virtues. In one section of the *Summa Theologiae*, though, he seems to treat martyrdom as a kind of gifted fortitude. In other words, whereas natural fortitude might enable one to face up to moral challenges in everyday life, infused fortitude could empower one to give one's life for one's faith. In classes that I teach, I sometimes have students discuss in small groups what infused natural virtues might be like. We usually come up with something like this:

INFUSED VIRTUES (CORRESPONDING TO THE NATURAL VIRTUES) THAT FLOW OUT FROM FAITH, HOPE, AND CHARITY	
Infused prudence	Founding and running an institution that gives charitable service
Infused justice	Dedicating one's life to the service of the poor
Infused fortitude	Giving one's life for one's faith
Infused temperance	Living out vows of poverty, chastity, and obedience

Contemporary Virtue Ethics

In recent decades, virtue ethics has arisen at least in part in reaction against excessively rule-based approaches. It has also arisen in part as a response to some modern versions of ethics that stress individual choice, personal values, and autonomous decision-making freed from the restraints of Tradition and social pressure. In contrast, virtue ethics has tried to reemphasize the deep and lasting importance of community, Tradition, formation, character, and even revelation. The morally mature Christian is the one whose character is continually being formed within the context of Christian community and Tradition. Without denying the significance of individuals, virtue ethics challenges tendencies to boil all morality down to an individual's personal choice. Many precious values are rooted in and passed down through Tradition as lived out in a community context. A community's values deserve no less respect and protection than those of individuals.

Rules remain important for virtue ethicists, but not in a fundamentalist or traditionalist manner. Rules are no substitute for personal character. Those who "put on Christ" (see Rom 13:14) by allowing themselves to be formed as Christian disciples are those most likely to be able to know the right thing to do and have the strength to do it in any given situation.

During the civil rights struggle in the United States in the 1960s, followers of Martin Luther King would receive training concerning how to react nonviolently no matter what law enforcement officials or others would do to provoke them. The ability to protest peacefully is not an inborn trait; it is an acquired virtue that people have to practice and develop. Aquinas might think, however, that Martin Luther King and many others also acted out of an infused fortitude that flowed out from their faith, hope, and charity, even to the point of giving up their lives for their fellow human beings.

In a virtue ethics approach, gifts humbly received trump any idea of morality as a personal achievement. Accepting oneself, faults and all, as a sinner who has been forgiven, and accepting others in the same fashion, can often be a more important key to moral growth than any self-improvement regimen.[16] Sin is a serious, negative reality that needs ever to be recognized and fought against, but the key tools for doing so are extraordinarily positive qualities: "The fruit of the Spirit is love, joy, peace, patience, kindness, generosity, faithfulness, gentleness, and self-control" (Gal 5:22–23).

Pacifist Activism

Leo Tolstoy and the Influence of His Interpretation of the Sermon on the Mount

Leo Tolstoy is a key figure in developing an approach to Christian morality based on the Sermon on the Mount that deeply influenced a range of twentieth-century Christian pacifists and political activists, including Mahatma Gandhi, Dorothy Day, and Martin Luther King. In his essay "My Religion," Tolstoy told of how one day, when he was translating the Sermon on the Mount (Matt 5—7) from the original Greek into Russian, he had an epiphany that came to him like a sudden flash. He came to think that the key to understanding not only the Sermon on the Mount, but all of the teaching of Jesus as well as the entire meaning of the New Testament was found in two lines in the Sermon on the Mount, where Jesus says,

> You have heard that it was said, 'An eye for an eye and a tooth for a tooth.' But I say to you, Do not resist an evil-doer. But if anyone strikes you on the right cheek, turn the other also. (Matt 5:38–39)

As Tolstoy saw it, the core principle of Christianity is to refuse to return evil for evil, but rather to always do good to everyone, even those who hate you. It does not matter what someone else does to you. You must always remain good. You must always respond with love and forgiveness. Many lines in the Sermon on the Mount can be read as supporting Tolstoy's view. Give away whatever you have to those who ask or are in need. Trust in God, and don't hoard away treasures in this life. Blessed are you when they persecute you. The old law says you shall not kill, but Jesus says, don't even be angry with your brother. Love your enemies. According to Tolstoy, Jesus not only taught this vision as his main message but he lived it as well. Jesus offered no resistance to those who arrested, interrogated, tortured, and killed him. While dying on the cross, Jesus prayed, "Father, forgive them; for they do not know what they are doing" (Luke 23:34).

Tolstoy thought that established Christian churches, including his own Russian Orthodox Church, taught many things that were wrong and often had their priorities backwards. He had little interest in conventional church dogmas or rituals. He contrasted true spirituality with conventional religion, seeking to follow Jesus by living simply and peacefully. He himself sought to give away his wealth, but he ran into the resistance of his wife on that point. He moved to one of his family's estates where he lived among the peasants. Tolstoy remained intellectually active, continuing to write as well as to correspond widely.

Tolstoy's sharp contrast between the true following of Jesus and the conventional teaching of the churches is, in my judgment, rather extreme and might even represent a form of spiritual elitism. Yet there remain many things about Tolstoy that all Christians can not only admire but receive as a positive influence.

Mahatma Gandhi

In 1908, Tolstoy wrote a long letter in response to an editorial that appeared in the Indian periodical *Free Hindustan* that had advocated combatting force with force.[17] Tolstoy's letter was translated by Gandhi from Russian into Gujarati and by others into numerous Indian dialects. Tolstoy described the British colonization of India as an irreligious system based on compulsion and violence. Tolstoy claimed that the ancient teachings of the great world religions all agreed on one principle, "namely, the enduring of injuries, insults, and violence of all kinds without resisting evil by evil."[18] Tolstoy urged that the Indian people refuse to cooperate with the British rule. Such passive resistance would include nonparticipation in the proceedings of the courts, in the payment of taxes, and in the violence perpetrated by the military.

Gandhi corresponded with Tolstoy for two years until the latter's death in 1910, and he considered Tolstoy to be his mentor. Both Tolstoy and Gandhi fought against secular antireligiousness, though neither of them were themselves religious in a conventional way. They both practiced an eclectic spirituality that drew upon the sacred texts and practices of a wide range of religions. Gandhi was a Hindu who found in the Sermon on the Mount one of the key texts of his own life philosophy. He lived a simple lifestyle in communities that replaced the caste system with human equality.

Gandhi began his independence movement using Tolstoy's strategy of "passive resistance" but gradually developed his own philosophy of "active non-violent resistance." He trained his followers never to respond with violence, but they would still confront the British directly with open civil disobedience that they considered to represent the use of "non-violent force." Gandhi called his own approach *satyagraha*, which could be translated as "insisting on truth" or, more commonly, "truth-force." The idea was to confront the oppressor face-to-face with the reality of their own violence and brutality. Gandhi's followers were willing to suffer peacefully the insults and physical injuries resulting from their confrontations with the British.

Christians can learn from Gandhi to consider not only the ethical challenges that exist within nations but also those that exist in how different nations relate with each other. They can also learn how the Sermon on the Mount helped to inspire a person to struggle for truth and justice in ways that are nonviolent and yet anything but passive.

Dorothy Day

The U.S. Catholic social activist and journalist Dorothy Day was directly influenced by the writings of Tolstoy as well as other Russian political thinkers. Day grew up in an Episcopalian family that did not place much focus on religion. In college, she became a Marxist who took the side of workers. When she converted to Catholicism, she rejected atheism but still brought along her intense concern for the rights of workers. Along with the French Catholic social thinker Peter Maurin, in the midst of the Depression, Day was cofounder of the Catholic Worker Movement as well as of its newspaper, *The Catholic Worker*. In her autobiography, *The Long Loneliness*, she names among the many factors leading to her religious conversion that she wanted to identify as much as possible with the poor.[19] In the New York of her time, Catholicism was the religion of the immigrant poor.

Day and Maurin tried to effect social change not only through their newspaper, but also in several other ways. They founded Houses of Hospitality that offered bread and soup to the unemployed and the poor. They rented halls to hold Round-Table Discussions that brought together people of various walks of life to get to know and learn from each other. They started agronomic universities, which were farms that also brought together rich and poor, priests and laypeople, trained and untrained workers, and farmers and city folk to live together and to share whatever they possessed both in intellectual knowledge and in practical skills.

Day took most seriously any words in the New Testament that were spoken directly by Jesus. She read the Sermon on the Mount as if it were directly addressed to her. She embraced pacifism, voluntary poverty, and a commitment to social change. Day not only wrote in support of workers, but she would join the picket lines with them, at times being thrown in jail. When the United States entered World War II, she firmly stood by her pacifist stance, a position for which she received much criticism and that caused the circulation of *The Catholic Worker* to drop off.

Although one could never say that anything about Day was conventional, she can be contrasted somewhat with Tolstoy and Gandhi by her intense embrace of the traditional beliefs and practices of her religion. If Tolstoy and Gandhi can be described as distinguishing clearly between "spirituality" and "religion," Day can be said to have practiced her faith in a way that her spirituality completely permeated her religion. Day attended Mass daily and frequently prayed the rosary. She would pray to St. Joseph, the father of Jesus, to help her find a location for a new Catholic Worker House, and when she would find it, she would believe that St. Joseph had helped her.

Many Catholics and others today remain devoted to Dorothy Day as a shining example of what Catholic faith can mean. She devoted her life to the working poor, living out a personal synthesis of traditional devotion, a simple lifestyle, and active nonviolent resistance. In 2000, then New York Cardinal John O'Connor instigated the cause for her canonization as a saint. In 2012, her cause was endorsed by the United States Conference of Catholic Bishops.

Martin Luther King

Civil rights leader and Baptist minister Martin Luther King was directly influenced by the writings of Tolstoy and Gandhi, as well as by Henry David Thoreau on civil disobedience. Like Gandhi, King and his followers practiced active nonviolent resistance. In one of his early sermons, King preached on the line "Love your enemies" from the Sermon on the Mount.[20] He said that this principle is basic to his own life philosophy and orientation, and he explicitly connected it with the practice of nonviolent resistance. The practice of loving your enemies, he said, contains within it the power to transform them. King also drew greatly upon the Christian spiritual heritage of those who had been slaves in the United States. Like Moses, King was on a mission from God to challenge the Pharaoh to set his people free. Like Jesus, he gave his life in the service of others.

King led many activities by which African Americans demanded their rights by occupying white-only lunch counters and by organized protests to secure the right to vote. As mentioned previously in the discussion of virtue ethics, King's followers underwent training sessions to develop the habit of responding nonviolently under any and all conditions. At times, they suffered physical beatings and imprisonment. King's movement provided critical pressure for the passing of the Civil Rights Act in 1964.

Black liberation theologian James Cone has rightly pointed out that many of the African Americans who followed King accepted nonviolent resistance more as a practical necessity than as an essential principle of love.[21] They were so overpowered by military and police that violent resistance could only have ended in their own massacre. In the writings of King, however, one encounters the voice of a man who believed first of all that nonviolence occupied a space near the core of the meaning of God's love, and that, secondarily, it also happened to be the only practical response in the situation.

King died as a martyr for the Civil Rights Movement. He is remembered today in the United States by a national holiday, Birthday of Martin Luther King Jr., observed on the third Monday of each January, close to his actual birthday on January 15. To Christians, he stands as an example of how faith and courage can fuel a social movement that effects real change.

Most Christians today are neither pacifists nor live by a radical social ethic. Not everyone agrees with Tolstoy's interpretation of the Sermon on the Mount or his estimation of its central importance for the meaning of Christianity. Many Christians consider his approach to be overly idealistic and utopian. For virtually all Christians, however, the figures discussed in this section stand as guiding lights who challenge them to think deeply about what they believe and how they live.

In this chapter, we have examined three major approaches to Christian ethics. Anyone acquiring a basic knowledge of Christianity should be familiar with the Ten Commandments, virtue ethics, and

Commandments, Virtues, Pacifist Activism

pacifist activism. Different approaches to Christian morality usually arise from different starting points and relative emphases. The following chapter will focus on Catholic social teaching.

FOR FURTHER REFLECTION

1. Do you think that the Ten Commandments remain a valuable way for Christian communities to hand on their moral teachings? Why or why not?

2. What in addition to the Ten Commandments is needed in order for Christian communities to hand on their moral teachings and practices?

3. Do you agree with Aristotle that the key to happiness lies in a virtuous life?

4. Describe how Aquinas adapts Aristotle's ideas about virtue into a specifically Christian framework.

5. Aquinas describes faith, hope, and love as explicitly Christian values. Do you think that people of other religions and also nonreligious people can possess virtues similar to faith, hope, and charity? If so, try to give examples.

6. What is contemporary virtue ethics? To what modern tendencies does a virtue ethic offer an alternative?

7. When you read the Sermon on the Mount, is there anything about it that hits you in the guts? Explain.

8. Do you think that Leo Tolstoy got it right in his interpretation of the Sermon on the Mount? Why or why not?

9. Do you consider yourself to be a pacifist? Why or why not?

10. What is active nonviolent resistance? How does it work? What impact can it have upon those who are perpetrating social injustices?

269

11. Does it seem to you to be a contradiction that Dorothy Day combined radical social activism with traditional religious devotion?

FOR FURTHER READING

Aquinas, Thomas. *Summa Theologiae*. Questions on the Virtues. II–II, QQ 1–170. Christian Ethereal Library, originally *Summa Theologica*. Translated by Fathers of the English Dominican Province. Benziger Bros. edition, 1947. http://www.ccel.org/ccel/aquinas/summa.SS.html.

Aristotle. *Nicomachean Ethics* (350 BCE). Translated by W. D. Ross, http://classics.mit.edu/Aristotle/nicomachaen.html.

Day, Dorothy. *Loaves and Fishes*. Maryknoll, NY: Orbis Books, 1997.

———. *The Long Loneliness*. New York: Harper and Brothers, 1952.

Gandhi, Mahatma. *Gandhi's Experiments with Truth: Essential Writings by and about Gandhi*. Edited by Richard L. Johnson. Lanham, MD: Lexington Books, 2006.

Luther, Martin. *The Large Catechism* (1530). Translated by F. Bente and W. H. T. Dan. In *Triglot Concordia: The Symbolical Books of the Ev. Lutheran Church*. St. Louis: Concordia Publishing House, 1921. http://www.creeds.net/lutheran/luther_large.htm.

McCarthy, David Matzko, and M. Therese Lysaught. *Gathered for the Journey: Moral Theology in Catholic Perspective*. Grand Rapids: Eerdmans, 2007.

Philibert, Paul J. *The Priesthood of the Faithful: Key to a Living Church*. Collegeville, MN: Liturgical Press, 2005.

Pieper, Josef. *Faith, Hope, Love*. San Francisco: Ignatius Press, 1997.

———. *The Four Cardinal Virtues*. Notre Dame, IN: University of Notre Dame Press, 1966.

Taylor, Charles. *A Secular Age*. Cambridge, MA: Harvard University Press, 2009.

Tolstoy, Leo. *The Kingdom of God is Within You*. Translated by Constance Garnett. Stilwell, KS: Digireads.com Publishing, 2005.

———. "A Letter to a Hindu; The Subjection of India—Its Cause and Cure." Available as a free e-book at http://www.gutenberg.org/files/7176/7176-h/7176-h.htm.

———. "My Religion." Available as a free e-book at http://www.gutenberg.org/files/43794/43794-h/43794-h.htm.

GLOSSARY

Acquired virtues: virtues attained through training and practice.

Active nonviolent resistance: a method of social action most associated with Gandhi and Martin Luther King that involves provocation through civil disobedience and a nonviolent response intended to raise the consciousness of the oppressor and bring about social change.

Agronomic universities: really farms, intended by the Catholic Worker movement to bring together people of various class and education levels to interact and learn from each other.

Character: a virtuous state of being resulting from formation and training.

Faith: for Aquinas, the intellectual virtue that enables one to accept what God has revealed.

Fortitude: the virtue by which one acts with moral courage.

Habit: an acquired pattern of behavior.

Hope: the virtue by which one remains open to ultimately good possibilities in the future; the opposite of despair.

Houses of hospitality: houses occupied by members of the Catholic Worker movement that offer food, supportive conversation, and other forms of help for the unemployed and the poor.

Infused virtues: virtues that come as gifts from outside oneself.

Interim ethic: a label given by some biblical scholars to the radical teaching in the Sermon on the Mount that seems to be designed for Christians who think that the end of the world is imminent.

Justice: the virtue by which one gives to each their due.

Love: according to Aquinas, God's all-embracing, all-including love is the highest form of love; through the supernatural virtue of love, human beings are enabled to share in the love of God.

Natural virtues: Aquinas's label for the basic human virtues as treated by Aristotle.

Pacifism: a belief or philosophy that violence is never an acceptable human course of action.

Prudence: the virtue that enables one to act according to practical reason.

Round-table discussions: public conversations promoted by the Catholic Worker movement to bring together people of various classes and educational backgrounds to create mutual understanding.

Satyagraha: "insisting on truth," or "truth-force," Gandhi's own label for his method of active nonviolent resistance.

Sermon on the Mount: Sermon given by Jesus in Matthew 5—7. In this textbook, the "Sermon on the Mount" names an approach to Christian morality focused on pacifism, simple living, and a radical social ethic.

State of grace: being connected with God's saving grace; being empowered by faith, hope, and charity.

State of sin: being shut off from the grace of God; a mode of life characterized by bad habits and denial of one's true condition; whether anyone is culpably in this condition is a judgment that must be left to God.

Supernatural virtues: faith, hope, and love when given as gifts from God that allow human beings to participate in God's own life.

Temperance: the virtue by which one moderates one's appetites.

The Ten Commandments: used in this textbook to name an approach to ethics that uses the Ten Commandments (1) to stress that Christian moral teaching comes ultimately from God and (2) to have categories for expressing in a clear and simple way what Christians are supposed to do and not do.

Vice: a morally bad habit.

Virtue: a morally good habit.

Virtue ethics: an approach to ethics that stresses the need for character formation within the context of a vibrant Christian community; a complement to normative ethics.

NOTES

1. See Exod 20:2–17; Deut 5:6–21.

2. As found in the *Catechism of the Catholic Church*, see http://www.vatican.va/archive/ccc_css/archive/catechism/command.htm. There is also a traditional Protestant version of the Ten Commandments that is slightly different in organization and numbering.

3. For a study of the meaning of the seventh commandment in the context of the Old Testament, see Robert Gnuse, *You Shall Not Steal* (Maryknoll, NY: Orbis Books, 1985 [republished by WIPF and Stock, 2011]).

4. Martin Luther, *Large Catechism*, http://bookofconcord.org/lc-3-ten commandments.php.

5. The *Baltimore Catechism* was originally issued in 1885. Quotes here are taken from the *Baltimore Catechism* (Revised Edition, 1941), http://www.catholicity.com/baltimore-catechism/lesson19.html. A later revision appeared in 1963. This catechism was used in the United States to educate more than 90 percent of Catholic children between 1910 and 1965.

6. Ibid.

7. The *Catechism of the Catholic Church* was first published in French in 1992. The first English edition was issued in 1994. In 1997, the official Latin edition was published with a few changes, most notably containing a clear rejection of the death penalty. This catechism is intended to be a resource for the entire Catholic Church.

8. Aquinas treats the topic of virtue in *Summa Theologiae*, II–II.

9. Points from Aristotle are drawn from the *Nicomachean Ethics*, book 2.

10. This chart is constructed from points made in prose by Aristotle in the *Nicomachean Ethics*, book 2.

11. The movement "Occupy Wall Street" could serve as an interesting subject of study concerning this point.

12. Thomas Aquinas, *Summa Theologiae*, II–II, Q 150, a 1, http://www.ccel.org/ccel/aquinas/summa.SS_Q150_A1.html. Note: Aquinas's advice about not abstaining from wine does not apply to those who suffer from alcoholism.

13. Thomas Aquinas, *Summa Theologiae*, II–II, Q 153, a 2, http://www.ccel.org/ccel/aquinas/summa.SS_Q153_A2.html.

14. See 1 Cor 13:13: "And now faith, hope, and love abide, these three; and the greatest of these is love."

15. Aquinas's use of the category of participation here, as well as the idea that something on a lower level can participate in something on a higher level, has parallels with the thought of Plato.

16. Paul J. Philibert, *The Priesthood of the Faithful: Key to a Living Church* (Collegeville, MN: Liturgical Press, 2005).

17. Leo Tolstoy, "A Letter to a Hindu; The Subjection of India—Its Cause and Cure." Available as a free e-book at http://www.gutenberg.org/files/7176/7176-h/7176-h.htm.

18. Ibid., chap. 3.

19. Dorothy Day, *From Union Square to Rome* (Maryknoll, NY: Orbis Books, 2006), 16–18. This point is also found in *The Long Loneliness* (New York: Harper and Brothers, 1952).

20. Martin Luther King, "Loving Your Enemies" (1957), http://www.ipoet.com/ARCHIVE/BEYOND/King-Jr/Loving-Your-Enemies.html.

21. James H. Cone, *Martin and Malcolm in America: A Dream or Nightmare?* (Maryknoll, NY: Orbis Books, 1991), 260.

Chapter 13

CATHOLIC SOCIAL TEACHING ON PEACE, SOCIAL JUSTICE, AND THE ENVIRONMENT

This chapter is devoted specifically to Catholic social teaching regarding matters of justice, peace, and the environment. Both the individual and social dimensions of morality are of immense importance and integrally related to each other. An individual cannot live a truly moral life without attending to the bigger picture of the world in which he or she lives. The better a society is, the more opportunities exist for individuals to participate in it in a meaningful way. And the more corrupt a society is, the harder it is for individuals to live morally good lives. All human beings are to some degree shaped and formed by the contexts of their lives.

Leo XIII's *Rerum Novarum*

Modern Catholic social teaching begins with an encyclical letter, *Rerum Novarum*, issued by Pope Leo XIII in 1891.[1] Leo was responding to the nineteenth-century economic and social crisis in Europe concerning the situation of the working class laborers. In the long wake of the Industrial Revolution, many workers were living under oppressive conditions. The Church was losing members to socialist movements that attempted to address these matters in a direct and radical manner. *Rerum Novarum* laid out basic principles that still guide Catholic social teaching today. It is remarkable both how immediately relevant many of his positions still are, as well as how outdated are other of his ideas.

275

On the one hand, Leo condemned "socialism," here meaning an economic system that rejects private ownership. Instead, he affirmed the ability to own property as a basic (though by no means absolute) human right. On the other hand, having affirmed ownership as well as a market economy as starting points, Leo placed serious conditions and qualifications upon economic activities that sharply distinguish what he was affirming from the then-reigning nineteenth-century model of *laissez-faire* ["leave it alone" or "anything goes"] capitalism. As Leo expressed it: "A small number of very rich men have been able to lay upon the teeming masses of the laboring poor a yoke little better than slavery itself" (no. 3). Perhaps to many contemporary people this sounds like a familiar idea, perhaps even a bit too close to home.

Catholic social teaching should not be said to offer a third way between socialism and capitalism because it does not endorse a particular system or paint a clear picture of what an alternative would look like. It is rather the case that Catholic social teaching rejects certain extremes while offering principles that can guide and critique a number of political, economic, and social arrangements.

Rerum Novarum Rejects Socialism

Leo attacked what he called "socialism" at its very roots. The word *socialist* has many meanings today, often being applied to countries that have high taxes and strong social welfare systems. What Leo condemned is closer to what people today think of as communism, whereby the state (said to represent the people) owns the means of production as well as all property.

Karl Marx (1818–83) had described and analyzed the alienation of the workers. He attributed their sufferings to the capitalist system by which the working class was exploited by the owning class. According to Marx, religion functioned as the opiate of the people, both expressing their suffering and dulling their pain somewhat. Yet religion also functioned as part of an ideological superstructure that held them back from doing anything about their situation as they awaited their heavenly reward in the next life. The tensions within this two-class society would ultimately be resolved by revolution, resulting in a utopian society. There would be no more countries,

276

classes, possessions, wars, or religion.[2] Work would become creative and free. People would give all they had and take only what they need. Marx put forth his views as a scientific prediction, but it is easy to interpret his views as offering something that comes very close to being a religious vision.

Leo's most basic criticism of socialism in *Rerum Novarum* is that its rejection of ownership is out of kilter with the fundamental nature of human beings, and for this reason, it will not work. Leo's claim stands within the Catholic Tradition of natural law theory with its assumption that God designed human beings with certain purposes in mind, which human beings can discern. His argument goes something like this: what distinguishes human beings from other animals is their ability to reason. Reason enables human beings to live in a way that connects the past, present, and future. They are able to make their own choices. They need to be able to plan and organize. They do not just live for today. For this reason, they need to be able to own property. It is not reasonable to think otherwise. Moreover, it is human nature to need to be motivated to work. It is appropriate that those who cultivate land and maintain it can claim it as their own. Leo remarked, "So strong and convincing are these arguments that it seems amazing that some should now be setting up anew certain obsolete opinions in opposition to what is here laid down" (no. 10).

Leo thought that the whole point of working is to earn some wages so that one can put aside some money and eventually be able to own one's own property and home. His own solution to the divisions between owners and workers was thus that everyone should have the opportunity to become an owner. Leo rejected the idea, however, that society should be completely without classes. He claimed that it would be impossible to reduce society to one equal level. People differ in capacity and skill, and unequal fortune is the necessary result of unequal condition. He taught further, however, that there should be harmony among the classes. He thought it was a great mistake to presume that the classes must naturally be hostile to each other. If socialism were implemented, the sources of wealth would soon run dry, and everyone would be leveled to the same depth of misery.

Rerum Novarum Places Moral Restraints upon Capitalism

After establishing his antisocialist credentials in the opening sections, Leo then uses most of the rest of the encyclical to outline qualifications that need to be made about capitalism. Ownership is a fundamental right that needs to be protected from the encroachment of the state, but it is not an absolute right. Leo cites Thomas Aquinas, who made a strong distinction between obligations of justice that should be enforced by law and obligations of charity that depended on the openness of people's hearts. Aquinas held that according to justice, people have a right to spend their money to address their own needs in a becoming manner, but it is an obligation of charity to give the remainder to those in need (no. 22).

Leo further cites Aquinas to explain that justice is not only individual and legal, but also distributive. Distributive justice addresses the overall distribution of wealth within a society. It is the duty of rulers and public administrators "to provide for the welfare and comfort of the working classes" (no. 33). For Leo, a key element in distributive justice lies in workers receiving a just wage. Although Leo sought some protections for women and children in the workplace, when it came to the subject of a just wage, he assumed that the worker is a man who is the head of a household. A just wage is enough for a frugal person to support a family as well as to save a bit from each paycheck to be able eventually to own one's own home. Leo did not simply trust the market on its own to determine the appropriate wages to be paid to workers. He did see the market as having an important role, however, as long as the workers have the right to bargain collectively. Leo endorsed in principle the right of workers to form unions and even, as a last resort, to strike. He strongly urged owners to do whatever was in their power to remove peremptorily the causes that might lead to a strike, including not only low wages but also long hours and harsh conditions.

Leo directly took issue with those who argued that workers had no right to strike because they had entered freely into a contract. He explains that work is not merely a choice but a necessity for those who want to eat and otherwise survive. Due to this necessity, workers are not always completely free when entering into agreements; rather, they can be pressured into accepting contracts that are unjust. Contracts that are unjust are not morally binding. In such cases, the government should not necessarily be expected to enforce existing contracts but rather to protect the rights of the workers.

Background of Modern Catholic Social Teaching

Rerum Novarum did not simply appear out of the blue. There is of course a history leading up to this encyclical, as well as a deep background—both Catholic and Protestant—found in Scripture and in Tradition, that speaks to social and economic concerns. Scripture and Tradition contain resources that have inspired the imaginations of social reformers. In the Old Testament, one encounters concern for social justice in the Law, Wisdom Writings, and Prophetic Books. In the New Testament, in Luke, Jesus says, "Blessed are you who are poor, / for yours is the kingdom of God," (6:20), as well as "but woe to you who are rich, / for you have received your consolation" (6:24). All four Gospels present Jesus as taking a few loaves of bread and a couple of fish and feeding thousands of people. In Acts of the Apostles, the earliest Christian community is depicted as sharing all goods in common.

The writings of the early Church fathers contain statements about material justice that can sound shocking to contemporary Christians. Ambrose of Milan (340–97) stated, "You are not making a gift of your possession to the poor person. You are handing over to him what is his."[3] John Chrysostom (347–407) explained that "the rich are in possession of the goods of the poor, even if they have acquired them honestly or inherited them legally."[4] Basil of Caesarea (330–70) agreed:

> The bread which you keep, belongs to the hungry; that coat which you preserve in your wardrobe, to the naked; those shoes which are rottting in your possession, to the shoeless; that gold which you have hidden in the ground, to the needy. Wherefore, as often as you were able to help others, and refused, so often did you do them wrong.[5]

Christian social thought became less radical and more complicated after the end of the fourth century when Christianity was accepted as the religion of the Roman Empire. The value of such developments can be debated. The obligation to give service and to help the poor, however, has remained an important dimension of Christian Life. Poverty has continued to be an important ideal in monastic life for those who took religious vows. An early reform movement led by Peter Waldo of Lyon (c. 1120–c. 1205) focused on simplicity and voluntary poverty. Francis of Assisi (1181/82–1226), the founder of the Franciscans, also had a radical and even dramatic focus on voluntary poverty as a holy practice. Many other Catholic religious orders and Protestant movements have since been founded to care for the poor.

Some of the Radical Reformers combined concern for justice with simple living and pacifism. Although some of the earliest Anabaptists in the 1520s and 1530s were violent revolutionaries, the Radical Reformers gradually came to blend their concern for social justice with nonviolence and simplicity of life. After a terrible defeat in Münster in 1535, the pacifist branch of the Anabaptists won out. The Sermon on the Mount functioned as an important text for the Radical Reformers, along with other texts that they thought represented the true words of Jesus. Christian communities such as the Church of the Brethren, the Religious Society of Friends (Quakers), and the Mennonites, including the Amish, are collectively known as the historic peace traditions. Today, Christians of many varieties look to the peace traditions as a source of inspiration.

Catholic Social Teaching Documents and Their Basic Principles

As previously mentioned, in Europe in the nineteenth century, during the Industrial Revolution, new forms of social problems emerged. The exploitation of workers in factories as well as the development of urban slums called for new ways of thinking about the rights of workers and their relationship with their employers. *Rerum Novarum* marks the beginning of a long line of modern

Catholic social teaching documents that offer a response to these problems.[6] Catholic social teaching has grown and expanded over the last 125 years. In 1931, Pius XI addressed a world divided into the communists, fascists, and liberal democrats. The encyclicals of Pope John XXIII, in the early 1960s, became yet more international in scope and included concerns about debt, human rights, and the need for peace in a nuclear age. The writings of Pope Paul VI, in the late 1960s and 1970s, addressed with urgency the lingering effects of colonialism as well as the growing gap between the rich nations and the poor nations of the world. John Paul II (r. 1978–2005) wrote during an era of great social change that included the fall of the Berlin wall. Benedict XVI and Francis have been writing, in a period of ever-increasing globalization with new threats and new opportunities, regarding matters of peace, economic justice, and the environment.

The following chart offers one selected point of focus for each of the Catholic social teaching documents listed. Many of these points of focus are found already in *Rerum Novarum*, and all of them are found in more than one document. I tried to select one significant point from each document as a focused way of organizing an overview of the principles of Catholic social teaching.

CATHOLIC SOCIAL TEACHING DOCUMENT		ONE SELECTED POINT OF FOCUS	
1891	*Rerum Novarum*	Leo XIII	Preferential Option for the Poor: ultimately in the interest of everyone
1931	*Quadragesimo Anno*	Pius XI	Subsidiarity: importance of various social bodies, especially the family
1961	*Mater et Magistra*	John XXIII	Common Good: requires a significant role for the government
1963	*Pacem in Terris*	John XXIII	Human Rights/Peace: linked with each other

Table continued next page

1965	Gaudium et Spes	Vatican II document	Consistent Ethic of Life: opposition to abortion, capital punishment, economic injustice all based on the protection of life
1967	Populorum Progressio	Paul VI	Human Development: must be rooted in an integral humanism
1981	Laborem Exercens	John Paul II	Dignity: each human person is of inestimable worth
1987	Sollicitudo Rei Socialis	John Paul II	Solidarity: being is deeper than having
1991	Centesimus Annus	John Paul II	Market Plus: a market starting point needs qualifications and limits
2009	Caritas in Veritate	Benedict XVI	Gratuitousness: charity must be linked with truth
2013	Evangelii Gaudium	Francis	Inclusion: share the joy of the gospel with everyone, especially the poor
2015	Laudato Si'	Francis	Sustainability: care for God's creation

Preferential Option for the Poor

Leo XIII did not use the exact phrase "preferential option for the poor," an expression associated with liberation theology, a theology that focused on social and economic injustice in Latin America.[7] The basic idea, however, is clearly present in *Rerum Novarum*. In the middle of his letter, Leo cited Jesus' strong warnings concerning the dangers facing the rich. He asserted firmly that it is no disgrace to be poor. Jesus himself was the son of a carpenter, and even a carpenter himself. Leo stated that the life of virtue that leads to eternal reward is equally open to the rich and the poor. But there is a special place in the heart of God for those who are poor, the thought of which should help the classes to live in harmony. Leo wrote,

> Nay, God Himself seems to incline rather to those who suffer misfortune; for Jesus Christ calls the poor "blessed"; He lovingly invites those in labor and grief to come to Him for solace; and He displays the tenderest charity toward the lowly and the oppressed. These reflections cannot fail to keep down the pride of the well-to-do, and to give heart to the unfortunate; to move the former to be generous and the latter to be moderate in their desires. Thus, the separation which pride would set up tends to disappear, nor will it be difficult to make rich and poor join hands in friendly concord. (no. 24)

I have found college students to be very engaged, sometimes negatively at first, by the idea of God's preferential option for the poor. Does God not love everyone? Does Christianity teach that rich people are bad? Does being poor make you a better person? The answers to these questions are, respectively, no, no, and no. It often takes quite a bit of discussion to establish that the preferential option for the poor does not stand in contradiction to the belief that God loves everyone.

To grasp the meaning of the preferential option of the poor, it can be helpful to get beyond any individualist presuppositions and to think in terms of all people as belonging to one human family. To an individualist, a preference in favor of one person or group can only mean a preference against another person or group. In contrast, Leo is really hoping that a society can ultimately be based upon love of God and love of neighbor. If one tries to think in terms of belonging to one human family, one can start by saying that some among us are at a disadvantage.[8] We care about our family, and we are not comfortable with the fact that so many among us are at such a disadvantage. From this standpoint, it is to everyone's advantage that all of us make a preferential option for the poor. This is a decision for the benefit of the whole family. It is ultimately in everyone's interest. We make a preferential option for the poor because we care about everyone. Those who are most in need have a special claim upon our attention.

The option for the poor requires empathy. Are you able in your heartfelt imagination to change places with the other person? Can you walk a mile in the others' shoes? How would you feel if you lived as part of an economically or culturally excluded group?

Taking the option for the poor can include trying to figure out the interests of the poor in political and economic matters and then voting, investing, and overall acting with those interests in mind. It can include making sure that, in some significant way, you remain in frequent contact and relationship with poor people, either through where you live or where you work or where you volunteer. It can also include a spiritual humility by which you cultivate a sense of your continuing dependence upon God and your solidarity with other people.

Subsidiarity

Subsidiarity is another concept found already in Leo XIII's *Rerum Novarum*, but which is only labeled later, in *Quadragesimo Anno* in 1931. Subsidiarity refers to the manner in which society is made up of different forms of communities on various levels. The needs of people who lack jobs and material goods cannot be addressed solely by anonymous government programs but require also face-to-face solutions implemented by associations on the local level.

Catholic social teaching does not limit its concern to the rights of individuals, but also includes the rights of these various types of groups and communities. On the one hand, subsidiarity protects both individuals and communities against the overreach of the state. On the other hand, subsidiarity also protects various groups and organizations against the overreach of claims to individual rights that would ignore or underplay the rights of the community. These communities can include neighborhoods, parishes, faith sharing groups, social organizations, labor unions, and many other types of associations. Foremost among these communities is the family. The family is the basic unit of a healthy society.

Subsidiarity has many practical implications. The principle does not offer immediate solutions to complex matters, but rather lends support for the rights and capacities of various types of community that can at times come into conflict with claims for individual rights. The right of an individual store owner to sell pornographic materials might be limited by the right of a community that does not want such business in its neighborhood. The so-called right to an abortion for an employee can be limited by the right to religious freedom of the owners of a business that includes medical insurance as part of compensation. Few cases that involve a conflict of rights are clear-cut or simple in today's complex world.

The Common Good

Catholic social teaching both affirms the rights of individuals as well as fights against any tendencies toward extreme forms of individualism. Individualism goes beyond simply valuing the dignity and rights of all individuals by insisting that the individual is the basic unit and measure of all values. In contrast, at the heart of Catholic social teaching is an endorsement of the common good, described by John XXIII in the 1961 *Mater et Magistra* as the sum total of the social conditions necessary to make it possible for all individuals to thrive as much as possible. There is a tendency in contemporary political discussion in the United States to assume that each individual should seek only their own interests and that a focus on the common good conflicts with individual rights. In Catholic social teaching, the dignity of each person and the value of the common good are thought to go hand in hand. Individuals and groups are expected to act with the common good in mind. A balance between individual rights and the rights of groups needs to be maintained.

Everyone is called to contribute to the common good, but the state has a special role. One cannot assume that a market economy, left to itself, will somehow automatically produce the most just society possible. The role of the state is a limited but very important one. The state should promote sufficient material production, the just distribution of wealth, and the rights of all citizens to participate meaningfully in public life.

Although Catholic social teaching recognizes legitimate debate when it comes to the size and particular role of the government, it does not see as debatable the basic claim that the government has a significant role to play in achieving social and economic justice.

Human Rights and Peace

The French Revolution supported individual rights in a way that up-ended traditional social arrangements and that challenged the role of the Church in society. For complex political reasons, the Catholic Church and what has become the quest for universal human rights have experienced significant points of conflict throughout the past two centuries. Still, there have also emerged significant points of overlap, since the quest for universal human rights has some clear and deep points of correspondence with traditional Christian teachings and values, such as respect for the dignity of each human person. Catholics made serious contributions to the writing of the 1948 United Nations Declaration of Human Rights.[9]

In his 1963 encyclical *Pacem in Terris*, John XXIII strongly endorsed universal human rights. This document was written just months after the October 1962 Cuban Missile Crisis, when the fate of the world stood in the balance of the faceoff between John F. Kennedy of the United States and Nikita Khrushchev of the Soviet Union. John XXIII played a significant role in mediating the resolution of this conflict. In *Pacem in Terris*, he called for the cessation of the arms race, the reduction of stockpiles, and the elimination of nuclear weapons. Moreover, he linked the achievement of peace with the need to promote social and economic justice among the nations.

Until the Second Vatican Council, official Catholic teaching recognized as valid only the "just war" approach to questions of war and peace. The initial development of "just war theory" is associated with Augustine in the early fifth century. It addressed the question of when it is legitimate to engage in a war. Over the centuries, a range of basic rules developed: the military should only be used by legitimate authority for a just cause and as a last resort; there must be a reason-able hope that victory can be achieved and that an improved situation can be brought about; there should be no more destruction than is necessary; and civilians should not be targeted.

The 1965 Vatican II document *Gaudium et Spes* continued support for the just war tradition, stating that "governments cannot be denied the right to legitimate defense once every means of peaceful settlement has been exhausted" and offering praise to those "who devote themselves to the military service of their country" (no. 79). It also, though, offered praise for "those who renounce the use of violence in the vindication of their rights" (no. 78). The Council thereby recognized some room for interpretation when it comes to applying Christian faith to situations of violence. Pacifists are now welcome!

More recent ethical discussion in Christian circles has been focusing on "just peace-building": What preventative measures can be taken in advance in order to avoid military conflict? When might it be legitimate to intervene militarily in response to the threat of genocide or the gross abuse of human rights?

Consistent Ethic of Life

Gaudium et Spes stated a principle that came to be labelled the "consistent ethic of life":

> Whatever is opposed to life itself, such as any type of murder, genocide, abortion, euthanasia or wilful self-destruction, whatever violates the integrity of the human person, such as mutilation, torments inflicted on body or mind, attempts to coerce the will itself; whatever insults human dignity, such as subhuman living conditions, arbitrary imprisonment, deportation, slavery, prostitution, the selling of women and children; as well as disgraceful working conditions, where men are treated as mere tools for profit, rather than as free and responsible persons; all these things and others of their like are infamies indeed. They poison human society, but they do more harm to those who practice them than those who suffer from the injury. Moreover, they are supreme dishonor to the Creator. (no. 27)

Some Catholics have tended to concentrate more on one set of these issues to the relative neglect of the other. One hears remarks sometimes about the "social justice Catholics" who may think that placing an emphasis on reproductive issues signals upside-down priorities. One also hears similar remarks made in reverse by those who see abortion and related issues as greatly surpassing in importance what they take to be vague teachings that are difficult to apply to actual problems of social and economic injustice. *Gaudium et Spes* delivered the message that these Catholics need to come together.[10] All of the issues mentioned above are deeply interrelated as matters of promoting life. They are all of great importance.

Human Development

In his 1967 encyclical *Populorum Progressio*, Paul VI argued forcefully that technological progress in itself means nothing apart from justice, peace, and the inclusion of peoples of various nations and races. Human development must include not only the material, but also the intellectual, social, and spiritual well-being of all.

Think about what success means in the life of an individual. As the song goes, "it's not about the money, money, money."[11] There are so many dimensions to life. There is your intellect, your feelings, your friendships, your experiences. There are the contributions you make to others, to those you know, to society in general. There is your relationship with God, the integrity of your own soul. A successful life is one that attends to various dimensions of meaning and various layers of connections with others.

Paul VI applied something like this idea of "success" to the world itself. Full human development goes beyond the material and the technical to include all people as well as all of the dimensions of life.

Dignity

The dignity of the human person has been a key theme throughout Catholic social teaching. In his 1981 encyclical *Laborem Exercens*, John Paul II developed this theme with a focus on the fundamental dignity of workers. Where Leo XIII had advocated that everyone become an owner, John Paul II recommended that everyone come to think of themselves as workers. He explained that there is an objective side to work, and different jobs command different salaries. He argued further, however, that the dignity of work comes from its subjective side, from the fact that the one doing the work is a person. According to John Paul II, whether you are a lawyer, CEO, housewife, investor, sanitation worker, or manager, you should think of yourself as a worker. Whatever it is that you do, that is how you make your contribution to the larger society. In spite of the fact that social classes remain, we should all cultivate an awareness of the dignity that we all share as workers.

Solidarity

No social or governmental system can work adequately apart from human solidarity. Solidarity refers to a deep sense of interconnectedness among a group of human beings. Human solidarity extends that interconnectedness to the entire human race. In Catholic social teaching, there is a need to appreciate that everyone belongs to one human family.

In *Sollicitudo Rei Socialis* (1987), John Paul II examined the moral failings of both the East and the West. In the East, he found material misery due to underdevelopment and a lack of human rights. In the West, he found what he called a "super-development" marked by materialism and consumerism. He lamented the tendency for people to define themselves more by what they have than by what they are. He contrasted "having"—possessing material goods and social status—with "being." "Being" is the fact that you are, that you exist. Your existence is a gift from God. When we define ourselves by "having," we stress those things that make us different from each other. When we look to the gift of our "being," we focus on something that we all share and that makes us alike. "Being" is deeper than "having." The problem in the West, as John Paul II saw it in 1987, is that the priorities were turned upside-down. He explained that it is not wrong to have, or even to want to have more. The problem arises when we value "having" more than "being," and thus lose our sense of solidarity and our need to share with all of those who are made in the image and likeness of God. Our desires to possess and to own should be shaped and honed by our love for God and for others.

Market Plus

In *Centesimus Annus* (1991), John Paul II addressed the new world situation after the fall of the Berlin Wall in 1989 and the following collapse of the Soviet bloc. Did this now mean that capitalism had won and Marxist communism had failed? To this question, John Paul II gave a carefully balanced response:

> The answer is obviously complex. If capitalism is understood as an economic system that recognizes the fundamental and positive role of business, the market, private property and the resulting responsibility for the means of production, as well as free human creativity in the economic sector, then the answer is certainly in the affirmative, even though it would perhaps be more appropriate to speak of a "business economy," "market economy," or simply "free economy." But if capitalism is understood as a system in which freedom in the economic sector is not circumscribed within a strong juridical framework that places it at the service of human freedom in its totality, and that sees it as a particular aspect of that freedom, the core of which is ethical and religious, then the reply is certainly negative.
>
> The Marxist solution has failed, but the realities of marginalization and exploitation remain in the world, especially the Third World, as does the reality of human alienation, especially in the more advanced countries. Against these phenomena the Church strongly raises her voice. (no. 42)

John Paul II's assessment is remarkably similar to basic ideas that Leo had outlined in *Rerum Novarum*. Marxist communism does not work. It is much better to affirm the role of private ownership and a market economy. The issues to which the Marxists direct us, however, remain present and serious. A market economy needs to be complemented by three things:

a. A significant role for the government;

b. A practice of subsidiarity that protects the rights not only of individuals but also of various types of community, including the family, churches, unions, and other social groupings;

c. A sense of solidarity that strives to express itself as a civilization of love.

Gratuitousness

Benedict XVI wrote what is perhaps the most philosophical of all the Catholic social teaching documents. In his 2009 *Caritas in Veritate*, he explained that even though the obligation of charity toward others goes beyond simple justice, it is still rooted in truth. It is not rooted in subjective whimsy. Both charity and truth are themselves gifts from God. Everything in each of our lives, including our life itself, is a gift from God. We are called to act both justly and with a loving gratuitousness. Hard work and personal responsibility may contribute greatly to the material success of an individual, a business, or a nation, but all should remember their ultimate dependency on the gracious gifts of God. The economic world itself needs to find the appropriate balance between profit and nonprofit approaches to the exchange of goods.

Inclusion

In his 2013 apostolic exhortation, *Evangelii Gaudium*, Pope Francis addressed a crucial theme in current Christian moral theology: inclusion. Inclusion is based upon the recognition, appreciation, and embrace of "the other." This theme takes on a special importance when seen against the background of the Euro-centrism that permeated the centuries of world colonization. "The other" exists apart from oneself and cannot be regarded simply as a piece of furniture within one's own egocentric universe. Others must be respected and loved in their own right, and even seen as placing legitimate demands upon us.[12]

Francis emphasizes how Christian missionary outreach must include everyone, especially those who are poor. The poor must be fully included in society. Christians are not to sit in judgment of others, for "one who accompanies others has to realize that each person's situation before God and their life in grace are mysteries which no one can fully know from without" (no. 172). In an interview, when asked about gay priests, Francis said, "Who am I to judge?" Francis's own personal outreach has included not only gays, but people with AIDS, prisoners, Muslim women, and the poorest of the poor. Those who cheer Francis on in his inclusion of "the other" often make a comparison with the way in which Jesus' teachings and example in the New Testament broke through social boundaries and extended the love of neighbor toward a universal horizon.

Sustainability: Care for the Environment

Ecological themes have been present in Catholic social teaching for over thirty years, but Francis has written the first papal encyclical directly devoted to these themes. In his 2015 *Laudato Si'*, he draws deeply upon Scripture and Tradition to argue that Christians need to respect the things of creation as having been made by God and as having their own purpose beyond the wishes of human beings. Francis recognizes that human beings occupy a special place in the cosmos, but he also acknowledges that some Christians have misinterpreted Christian sources to justify their harsh "dominion" over the earth. Francis teaches that human beings are called to care about and to care for the things that God has made.

Francis accepts the scientific consensus that human beings must take responsibility for climate change. He urges people of various worldviews to come together to address this situation in a serious manner. Francis connects the ecological crisis with modern individualism and a self-centered culture of instant gratification. He connects possible solutions to the ecological crisis with the option for the poor because, he claims, it is the poor who are hurt most immediately and most deeply by climate change.

Ultimately, argues Francis, everything is connected, everything is related. Throughout the encyclical, he draws upon traditional themes of Catholic social teaching, such as solidarity, human dignity, universal rights, gratuitousness, and inclusion, to make his case for how and why human beings can care for the environment and improve human social conditions at the same time. He highlights especially the dangers of unfettered capitalism with its quest for profits without sufficient regard for the consequences for either the poor or the environment. He urges the human race to experience an "ecological conversion" and to do it now (no. 217).

Pope Francis's theme that everything is connected speaks directly to one of the main themes of this textbook. As we conclude this three-chapter segment, we realize that Christian Life can best be understood within the context of a larger discussion that includes Scripture, Tradition, and Sacraments.

FOR FURTHER REFLECTION

1. Why do some people say that Church leaders should restrict their teachings to religious matters and not address political and economic matters that are beyond their competence? What are your own thoughts about this?

2. What are some of the traditional moral criteria for judging whether or not a particular war is just? Can there ever really be such a thing as a just war?

3. What is meant by "socialism" in *Rerum Novarum*? On what grounds does Leo XIII reject socialism?

4. Explain some of the limits and qualifications that Leo places upon the capitalism of his time.

5. What is the preferential option for the poor?

6. How can the preferential option for the poor be considered to be in the interest of everyone?

7. Explain what John Paul II meant when he said that "being" is deeper than "having."

8. Explain John Paul II's response to the question of whether the collapse of the Soviet bloc meant that capitalism had won and Marxist communism had lost.

9. What three things does John Paul II think a society needs to complement its affirmation of a market economy?

10. What does Pope Benedict mean when he says that the obligation to charity is grounded in truth?

11. Is Pope Francis right to think that care for the environment represents a matter of utmost urgency for our time?

FOR FURTHER READING

Compendium of the Social Doctrine of the Church. Washington, DC: United States Conference of Catholic Bishops, 2005.

Himes, Kenneth, ed. *Modern Catholic Social Teaching: Commentaries and Interpretations*. Washington, DC: Georgetown University Press, 2005.

———. *101 Questions & Answers on Catholic Social Teaching*. 2nd Edition. Mahwah, NJ: Paulist Press, 2013.

Marx, Karl. *Karl Marx: Selected Writings*. 2nd Edition. Edited by David McLellan. Oxford: Oxford University Press, 2000.

Misner, Paul. *Social Catholicism in Europe: From the Onset of Industrialization to the First World War*. New York: Crossroad, 1991.

O'Brien, David J., and Thomas A. Shannon. *Catholic Social Thought: The Documentary Heritage*. Expanded edition. Maryknoll, NY: Orbis Books, 2010.

Sullivan, Susan Crawford, and Ron Pagnucco, eds. *A Vision of Justice: Engaging Catholic Social Teaching on the College Campus*. Collegeville, MN: Liturgical Press/Michael Glazier, 2014.

GLOSSARY

Being and having: John Paul II's point of contrast referring to the extent to which one's most basic identity stems more from either an appreciation of one's life as a gift from God or from an assessment of one's material and social status.

Catholic social teaching: a body of moral teaching focused on social issues found in Catholic teaching documents issued mainly by popes and by episcopal conferences.

Common good: the sum total of the social conditions necessary to make it possible for all individuals to thrive as much as possible. A vision of the common good is often named as something that a society based on individualism lacks.

Consistent ethic of life: an approach to Christian morality that stresses how a range of issues such as abortion, capital punishments, and economic injustice are bound together by being based on the protection of life.

Gratuitousness: a quality of being rooted completely in freedom, of gifts given without obligation.

Inclusion: a moral principle based upon the recognition, appreciation, and embrace of "the other."

Just War theory: starting with St. Augustine, a traditional list of criteria and arguments addressing when a war can be morally justified.

***Laissez-faire* capitalism:** a theory based on the belief that the freedom of the market is the top priority economically and that the interference of government only creates problems. Those who support the morality of *laissez-faire* capitalism argue that only the market forces by themselves can achieve what is most productive and ultimately what is most fair.

Market Plus: endorsement of a market starting point for an economy along with clear qualifications and conditions attached. This approach reflects Catholic social teaching in its rejection of *laissez-faire* capitalism.

Natural law theory: a classical approach to Christian morality that discerns the will of God in the design of creation as well as in the accepted customs of civilized cultures.

Preferential option for the poor: the belief that everyone should try to discern the interests of the poor and act in favor of those interests. It includes the effort to maintain real relationships with poor people.

It is based on the belief that God takes a special interest in the poor and all who are in need, and there is no disgrace in being poor.

Social encyclical: a letter circulated by the pope specifically to address social issues, starting with Leo XIII's *Rerum Novarum*.

Socialism: as used by Leo XIII in *Rerum Novarum*, an economic system based on the rejection of private ownership and the transference of all power to the government, akin to totalitarian communism. In the contemporary world, "socialism" more often refers to an economic system requiring high taxes and offering many social benefits.

Solidarity: a deep sense of interconnectedness with others; the interconnectedness of all human beings; thinking, feeling, and acting as part of one human family.

Subsidiarity: a principle in Catholic social teaching that highlights the existence of various forms of community in between the individual and the large, anonymous state. Not only individuals, but also families, churches, neighborhoods, unions, and various social and political groups exist prior to the state and have rights. An important dimension of enabling social opportunities and of addressing social problems lies in the ability to engage these things on the lowest level possible, especially the level of face-to-face.

Sustainability: a quality of environmental practices that rely upon renewable sources for materials and energy.

NOTES

1. Many papal encyclicals as well as other Catholic social teaching documents will be discussed in this chapter. The best way to access an encyclical online is to search for the Latin title. The official versions are all posted at the Vatican website, www.vatican.va.

2. In classes, I often have my students analyze the John Lennon song, "Imagine." John Lennon, vocal performance of "Imagine," by John Lennon, recorded May–July 1971, on *Imagine*, Apple.

3. *De Nabute*, c. 12, n. 53: *PL* 14. 747; as quoted in Pope Paul VI, *Populorum Progressio*, no. 23, http://w2.vatican.va/content/paul-vi/en/encyclicals/documents/hf_p-vi_enc_26031967_populorum.html.

4. *De Lazio Concio* 2, 4 *Patrologia Graeca* 48: 987–88; as quoted in Paul Wadell, *Happiness and the Christian Moral Life: An Introduction to Christian Ethics* (Lanham, MD: Rowman and Littlefield Publishers, 2008), 243.

5. *Homilia*, in *Illud Lucae Patrologia Graeca* 31: 276–77; as quoted in Charles Avila, *Ownership: Early Christian Teaching* (Maryknoll, NY: Orbis Books, 1983), 50.

6. A history of Catholic responses to the new forms of social problems, responses that influenced *Rerum Novarum*, can be found in Paul Misner, *Social Catholicism in Europe: From the Onset of Industrialization to the First World War* (New York: Crossroad, 1991).

7. Liberation theology has since spread to include various particular regions and movements, such as Asian, African, Black, and Women's liberation theology, to name just a few.

8. I first got this idea from Roberto S. Goizueta, *Caminemos con Jesús: Toward a Hispanic/Latino Theology of Accompaniment* (Maryknoll, NY: Orbis Books), 175–91.

9. Drew Christiansen, "Commentary on *Pacem in terris* (Peace on Earth)," in *Modern Catholic Social Teaching: Commentaries and Interpretations*, ed. Kenneth R. Himes (Washington, DC: Georgetown University Press, 2005), 235–36.

10. The consistent ethic of life is most associated with the late Cardinal Joseph Bernardin, former Archbishop of Chicago. See *Catholic Common Ground Initiative: Foundational Documents* (New York: Crossroad, 1997).

11. Jessie J., vocal performance of "Price Tag," by Bobby Ray Simmons Jr., Lukasz Gottwald, Bobby Simmons, Jessica Cornish, Claude Kelly, recorded 2010, released January 25, 2011, on *Who You Are*, Lava Island.

12. The concept of "the other" in contemporary philosophy is most associated with the work of the Jewish philosopher Emmanuel Levinas. See *Totality and Infinity: An Essay on Exteriority*, trans. Alphonso Lingis (Pittsburgh, PA: Duquesne University Press, 1969). See also *Otherwise than Being or Beyond Essence*, trans. Alphonso Lingis (Dordrecht and Boston, MA: Kluwer Academic Publishers, 1978).

INDEX